WITHDRAWN

Unbodied Hope

Unbodied Hope

Narcissism and the Modern Novel

Lawrence Thornton

Lewisburg
Bucknell University Press
London and Toronto: Associated University Presses

Associated University Presses
440 Forsgate Drive
Cranbury, NJ 08512

Associated University Presses
25 Sicilian Avenue
London WC1A 2QH, England

Associated University Presses
2133 Royal Windsor Drive
Unit 1
Mississauga, Ontario
Canada L5J 1K5

Library of Congress Cataloging in Publication Data

Thornton, Lawrence, 1937–
   Unbodied hope: narcissism and the modern novel.

   Bibliography: p.
   Includes index.
   1. Fiction—19th century—History and criticism.
2. Fiction—20th century—History and criticism.
3. Narcissism in literature.   I. Title.
PN3499.T48   1984   809.3'9353   83-43104
ISBN 0-8387-5065-6

Printed in the United States of America

For Toni

There was a pool, silver with shining water,
To which no shepherds came, no goats, no cattle,
Whose glass no bird, no beast, no falling leaf
Had ever troubled. Grass grew all around it,
Green from the nearby water, and with shadow
No sun burned hotly down on. Here Narcissus,
Worn from the heat of hunting, came to rest
Finding the place delightful, and the spring
Refreshing for the thirsty. As he tried
To quench his thirst, inside him, deep within him,
Another thirst was growing, for he saw
An image in the pool, and fell in love
With that unbodied hope, and found a substance
In what was only shadow. He looks in wonder,
Charmed by himself, spell-bound, and no more moving
Than any marble statue. Lying prone
He sees his eyes, twin stars, and locks as comely
As those of Bacchus or the god Apollo,
Smooth cheeks, and ivory neck, and the bright beauty
Of countenance, and a flush of color rising
In the fair whiteness. Everything attracts him
That makes him so attractive. Foolish boy,
He wants himself; the loved becomes the lover,
The seeker sought, the kindler burns. How often
He tries to kiss the image in the water,
Dips in his arms to embrace the boy he sees there,
And finds the boy, himself, elusive always,
Not knowing what he sees, but burning for it,
The same delusion mocking his eyes and teasing.
Why try to catch an always fleeing image,
Poor credulous youngster? What you seek is nowhere,
And if you turn away, you will take with you
The boy you love. The vision is only shadow,
Only reflection, lacking any substance.
It comes with you, it stays with you, it goes
Away with you, if you can go away.

—Ovid, *Metamorphoses* 3.410–437
(translated by Rolfe Humphries)

Contents

Preface

This book explores two forms of narcissism in an attempt to illuminate the theology of the self and attendant questions of identity which have concerned a wide range of novelists interested in the personal and social costs of self-love. It accepts the tradition of nihilistic thought which emerged in the late nineteenth century as a central, formative influence, and posits Narcissus as a vector through whom this theology passes from late Romanticism to the Modern and Post-Modern periods. For my purposes these two forms are best treated through identification with Nietzsche's Apollonian and Dionysian esthetics ("art realms," as he called them), based on attitudes which correspond closely with narcissistic illusions regarding the self. In my adaptation of Nietzsche's paradigms, the drives of the Apollonian narcissist are revealed in his attempt to create a new version of himself in the naive belief that he can transcend his present identity and fulfill himself within a heroic context. Flaubert, Chopin, Conrad, Ford, Fitzgerald, and Durrell explore various permutations of Apollonian desire. While his Dionysian counterpart shares a compulsion for the new, his agenda for change is markedly violent. As Gide, Mann, and Hawkes show, Dionysian narcissism is manifested in a sophisticated, dark desire for omnipotence and mastery. In each case, self-love animates desires which reveal a will to power virtually identical with Nietzsche's celebrated concept. Like Narcissus, the characters I consider attempt to give form to an imaginative shadow in order to incarnate a fictive model of the self in reality. Their attempts, however, are anything but benign, for the narcissist's potent imaginative capabilities eventually overwhelm them.

The collective fate of the characters I discuss is embodied in the soothsayer Tiresias's prophecy that Narcissus would live only until the moment he saw his reflection in the pool. My

9

argument concentrates on the point of contact between Narcissus's fantasy of himself and Tiresias's prediction that the
youth's self-image, once perceived, would become his own
memento mori. As we will see, the mirror of the self at once lies
and tells a truth the characters do not seek. They are not what
they see, yet what they see seals them off from life, most often
by death, but for those who continue to live, by despair, accidia,
psychic paralysis. A curse shimmers on the surface of Narcissus's pool, for the cost of self-love is to lose the self as the
narcissist stares through the counterfeit image into the void—a
process that makes these novels among the most disturbing of
the Modern and Post-Modern periods because it questions the
existence of the sanctified self.

My attempt to clarify these problems has three focal points.
First, the idea of the narcissist as artist permeates all the novels.
Each of the characters imaginatively recreates himself in the
image of a model drawn from his reading or from cultural codes.
In the exchange of his identity for the model's, he locks himself
into a fantasy world which can never be actualized. Second, this
exchange is motivated by fantasies of love or power generally
aligned with the fixed world of Romance. Though he consciously
functions as if his desire is directed outward to the embodiment
of a Romantic ideal (Rodolphe for Emma Bovary, Daisy for
Gatsby), others are only mirrors for the narcissist. Third, there
are important social implications in narcissistic behavior.
Caught in the stale world of routine, the narcissist compulsively
seeks ᴜo transcend his condition, and once he adapts a persona
he insures his alienation from society. Imitation forces him into
actions which inevitably lead to rejection because his views
threaten the values, traditions, and sometimes the very structures of the world he reluctantly inhabits.

When I began to write this book my intention was to include
as many works as possible that would illustrate the problem of
narcissism. My desire to fully document my argument, and to
forestall criticism by readers who might object that the canon is
either too limited or quirky, led to a list of writers much longer
than appears here. George Eliot and Proust are examples of the
many writers who might have been included—as well as contem-
poraries like Genet, Isherwood, Fowles, and Mailer. Although I
allude to other writers who provide suggestive analogies, my
focus is on Flaubert, Chopin, Conrad, Fitzgerald, Ford, Durrell,
Gide, Mann, and Hawkes. To some extent I have followed my

own interests, but my choices were made, in each case, from the belief that they would best illustrate the theme of narcissism from a Post-Romantic perspective while at the same time convey a wider, cultural response to the theme at specific historical junctures in European and American literature. Flaubert, for example, is central because he saw the problem of self-reflection afflicting the whole of the bourgeoisie in nineteenth-century France. Gide was chosen because *The Immoralist* expresses turn-of-the-century attitudes towards Nietzschean individuality which affected at least a generation of Europeans and Americans. The connections with German idealistic thought, especially that of Wagner and Nietzsche, made *Death in Venice* an essential choice. Similar considerations guided my inclusion of the others.

Each of the nine novels has been dealt with in depth in the conviction that only through extended analysis can the complexity of narcissism as a literary theme be clearly and adequately charted. My aim was to build up a model from chapter to chapter which would emerge in the conclusion in such a way as to not only illustrate the frame concepts, but also leave the reader with a gestalt, a sense of the theme which could then be further illustrated by other texts.

Now that I have outlined the substance of my book, and provided a rationale for the selections, I would like to offer a brief overview of its separate chapters. In chapter 1, I describe the central elements of narcissistic identity which enable me to make preliminary observations about the formation of self-images. Each of the subsequent chapters then treats a theoretical aspect of narcissism while providing a detailed reading of a given text.

Chapter 2 is devoted to Flaubert's analysis of the ways received ideas progressively erode Emma Bovary's sense of reality until all hope of self-knowledge is negated. Because this is the first interpretation I present of a narcissistic character, I consider in detail the twinned themes of homosexuality and auto-eroticism which Flaubert employs in order to reveal some of the more complex aspects of self-absorption. Variations of these themes appear in all of the novels, but they will be especially relevant later on to my discussions of Gide and Mann in Part II.

In the third chapter, the focus shifts from the inner world of Emma's consciousness to a consideration of how Romantic ideals reflect a culture's sense of itself. Chopin's Edna Pontellier has been justly called an American Bovary, but Chopin shapes the materials she adapted from Flaubert to political ends. Edna's susceptibility to the lures of Romanticism is identical to Emma's, but Chopin exposes in far more detail than Flaubert the devastating social consequences of a naive response to these fantasies. In the course of *The Awakening* she demonstrates how Edna is partly demystified once she realizes that her old notions serve only to oppress women by submerging them in traditional Creole values towards sex and marriage which deprive them of individual identity. Despite her awareness, Edna's fascination with her new self leads her into a spiritual quandary, for her independence leaves her without a context to live in, and death becomes the only alternative to a return to her former oppression.

The next four chapters on Conrad, Ford, Fitzgerald, and Durrell explore topics related to those raised in my analyses of Flaubert and Chopin. However, each of these novelists presents a discrete set of problems which broaden the range of my investigation. For example, in chapter 4, I consider how Conrad explores the ethical dimension of narcissism as he examines the tensions created between the demands of Jim's fantasies and the legitimate needs of society. At the same time, Conrad discloses the finite nature of the narcissist's vision in Stein's famous speech on the destructive element which reveals that survival in the dream of the self can only be temporary.

Although *The Good Soldier* takes us back to the world of chivalric romance by way of Edward's commitment to medieval ideals of behavior, Ford's thematic interests are not altogether different from Conrad's. He too calls attention to the social costs of self-absorption through his illustration of the suffering that results from Edward's forcing Leonora and Nancy to conform to his preconceived ideas about them. This manipulative aspect of narcissism will become more pronounced as we move from the Apollonian to the Dionysian mode of identity.

These problems take an interesting turn in chapter 6, where the chronic sentimentality of Fitzgerald's own world view reveals a confusion of life and art necessitating a lengthy discussion of the author's personal investment in Nick and Gatsby. My conclusions about *The Great Gatsby* are unorthodox, for I believe that Fitzgerald's novel is more seriously compromised by his inability to see beyond the allures of Romanticism than has previously been noticed.

Chapter 7 concludes Part I with an investigation of Durrell's *The Alexandria Quartet,* where we find a tentative solution to the problems that have blighted the protagonists of the previous novels. Durrell's four volumes slowly disclose how the deceptive worlds of mirrors, masks, and palimpsests (the apparatus of narcissism also apparent in Flaubert, Gide, Mann, and Hawkes) are transcended by Darley and Clea through sympathetic relation to each other and to the natural world.

In Part II, I take up the consequences of Dionysian self-concepts and world-views. Both Gide and Mann analyze the processes of self-destruction in Michel and Aschenbach who consciously accept decadence as a means to achieve a transcendent goal. Gide shows that reality filtered through a Nietzschean lens encourages self-indulgence to the point where Michel finds himself in imminent danger of becoming lost in the recesses of his own psyche. And Mann goes one step further: *Death in Venice* becomes a sustained meditation on the "romantic as morbid and antagonistic to life." In Aschenbach, perhaps more than in any of the other characters, death is the inevitable conclusion to narcissistic longing.

Chapter 10, devoted to Hawkes's *The Blood Oranges,* focuses on the extraordinarily imaginative constructions of Cyril, whose attempt to create a "terrestrial paradise" similar to the one Ford's Dowell longs for ends in death and isolation. *The Blood Oranges* brings together the Apollonian and Dionysian strands of narcissism and thus prepares the way for the conclusion, which takes us back to Nietzsche through an examination of the nihilistic implications of narcissistic consciousness.

The book ends not with easy answers or a neat schema, but with the suggestion that what we have been observing in these novels is really a double absence. By using Beckett's *Krapp's Last Tape* as a synecdoche of narcissistic desire, we see that the vacuity of the narcissist's quest, the impossibility of actualizing the fantasy self, corresponds to the absence of a life that can be lived in reality. In Beckett's play, Krapp has willfully reduced the experience of being human to experiencing the self in a darkened room. The solitary figure alone in that room forces himself upon us as a symbol of the malaise we have felt growing in our culture from the time of Nietzsche's revolutionary pronouncements about the self to the general cultural crisis which Christopher Lasch documents in *The Culture of Narcissism.*

L. T.

Acknowledgments

Beyond the immediate scholarly obligations acknowledged in the footnotes, I must single out four individuals who provided even more important stimuli. To Hugh Kenner, who has offered an example to follow and admire, I owe unrepayable debts. Ian Watt and Herbert Lindenberger taught me how to negotiate the laybrinth of critical theory. But my greatest debt is to Toni Clark, my wife, whose critical perceptions and support during the years the book was being written made it far better than it otherwise would have been.

I am grateful to the following publishers in the United States and England for permission to use copyrighted material:

E. P. Dutton, Inc., for permission to quote from *The Alexandria Quartet* by Lawrence Durrell, copyright 1961;

Faber and Faber Publishers, for non-exclusive world rights to quotations from *The Alexandria Quartet;*

W. W. Norton, Inc., for permission to quote from *The Awakening* by Kate Chopin, ed. by Margaret Culley, Norton Critical Edition, copyright 1976;

New Directions Publishing Corporation for permission to quote from *The Blood Oranges* by John Hawkes, copyright 1971 by John Hawkes;

Alfred A. Knopf, Inc., for permission to quote from "Death in Venice" by Thomas Mann in *Stories of Three Decades*, trans. by H. T. Lowe-Porter, 1936;

Alfred A. Knopf, Inc., for permission to quote from *The Good Soldier* by Ford Madox Ford, copyright 1955;

Janice Biala for nonexclusive world rights to quotations from *The Good Soldier;*

Charles Scribner's Sons for permission to quote from *The Great Gatsby* by F. Scott Fitzgerald, copyright 1925 Charles Scribner's Sons, copyright renewed 1953;

Harold Ober Associates, Inc., for non-exclusive world rights to quotations from *The Great Gatsby* by F. Scott Fitzgerald;

The Bodley Head for permission to quote from *The Great Gatsby* by F. Scott Fitzgerald;

Alfred A. Knopf, Inc., for permission to quote from *The Immoralist* by André Gide, trans. by Richard Howard, copyright 1970;

Macmillan Publishing Company for non-exclusive world rights to quotations from *The Immoralist* by André Gide;

The Estate of Joseph Conrad for permission to quote from *Lord Jim;*

W. W. Norton, Inc., for permission to quote from *Lord Jim* by Joseph Conrad, ed. by Thomas Moser, Norton Critical Edition, 1968;

W. W. Norton, Inc., for permission to quote from *Madame Bovary* by Gustave Flaubert, translated by Paul de Man, Norton Critical Edition, copyright 1965;

Indiana University Press for permission to quote from Ovid's *Metamorphoses* trans. by Rolfe Humphries, copyright 1957.

I am also grateful to the following journals for permission to reprint articles that originally appeared in their pages:

American Literature, for permission to reprint "*The Awakening:* A Political Romance," *American Literature* 52 (May 1980), 2:50–67, copyright 1980, by Duke University Press (Durham NC);

Deus Loci, for permission to reprint "Narcissism and Selflessness in *The Alexandria Quartet,*" *Deus Loci,* 1:4 (June 1978), 3–21, copyright 1978;

PMLA for "'The Fairest of Them All': Modes of Vision in *Madame Bovary,*" 93 (1978), pp. 982–92, reprinted by permission of the Modern Language Association of America.

Unbodied Hope

Part I
The Theology of Self

1
Narcissistic Consciousness

Then we beginne, & lett none hope to hisse us,
The play wee play is Ovid's own Narcissus.
—*Narcissus: A Twelfe Night Merriment*

Ovid's Narcissus, who "fell in love/ With that unbodied hope, and found a substance/ In what was only shadow", is embedded in the western imagination, his name synonymous with psychic retreat into the labyrinth of willed isolation where shadow is mistaken for substance and where the self flickers, like a shadow in Plato's cave, on the imagination's retina. Few myths exert such a strong hold on the mind; fewer still have been powerful enough to capture the attention of poets, novelists, philosophers, and psychoanalysts. But there is no mystery in this appeal. Of all the myths that found their way into the Greek and Roman mind, none more perfectly symbolizes the core of human identity, the self. What has been made of Narcissus as a symbol of the self from classical to modern times offers a history of what mankind has felt itself to be.

Before his appearance in *The Metamorphoses*, Narcissus had turned up, as far as we know, in minor writers and mythological abstracts. But it remained for Ovid to fully realize Narcissus; of all the early writers drawn to the myth, Ovid is the only one who describes his conception, birth, death, funeral and shadowy afterlife, and it is Ovid's version which has been the source for subsequent writers.[1] For Ovid and those who wrote before him, Narcissus exemplified the illusory nature of this world's pleasures. Later, as Paul Zweig has ably shown in *The Heresy of Self-Love*, Narcissus's significance became more closely associated with the promises and delusions of individual identity. Medieval iconographers rendered his obsession as a type of vanity, while the troubadours of the courts of love spiritualized his self-indulgence so that he embodied the essense of "Daun Cupido."[2] After Provence, self-love eventually achieved "philosophical prestige" in the writings of Montaigne, Spinoza, and Rousseau. For the social philosophers of the eighteenth and nineteenth centuries, Narcissus was a heroic figure whose obsession defied what they believed to be the alienating thrust of increasingly complex societies. And during the Romantic period philsophers and poets alike could see some of their most central concerns inscribed in the inward-turning gaze of Ovid's youth. Zweig, then, is undoubtedly right when he argues that "the heresy of self-love . . . has become a part of our cultural traditions, always condemned and yet central to our most familiar values" (p. v).

It will be apparent shortly that Zweig's interests in the consequences of narcissism are far from my own, but his book is extremely valuable for the historical context it provides. In the next paragraph I want to briefly summarize his conclusions regarding Narcissus's reception in western culture in order to dramatize a major shift which occurred in the latter part of the nineteenth century.

As Zweig sees it, within the cultural traditions of the west from the second to the nineteenth century the subversive nature of individualism had an heroic cast. Whether they were poets, philosophers, or religious thinkers, those who accepted the "ordeal of solitary self-inspection" were aware that their goals of "spiritual perfection" receded before them, yet they continued to explore in the hope of eventually discovering the "true self" which would allow them to transpose their lives into "the permanence of that image" (p. 182). Their common task was to recover their own displaced identities, and this collective feeling was neatly summarized by Kierkegaard when he wrote that "My present life is like a deformed counterfeit of an original edition of my true self" (p. 186). While the ways to the true self were various, the goal was identical: "the Great Work was the regeneration of the ego" (p. 219), whose cultivation would eventually free it from its prison from which it could then journey back to the world. This strikingly positive view of the virtues of the inward journey led to the heart of the Romantic period where Narcissus became a poet-hero who attempted to free the true self in order to discover his individuality, which Kierkegaard called "the paradoxical vessel of God on earth" (p. 202). Rousseau provides an interesting and more detailed description of this demi-god in his comment about the experience of isolation: "What do we enjoy at such a moment? Nothing outside us, nothing if not ourselves and our existence; as long as this feeling continues, we are self-sufficient, like God" (p. 164). Although the self and not mankind occupied the center of the early nineteenth-century world which was "shaped by the pleasures and the character of a single imagination," Zweig optimistically sees the microcosm of the true self containing the macrocosm of society (p. 165). By emphasizing the self love which affirms the reality of the inner self, and which at the same time discovers the self's relation to the macrocosm, narcissism, as Zweig defines it, foregrounds a central tenet of Romantic thought. And this is where Zweig's investigation ends, in the heart of Romanticism, just as it had begun to darken in the fertile thought of Baudelaire.

In beginning my study on the far side of Romanticism, in the midst of the intellectual ferment generated during the *fin-de-siècle* by Nietzsche's revolutionary ideals, my approach to narcissism will necessarily differ considerably from Zweig's. I say necessarily because my analysis is not offered as a counter argument to Zweig's or a difference of opinion as to how we should valuate narcissism, but because the nature of self-inspection changed dramatically from the Romantic to the Post-Romantic period dominated by Nietzsche. To account adequately for this change from the period Zweig investigates requires both a new terminology and a new conceptual system. It is my position that Nietzsche's attitudes towards the self and his central metaphors in *The Birth of Tragedy* provide a locus for a considerably different view of narcissism. Simply put, Nietzsche's impact on the problems of introspection and the nature of the self from the late nineteenth century to the present *altered both the substance of narcissism and its ideals* as they are presented in Post-Romantic, Modern and Post-Modern fictions.

From about the time of the death of Baudelaire in 1867 to the 1890s, a series of revolutionary changes dominated the European intellectual scene. In literature, art, philosophy, and the biological sciences, the old-guard was being overthrown by new spokesmen and new movements whose common goals were to replace inadequate received ideas. Amidst the search for a new relevance in all fields of thought and action, innumerable declarations, manifestos, and denunciations filled the air. The last quarter of the nineteenth century was thus ripe for the radical ideals of Nietzsche, whose place in the history of the readjustment of artistic and philosophical values can be precisely dated. Before May 1888 Nietzsche was relatively unknown, but his obscurity was forever banished when his work became the focus of a series of lectures presented by the Danish critic Georg Brandes. Almost immediately, the impact of the Brandes lectures spread through Scandinavian and German thinkers to Europe at large, and it is interesting that Nietzsche himself foresaw the effect of his ideas in letters written to Strindberg and Brandes in late 1888. In November, for example, he described the imminent spread of his "revaluation of all values," and he was so convinced of their importance that he could make this prediction: "I swear that in two years time the whole world will be in convulsions, I am sheer destiny." A month later he told Strindberg that he was strong enough "to cleave the history of mankind in two." And he was right, at least for the time being. As the new spokesman for the *avant garde,* his repudiations of traditional morality, his aristocratic radicalism, and his disdain for the century's received ideas evoked a sympathetic response from the intellectuals of the *fin-de-siècle* and the Great War which decisively influenced early Modernism.[3]

The Birth of Tragedy carried the weight of this influence, for it was at once a counter-doctrine, a philosophy of life, a new myth and a new ritual talismanic of a time's innermost desires. Through Dionysus, as Franz Kuna points out, Nietzsche "fed the sense of confrontation with anarchistic forces; beneath the surface of modern life, dominated by knowledge and science, he discerned vital energies which were wild, primitive and completely merciless. At the appropriate hour, man, he proposed, would raise himself to titanic proportions and conquer his civilization; the vital forces will be released in revenge, and produce a new barbarism."[4] The changes which Nietzsche helped to force in the traditional ways man perceived himself and his relation to society were enormous, and many of them lie beyond the scope of this book's argument. But the major area of significance for literature lay in the way Nietzsche responded to his Romantic heritage. In *The Birth of Tragedy* Nietzsche took over the Romantic exaltation of art and the imagination; he also adapted the Romantic myth of the self. But it would be a mistake to see in this appropriation of ideals a continuation of Romantic principles. As Walter Kaufman reminds us, "the 'romantic' was precisely what he opposed."[5] *The Birth of Tragedy* works a profound change on the positivist Romantic beliefs in self-expression and self-realization by turning them on their head; in the new agenda of Apollo and Dionysus, knowledge of the self became an end in itself.

We can begin to approach the philosophical substance of Nietzsche's "revaluation of all values" by turning to Martin Heidegger's view of Nietzsche as a metaphysician, the last in a long line beginning with Plato.[6] Even a cursory reading of Nietzsche shows that his thought was bound up with dualisms that have plagued philosophy from Plato to Kant, and that previous distinctions about man's dual nature made from Platonic, Christian, and Kantian perspectives had in common for him a nostalgic desire for the "other-worldly." Nietzsche's writings are not intended to justify various moral ideals of the past; they are intended to show forth a unifying principle underlying past assumptions which he sees as false. As far as morality is concerned, Nietzsche argues that the desire for a unifying principle to guide man's actions springs not from some abstract respect for man, but that the demand or hope in morality embodies what might be called desperation on the part of those who are spiritually weak and need protection from themselves and from those who are stronger. From his point of view all values, especially those with a moral tinge, are aimed at maximizing the individual's personal power. To deny this "will to power" is only a deception on the part of the weak, maintained against all odds in an attempt to shore up their weakness at some cost to those who are stronger. That Nietzsche addressed serious ontological crises in his revaluation of the past, and in doing so provided the modern age with a new model of the independent man living in and for himself, freed of the illusions of the past, is indisputable. But inscribed in the center of the new man's nature are precisely those characteristics of self-love which another new man, Freud, called narcissistic. Freud distinguished between primary, or neurotic narcissism, and secondary, or healthy self-love. Wherever we feel the influence of Nietzsche's thought in modern literature, we should be altered to the foregrounding of the destructive myth of the self emanating from primary narcissism which is manifested in the problematics of the fictional characters' relationships to reality.

Beginning with Nietzche, Narcissus loses the ascetic features Zweig perceives in earlier writing, appearing instead as a grinning and sometimes diabolical Greek mask whose dual faces of

Apollo and Dionysus are completely divorced from the more innocent Narcissus of earlier times. To put it another way, if the figure of Narcissus in Pre-Romantic and Romantic literature was of the poet-hero, that of the Post-Romantic era is analogous to Yeats's "rough beast." In the earlier canon, Narcissus represents the true self aligned with the spirit of man and God, and the condemned nature of his self-inspection, which Zweig calls subversive individualism, could eventually transcend the individual and promote his reintegration with society. With Nietzsche, Narcissus is intent not on restructing the old order, but on its destruction in acts which reveal the terrible power of the isolated ego. The hero-poet has become an anarchist whose self-realization demands apocalypse. In this new Narcissus it is easy to see how the melioristic inner search of the Romantics was abandoned at the site of Zweig's conclusion in the mid-nineteenth century.

This shift in the nature of narcissism finds support in Malcolm Bradbury's well-known essay on modernism where he argues that Nietzsche's work does indeed grown out of the Romantic period, but that it should be viewed as a "realignment of thought."[7] As I see it, *The Birth of Tragedy* reifies this realignment, for in this work the moral thrust of Romantic thought is replaced by nihilism which embodies what Trilling calls "a bitter line of hostility to civilization . . . a disenchantment with culture itself."[8] It presents life and the future as dark, blind, and chaotic, a "destructive stream of passion tending to sweep away everything in its path, including man's rational cosmologies and the fossilized structure of civilization itself."[9] Nietzsche justifies such destruction under the sign of the Self metaphorically projected into the figure of Dionysus, and it is in the metaphor that we find further crucial relevance to Nietzsche's place in the history of the new Narcissus. By creating Dionysus as a type of the new man, Nietzsche is at the same time admitting that the ego is no longer sufficient in and for itself as it was, say, for the Romantics; Nietzsche's ego achieves its destructive powers by incorporating an ideal Other, an *imagined* self. In the guise of Dionysus we see the new Narcissus as he appears in each of the novels analyzed in this book. Like Dionysus, Narcissus is an artist, a self-creator. Leaving aside for the time being the question of self-actualization, one sees that to create the self only *for* the self leads directly to the most disturbing feature of the novels I have chosen, for as this Nietzschean process is worked out in a variety of fictions we confront a virtual absence created by self-desire. We will see that what was once an inward, honest search for the configurations of the self becomes, in the modern novel, and following Nietzsche's example, a desire to find the self in an ideal Other who represents for the characters, as Dionysus does for Nietzsche, the ideal self.

In the remaining pages of this chapter I want to show how Nietzsche's insistence on the virtues of an unbounded will illuminates the conceptions of self that interested a wide variety of modern novelists beginning with Flaubert, who anticipated the effects of Nietzschean self-love. I will have a good deal to say about how Nietzsche's contempt for traditional values is repeated by narcissistic characters whose spiritual predicament is symbolized by the desert in *The Immoralist* in which Gide's Michel finds himself physically and psychically stalled. To facilitate my discussions of these and other aspects of the novels, I have freely adapted Nietzsche's key concepts of Apollonian and Dionysian modes of consciousness as a convenient means of discriminating between the two forms of narcissism that interest me. There is also another, equally important connection between Nietzsche's thought and that of the novelists I have chosen; Emma Bovary, Edna Pontellier, Michel and the others clearly belong with Nietzsche's "few," those he calls in *The Genealogy of Morals* "opposite men," "free thinkers," "attempters," "wanderers," "immoralists." Like Nietzsche and his privileged group, they too opt for an aristocratic morality which is opposed to the values of the "herd." But this anticipates the argument that follows. By attending to the opening sections of *The Birth of Tragedy,* we can begin to approach those modes of consciousness that are my principal concerns. Once the Apollonian and Dionysian attitudes towards the self are defined and illustrated by examples from *Ulysses* and *Under the Volcano,* I can then offer a theoretical model of narcissism which will be applied in the following chapters.

In *The Birth of Tragedy* Nietzsche sees Apollo as the god of esthetic form and ethical balance whose Olympian world is associated with light, stability, and idealistic dreams. Dionysus responds to a different order of values associated with the lower, chthonic world, wild nature, darkness, excess. Although the two modes are discrete, a constant sympathetic relationship obtains between visionary Apollo and rhapsodic Dionysus so that the restraint and nobility of Apollo is counterpointed by the oblivion of Dionysus, and Apollo's illusory belief in transcendence is matched by Dionysus's ecstatic death.[10] "To reach a closer understanding of both these tendencies," writes Nietzsche, "let us begin by viewing them as separate art realms of dream and intoxication, two physiological phenomena standing toward one another in much the same relationship as the Apollonian and Dionysian."[11] As the "god of light," Apollo "reigns . . . over the fair illusion of our inner world of fantasy." He is thus the god of illusion which is the unconscious creation of dream and the conscious creation of art. On the other hand, the beauty of illusion is contrasted to "Dionysiac rapture, whose closest analogy is furnished by physical intoxication,"[12] and whose ultimate expression can be found in the celebrations of the Dionysiac barbarians whose "central concern . . . was . . . a complete sexual promiscuity overriding any form of established tribal law."[13]

Now when Nietzsche goes on to say that "whenever we encounter 'naiveté' in art, we are face to face with the ripest fruit of Apollonian culture—which must always triumph first over titans, kill monsters, and overcome the somber contemplation of actuality, the intense susceptibility of suffering, by means of illusions strenuously and zestfully entertained,"[14] he provides a working definition of those forces driving the naive Romantics I discuss in Part I. Moreover, his point that "the naive work of art . . . is merely the illusion of an illusion" describes the central problem of the narcissist who defines himself in terms of models drawn from his reading or from received ideas enshrined in cultural codes. Flaubert, Chopin, Conrad, Ford, Fitzgerald, and Durrell create complex ironic responses to narcissism by exploring the consequences of these Apollonian traits as their characters strive idealistically towards a vision of the self that they believe is uniquely individual and ethical. In addition, the imaginative tasks they set for themselves coincide with Nietzsche's view of the naive belief underlying Apollonian culture which holds that illusion can "overcome the somber contemplation of actuality." The Apollonian narcissist is, before everything else, an artist dedicated to transforming himself and anything in his environment that can contribute to his personal fiction.

In an essay on Nietzsche aptly titled "Man as His Own Creator," Karl Jaspers observes that "creation, which Nietzsche substitutes for existential freedom as the sole immanent actualization of his kind of freedom, ends within itself or is lost, since it has only itself to depend on."[15] But Nietzsche attempts to deny the void created through solipsism by deifying creativity, making it an absolute: "[T]he creative good," he says, "is *the highest good of all*." It is so because in art Nietzsche sees a stark symbol of the will to power. Creating forms out of nothingness is analogous to the Nietzschean quest embodied in becoming a new man free of traditional ethical restraints, but the nature of his self-interest discloses itself when he admits that "all great love still wishes to create—the object of its love!"[16] This link between creativity and narcissism can be traced in the pervasive motif of the artist informing all the novels I discuss. Consider, for example, *Lord Jim*. As soon as we begin to feel confident that Jim's character has emerged from the mists surrounding him, Conrad obscures the outlines of his hero: "he was a finished artist," Marlow asserts, "a gifted poor devil with the faculty of swift and forestalling vision." Marlow's comment refers specifically to Jim's disastrous imaginative response to the *Patna*'s accident, but it also illuminates general problems of imagination and art. Let me risk the obvious by pointing out that art is the shared vocation of Aschenbach, Darley, and Clea, that Michel is a revisionist historian, Dowell a gifted diarist, Emma, Edna, Jim, and Gatsby visionaries, and Cyril an oral poet. In each case (and I do not think it matters whether their art is externalized or remains locked up in their imaginations) they approach raw experience with the aim of transforming it until it achieves a correspondence with an inner vision which, ironically, entirely misses reality. In other words, they are finished artists of naive Romance, creating alternative fictional worlds for themselves totally devoid of any sign of fortuity. Convinced that the reality which denies them actualization can be creatively re-structured, they see their gift from a dual perspective; while it allows them to imaginatively harrow hell, it always leads to disaster.

This process is anything but simple, as we can see by placing it within a larger context—the modern, displaced version of the myth of Narcissus. In Ovid "the loved becomes the lover,/ The seeker sought, the kindler burns." Here, the character longs for an image of another which he believes mirrors his own. René Girard addresses a similar idea when he argues that Don Quixote and Emma Bovary passively respond to the models of their own desire: "The disciple pursues objects which are determined for him, or at least seem to be determined for him, by the model. . . . From the moment the mediator's influence is felt, the sense of reality is lost and judgement paralyzed."[17] In the novels I examine the situation involves more deceit than Girard notices. While his view must be seriously considered, I would argue that what is really at issue here is a reversal of the process he describes: the character's attraction to his own image in the model sets up something like an imaginative magnetic field in which the model is drawn into the character's consciousness. This attraction can be expressed in a spatial paradigm. Imagine one of our characters on the extreme left-hand side of a rectangle—Emma lounging in her drawing-room, say, or Jim walking along the river in Patusan. On the right-hand side imagine the model—one of Emma's legion of adulteresses, or someone like the French lieutenant. The "finished artist" sees the model on the far side, and through an act of mind closes the distance separating them. At this moment, they *think* that they become exactly "like" the model, having shed their old identity through a kind of psychic molting (of this tendency to think metaphorically, more later). Once they possess the model, they live out their conceptions of its qualities. This is where the "sense of reality is lost" because the characters now exist solely within a matrix of language which has only a referential relation to reality; that is, *metaphor* replaces concrete *experience* as the characters' chief goal. Thinking of themselves in the language of Romance, in which signifiers refer only to other signifiers within the realm of received ideas, their common desire is to bind their lives to that series of images and codes they bless with the status of originality. In this way, the Apollonian characters enter into their conception of the real only after they have enclosed their lives in quotation marks.

What is involved here is very much like the exchange that takes place in metaphorical substitution, and two examples can be culled from the early sections of *Madame Bovary* and *Lord Jim*. As an adolescent at the convent, Emma is exposed to sentimental literature which presents women in absurdly stylized attitudes. After identifying herself with this generic type (a mix of stock Romantic images and gossip about society women lauded in the pages of her slick magazines), the only addition to Emma's self-image comes when she imagines herself the equal of famous adulteresses she has read about. In the case of Conrad's Jim the process is even simpler. We only have to go as far into the novel as the first few pages to see Jim's fateful encounter with "light literature." Already susceptible to heroics, once Jim has mentally experienced the adventures of Mr. Midshipman Easy and those of other characters of the type, his self-image is fixed and strong enough to survive even the humiliation of his lack of nerve after the *Patna*'s accident. Similar examples could be presented from the other novels, but these are sufficient to generalize from. What they suggest is that the Apollonian novel reveals its sources in residues of received ideas. These functions are clearly illustrated in the "Nausicaa" episode of *Ulysses,* which I present here (limiting it to the first half devoted to Gerty Mac-Dowell) as a more detailed demonstration of how the Apollonian consciousness shapes its responses to the external world. But before examining the fiction Gerty constructs for herself and Bloom, I want to call attention to two problems.

Because she is an assemblage of snippets from fiction, poetry, and popular codes, Gerty presents a difficulty which requires ideas about character which will be much different from those we confidently bring to a reading of, say, Dostoevski, James, or Faulkner. In fact, it can be argued that Gerty does not have an individual character, the whole tissue of her conscious and unconscious life consisting of identifications with received ideas.[18] Thus, Joyce's irony (and that of the other novelists except Fitzgerald) forces the reader into a primary relationship with an absence since Gerty disappears into what she has read, her human features obliterated by her narrative role.

The second problem is an extension of the first. Gerty responds to nothing as it is; identities of things in the world and of other human beings are changed in her consciousness (re-created) until they correspond with familiar classifications. For example, in "Nausicaa" Bloom is altogether another character than he is in the previous chapters, becoming himself only after Gerty limps off the scene and the narrative enters his consciousness once again. In the Apollonian novel, the protagonists are ghosts of other literary characters, while those with whom they have the most intimate contact are stripped of their independent existence to fulfill the exigencies of the Romantic plot generated by the protagonist. In this way the narcissist's quest for fulfillment is, as Todorov points out, really a quest for an absence, for what is desired cannot be realized outside the imagination.[19] The ambiguities which arise when we consider narcissistic identity and objects of desire will be explored in the following chapters and returned to in the Conclusion where I

suggest further implications from perspectives opened by recent
critical theory. But now I want to show how Joyce deals with
these materials in "Nausicaa."

The sensation of certain predetermined emotions is Gerty's
nirvana (or rather being aware of herself in the midst of such
experience), and we sense her excitement as she begins to respond to Bloom who is watching her from the promenade: "Till
then they had only exchanged glances of the most casual but
now under the brim of her new hat she ventured a look at him
and the face that met her gaze there in the twilight, wan and
strangely drawn, seemed to her the saddest she had ever seen."[20]
Bloom is already being metamorphosed as this Dublin Circe
fixes him in the language of romantic cliché: "His eyes burned
into her [and] she could see at once by his dark eyes and his pale
intellectual face that he was a foreigner, the image of the photo
she had of Martin Harvey, the *matinée* idol" (p. 357). Mimesis
such as this is one of the most common gestures available to the
Apollonian. Chopin's Edna Pontellier comes to mind immediately as an example, for she performs the same transformation on Robert Lebrun in relation to her picture of a great
tragedian. And in a slightly more complex way, the motif is
repeated when Justine attempts to commune with herself
through the picture she paints of Clea.

These two sentences graph Gerty's creative response to reality by highlighting not only her habits of thought, but also the
means by which predetermined attributes are attached to the
object of the narcissist's desire. What takes place here corresponds to Henry James's reflection in the Preface to *The Portrait
of a Lady* on the genesis of Turgenev's fictional characters: "It
began for him almost always with the vision of some person or
persons, who hovered before him, soliciting him, as the active or
passive figure, interesting him and appealing to him just as they
were and by what they were. He saw them, in that fashion, as
disponibles. . . ."[21] That is what happens to Bloom as Gerty sizes
him up; he is there *en disponibilité,* unattached, to be fitted into
the narrative generated by Gerty once she has sorted through
her classifications. In fact, such a process has already begun,
and as it continues Bloom is brought rapidly closer to the fictions
Gerty has stored in her mind. But first his nose must be fitted
into the developing picture of the strange foreigner who wanders
through the pages of popular Romantic fiction. Unfortunately,
Gerty is not quite sure whether it is "aquiline" or "slightly

retroussé." No matter; she continues, knowing that she can revise later. What is most important to her now is getting the plot right: "He was in deep mourning, she could see that, and the story of a haunting sorrow was written on his face" (p. 357). With her theme thus established, Gerty places Bloom firmly in the Ur-plot of popular Romance in language appropriately attuned to the most outrageous levels of *kitsch*. Reggy Wylie fades out of her memory, for "Here was that of which she had so often dreamed" (p. 358). Convinced that Bloom "was like no one else," the "girlwoman's" heart goes out to her "dreamhusband." Suffering, sin, even allegiance to protestantism—none matters for this "womanly woman" who could "make him forget the memory of the past." At which point Gerty reaches her stylistic apogee and threatens to destroy language altogether: "Then mayhap he would embrace her gently, like a real man, crushing her soft body to him and love her, his ownest girlie, for herself alone."

But an apogee of another sort animates the conclusion of Gerty's section of "Nausicaa." Bloom's eyes, widening for reasons other than those Gerty imagines, were "drinking in her every contour, literally worshipping at her shrine" (p. 361). Such adulation Gerty accepts as her due: "It is for you, Gertrude MacDowell, and you know it" (p. 362). Having reached the deep structure of her own fiction, and knowing the direction of its plot, Gerty pauses to improve incidental details: "How moving the scene there in the gathering twilight, the last glimpse of Erin, the touching chime of those evening bells and at the same time a bat flew forth from the ivied belfry through the dusk, hither, thither, with a tiny lost cry" (p. 363). Then more revisions occur to her. Maybe Bloom is married, or a widowed nobleman, or mourning an "old flame" from the "days beyond recall" (p. 364). Whatever the case, it is Gerty MacDowell who now elicits "whitehot passion" from him as she exposes her bloomers ("there was no one to see only him"). As the fireworks fill the sky above Erin at the moment her "nainsook knickers, the fabric that caresses the skin" (p. 366) peep out of the darkness, Gerty's erotic fantasy goes the way of Bloom's and the coda draws together all that she has created: "Their souls met in a last lingering glance and the eyes that reached her heart, full of a strange shining, hung enraptured on her sweet flowerlike face. She half smiled at him wanly, a sweet forgiving smile, a smile that verged on tears, and then they parted" (p. 367).

Gerty's fiction generated by Leopold Bloom, advertising canvasser *en disponibilité,* has precise analogues not only to the opera scene in *Madame Bovary* (with Bloom playing the part of Lagardy to Gerty's Emma), but also to Edna Pontellier's fantasy devoted to the trip into the Baratarian Isles with Robert Lebrun, the night at Nauheim when Edward Ashburnham "talks" to Nancy Rufford in the dark during the orchestra recital, Gatsby's stroll with Daisy along the mythical sidewalk, and Darley's constructions regarding Justine. In *Clea* Darley neatly sums up the process: "I saw now that my own Justine had indeed been an illusionist's creation, raised upon the faulty armature of misinterpreted words, actions, gestures."[22] And so, in addition to its wonderful parody of romantic *kitsch,* "Nausicaa" illustrates the single most important aspect of narcissistic consciousness; although the characters believe they are realistically assessing themselves and the objects of their desires, these assessments are founded on that most unreliable source, naive Romanticism. The paradox that thus emerges of an absence speaking to an absence foregrounds a serious philosophical problem that binds together all the novels focused on the Apollonian quest.

Dionysian consciousness is formed more ambiguously. Although Michel, Aschenbach, and Cyril may be aided in their quests by a model, the Dionysian's identity depends more on a gradual accretion of images and ideas than did the Apollonians'. For example, Michel takes the young barbarian king Athalaric as an ideal, Aschenbach is drawn to the figure of Dionysus, Cyril to a satyr, but the overriding thrust of their imaginative experience is always towards an ambience, some atmosphere of power or potency associated with, but not limited to, such models. Both types of narcissism shut the characters off from anything beyond their own sensations, but the Dionysian dreams of omnipotence experienced through a new sensation of being, which is considerably different from the Apollonian's desire for fulfillment of the self within the plot of heroic love or heroic action. And it is possible to make finer distinctions. Whereas the Apollonian is engaged in a static enterprise (the generic model does not change shape), the Dionysian's is dynamic, capable of changing to incorporate new materials that come into his field of view. This difference between an aura and a fixed idea suggests that the Dionysian's desire to break with the past is far more Nietzschean that his Apollonian counterpart's, but the result is the same. In *The Immoralist, Death in Venice,* and *The Blood*

Oranges the Nietzschean superman becomes lost within himself and therefore blighted in his ability to connect with anything outside his own will. This destructiveness is brilliantly illuminated in *Under the Volcano,* where Malcom Lowry's Consul can be taken as a guide to the Dionysian's psychic underworld.

Geoffrey Firmin is a poet, scholar, war hero, and alcoholic whose fascination with the occult has led him to see himself variously as a magus, an adept in the hermeneutic lore of the Cabbala, and as a black magician. He rationalizes his ruined life by thinking that his magical powers have been lost through alcoholism, but Lowry shows us that at the deepest levels of consciousness the Consul is aware that his anguish is founded on an inability to love.[23] Yet it is the Consul's guilt that distinguishes him from Michel, Aschenbach, and Cyril by keeping him within the stream of humanity even as that guilt forces him to continue drinking. As with the characters of Gide, Mann, and Hawkes, his destruction is self-imposed, but in his case we see a decent man unable to overcome what he calls "this dreadful tyranny of self," which nullifies his ability to exist in relation to others. In *Under the Volcano,* only slightly less than in *The Immoralist, Death in Venice,* and *The Blood Oranges,* Nietzsche's will to power is defeated, as Jaspers says, "within itself."

What drives the Dionysian narcissist comes up from below, from the darkest, normally most inaccessible areas of the psyche, so that the Consul's fascination with what is under the volcano may thus be seen as representative of the chthonic forces affecting Michel, Aschenbach, and Cyril.[24] *Under the Volcano* is dominated by the barranca in Quauhnahuac, the old silver and iron mines beneath the town, and constant references to the abyss.[25] In addition, chthonic forces are felt in the constant allusions to the sea, which isolates the action in Lowry's novel just as it does in the others I discuss in Part II. There are also gardens fallen into ruin which become types of the encompassing forest, reminiscent of Dante's "selva oscura," a sign of the characters' blindness and site of the death of the Consul and his wife, Yvonne. As Douglas Day puts it, the chthonic imagery is "archetypally demonic in nature: that is, it employs the traditional affirmative apocalyptic images of the Mount of Perfection, the fertile valley, the cleansing stream or fountain, and the blossoming garden, but employs them in an inverted, ironic form. . . . It is of a world turned upside down that Lowry writes."[26] And I would add that he writes especially of this world as it is manifested in the cantinas where the Consul drinks. In these symbolic hell-mouths Lowry explores the Nietzschean void where the concomitants of the will to power are seen as the solitude of self-consciousness, spiritual homelessness, nihilism.

In the Consul we find a man whose inability to love has made unity abhorrent to him and who resolutely defies anyone who would help. Even during those few lucid moments when a kind of sobriety clarifies the once fine mind now disintegrated by mescal, the Consul's remorseful thoughts about his estranged wife are silenced by his conviction of his irremediable separateness. All of this is prefigured in the novel's epigraphs. If man desires "deliverance," if he "unceasingly strives upward," he can be saved; if not, his effective will subsumed by accidia, he slides helplessly towards damnation. At the end of *The Immoralist* Michel's spiritual paralysis exemplifies just this blighted will. Aschenbach passively waits for his own death at the conclusion of *Death in Venice,* and Cyril is left alone in his crumbling villa, fantasizing that a new woman may come along to revive the ambience of his sensual dream. In each case, the will to power leaves the characters stranded within their own psyches, each having, in effect, worn out the self in an attempt to experience it in Nietzschean terms.

Lowry has written that "the mood and tone of [*Under the Volcano*] as well as the slow, tragic rhythm of Mexico itself"[27] revolve around themes of silence and isolation first announced by the Consul's friend, Dr. Vigil: "Did you never go to church for the bereaved here . . . where is the Virgin for those who have nobody with?"[28] Vigil's question shifts the allusive context of the scene from Dante to the culture of Mexico itself, for the patron saint evoked in his broken syntax is the Virgin of Guadalupe whom Lowry removes from the church to the cantina Bella Vista behind whose swinging doors the Consul sees "all mystery, all hope, all disappointment . . . all disaster," and an "old woman, who was sitting in the shade at the bar's one table."[29] Thus the state of the Consul's soul is expressed in the atmosphere of the cantina presided over by the old woman whose presence offers him communion with others who have chosen the inner world. The solitude which the Consul embraces here is similar to that of the Mexican whom Octavio Paz speaks of eloquently when he says "he has forgotten the word that ties him to all those forces through which life manifests itself."[30] The novel's refrain, "No se puede vivir sin amar," one cannot live without loving, gives the word both the Mexican and the Consul have forgotten, and this condition, which both Lowry and Paz saw clearly, reverberates ironically with the concepts that inhere in Nietzsche's "outsider."

The plot of *Under the Volcano* leads inexorably to the cantina called the Farolito. There, the terrain of the novel has narrowed to an "inner room" in which "a voice softly spoke to him: '¿Quiere Maria?'" At this point, the cantina is metamorphosed into a dingy backroom bordello:

> At first he saw only the shapely legs of the girl who was leading him, now by the constricted power of aching flesh alone, of pathetic trembling yet brutal lust, through the little glass-paned rooms, that grew smaller and smaller, darker and darker, until by the mingitorio, the "senores," out of whose evil-smelling gloom broke a sinister chuckle, there was merely a lightless annex no larger than a cupboard in which two men whose faces he couldn't see either were sitting, drinking or plotting.[31]

There is no doubt, as Day makes clear, that on one level of meaning the Farolito is a type of the mythic labyrinth, but the Consul is not so much confronted by a minotaur as he is by an image of man's solitude that mirrors his own. And shortly after this dimly perceived epiphany the "final frontier of consciousness" is passed over when the Consul is shot by the Chief of Rostrums and his body tossed into the barranca.

If the "dreadful tyranny of self" makes the Consul sound like a victim, we should not forget that he encourages such a view, and we misread Lowry if we see the Consul in total despair over his condition. Elsewhere in *Under the Volcano* he proclaims vindictively, "I love hell," and virtually every gesture he makes is calculated to keep him there. Although he is the most self-aware character I discuss, the Consul vividly illustrates a shared flaw. Ralph Harper, in his study of nineteenth-century nihilism, illuminates this common ground when he remarks that "[Nietzsche exemplifies] a certain type of man who may want love and yet be unable to give or accept it. What they want is recognition of themselves, and it is little wonder that their frustration should conclude in estrangement."[32] Harper's observation remembers that the pretense of love provides the narcissist with a protective covering, or justification, for self-indulgence.

In each novel we find that the conditions the protagonists impose on their love are impossible for others to live up to. Daisy's remark to Gatsby, "You want too much!", offers a neat illustration which can be side-lighted by Freud's observation that the needs of the narcissist do not "lie in the direction of loving, but of being loved."[33] Freud would call this a problem of projection; Jaspers would say that it illustrates the sterility of the will to power. Either way, nihilism becomes a function of narcissism since there is no meaning outside the character's consciousness.

The foregoing comments lead to a further equation. Romance can be seen as the literary equivalent of narcissism in that it denies fortuity and foregrounds idealism. In *Middlemarch,* George Eliot refines this notion when she observes that "we are all of us born in moral stupidity, taking the world as an udder to feed our supreme selves."[34] Except for Fitzgerald, who believed in the supreme self, the novelists present realistic critiques of "moral stupidity" by making us aware of the irresolvable claims of Romance through a double narrative perspective. While they develop realistic portraits of their characters within complex social settings, the characters themselves are in quite another world, that of Romance. These two perspectives are in a constant abrasive dialectical relationship to each other. On the one hand, the novelists ironically unmask the "infantile and irrational basis of illusion" in their characters."[35] On the other hand, the characters' commitment to romantic fantasy turns their lives into a series of wish fulfillments within an overall context that bears a striking resemblance to dreams.[36] What I call the inner text follows a line of regressive development, a retreat from the adult world towards immature conceptions of the self.[37] The outer text, which structures the characters' lives within an ironic world, undercuts these fantasies by emphasizing the stasis of "moral stupidity" from the perspective of a responsible moral position in adult society. As Erich Auerbach has shown in the case of *Madame Bovary,* Flaubert's language "unmasks stupidity by pure statement," and this language therefore "has a part in that reality of the 'intelligent' which otherwise never appears in the book."[38] These tensions between outer and inner texts, between ironic assessment of human experience and indulgence in the dream-like world of romance, show that while the narcissist is busily at work on the creation of self, the psychological processes we have observed reveal a "regressive disintegration of the self."[39]

Now that an overview of the problems we will encounter has been established, I want to focus more directly on certain clinical aspects of narcissism which will come into play in the rest of this book. Let me begin with an observation of Freud's. "The ego is in its very essence a subject," he writes:

> How can it be made into an object? Well, there is no doubt that it can be. The ego can take itself as an object, can treat itself like other objects, can observe itself, criticize itself, and do Heaven knows what with itself. In this, one part of the ego is setting itself over against the rest. So the ego can be split; it splits itself during a number of its functions—temporarily at least.[40]

The ego's relationship to itself thus involves, paradoxically, a movement away from self until sufficient distance has been established to allow it to enter into what Robert Rogers calls "a relationship of self to self in which one's self is regarded as though it were another person."[41] While all of the novels exemplify these aspects of the ego's functions, three of them— *Madame Bovary, Justine,* and *The Blood Oranges*—present almost clinical examples of narcissism. In *The Blood Oranges* Cyril, Hawkes' "sex-singer," sees everyone as an extension of his ego; even the natural world exists for him primarily to foster his sensuality. The theme of narcissism in *Madame Bovary* and *Justine* is initially linked to a series of mirror images which vividly illustrate Freud's premise that "the ego can take itself as an object." Emma's response to her mirrored image following her seduction by Rodolphe dramatizes the splitting of her ego which eventually leads to disaster, just as in *The Alexandria Quartet* Justine's fascination with her images in a dress-maker's multiple mirrors announces the motif of multiple personality on which Durrell bases his narrative strategy in all four volumes of the *Quartet.*

Jacques Lacan's incisive analysis of the beguiling effect of mirrors leads to an even more complex understanding of how the ego objectifies itself. Arguing that one of the basic psychoanalytic premises regarding narcissism posits that self-love compensates for a weak self-image, Lacan points out that the way to defeat this negative view of the self lies in developing a persona which can be unequivocally respected. After demonstrating that the child achieves a powerful sense of unity through its fascination with mirrors, Lacan observes that when the child sees itself

within a totally unified world the rejection of reality is both
natural and inevitable.[42] The relevance of his theory to *Madame
Bovary* (and to the other novels as well) should be apparent.
What Emma sees in the mirror is the ego as object, but it is an
object embellished with the desirable features of her models:
that is, she sees the heroines of her books, sees herself now
transposed to the unproblematic fantasy world of adulterous
women. Thus the function of models for the narcissist responds
exactly to Lacan's perceptions regarding the development of a
persona in the child fascinated by mirrors. Each instance illustrates Michael Balint's notion that narcissists "are desperately
dependent on their environment, and their narcissism can be
preserved only on the condition that their environment is willing, or can be forced, to look after them."[43] This precarious
relation to their environments assumes considerable ironic importance in the novels, for not only do the narcissists lose their
self-esteem when the imaginative environment ceases to function, they also lose their reason for being, as we see in the
conclusions to *Madame Bovary, The Awakening, Lord Jim, The
Good Soldier,* and *The Great Gatsby.*

    Two other contemporary psychoanalysts, Heinz Kohut and
Otto Kernberg, have also developed theories which can be applied to the novels under consideration. Kohut's interest in "patients who remain . . . fixated on archaic grandiose self-
configurations and/or on archaic, over-estimated narcissistically
cathected objects" leads to two particularly helpful observations. Arguing that "these archaic configurations have not become integrated with the rest of the personality," Kohut goes on
to cite two major consequences: "(a) the adult personality and its
mature functions are impoverished because they are deprived of
the energies that are invested in the ancient structure, and/or
(b) the adult, realistic activities of the patients are hampered by
the breakthrough and intrusion of the archaic structures and of
their archaic claims."[44] Some of this material will be familiar
from my earlier comments about the static aspects of Apollonian
consciousness, but Kohut offers us a new, structural perspective
to consider. Put briefly, "mature functions" are eroded by the
idealistic content of the characters' reading, or any other source
governing their behavior. This is particularly evident in cases
involving romantic concepts of love or heroic action which encourage child-like fantasies that by their very nature cannot ac-
comodate change, idiosyncracy, or fortuity. Gerty, for example,

experiences an adolescent sexual fantasy. Sex only peeps out from under her skirt and sexual feeling (symbolically disguised by her knickers) is displaced by a linguistic substitute. On the other hand, Bloom's experience, though onanistic, is maturely sexual, binding mind and body, while Gerty's is altogether imaginative. In this way, the archaic object (romantic *kitsch*) will always prevent Gerty's mature functions because her energies are literally exhausted by her emotional and imaginative invest-ment in fantasy material. And this leads to Kohut's second point. Because she is addicted to seeing men *en disponibilité*, any "realistic activities" she may have, any encounters with real men who seem even slightly attractive, will be interdicted by her "archaic structures," those classifications fixed in her conscious-ness.

Otto Kernberg's evaluation of "pathological narcissism" goes beyond Kohut's structural paradigm by confronting the psychic costs of narcissism. In the course of his exhaustive analysis of "The Subjective Experience of Emptiness," Kernberg narrows his discussion to

> patients with narcissistic personality structures—that is those who present the development of pathological narcissism characterized by the establishment of a pathological, grandi-ose self and a serious deterioration of all their internalized object relations. In contrast to . . . depressive and schizoid patients . . . these narcissistic patients' experience of emp-tiness is characterized by the addition of strong feelings of boredom and restlessness. They do not have available certain aspects of the capacity for human relationships which are pre-served . . . by schizoid, and (even more so) by depressive patients. Patients with depressive personality, and even schizoid patients, are able to empathize deeply with human feelings and experiences involving other people, and may feel painfully excluded from and yet able to empathize with love and emotion involving others.[45]

Gide's Michel immediately comes to mind. "Something in my will has been broken," he admits, and we see him ultimately incapable of feeling anything, even for himself. A similar situa-tion occurs at the end of *The Blood Oranges* when Cyril, having exhausted his relationship with Catherine (and having been abandoned by his wife, Fiona), assumes a passive role in which his depleted energies are disguised for him by his characteristic rhetoric, but not from Hawkes's readers. Much the same can be said of the end of *Death in Venice*. Immobilized on the beach, Aschenbach passively watches Tadzio who long ago lost his status as object and has now become a sign of Aschenbach's death. But what I want to stress here goes beyond the way these specific instances echo Kernberg. His assessment forcefully leads us back to the consequences of Nietzschean man who overreaches either as Apollo or Dionysus, and demonstrates that the absence of "the capacity for human relationships" is a likely consequence of the will to power.

This introduction to how narcissistic consciousness is formed and to some of the ways it operates in modern novels sets out the parameters for the following chapters. Before testing these ideas against *Madame Bovary,* I want to focus briefly on the last page of *The Alexandria Quartet* where Clea writes to Darley, assuring him that she is "a real human being, an artist at last." Durrell means for us to understand that art has now become a *function* of her humanity, and no longer provides the means to snare her in self-love. These words summarize much of the preceding argument and lead us back to the fundamental notion that the narcissist's defeat springs from a tragic conflation of art and essence. This confusion is resolved only in the *Quartet,* where the narcissist's destructive art is escaped by Darley and Clea once they are capable of moving beyond the demands of ego-libido to the un–self-conscious world of relation. Alexandria can thus be seen as a vortex of self-indulgence and as a metaphor of the narcissist's consciousness. Like all those who choose the ego over others as love-object, Emma Bovary dreamed of a Parisian equivalent of Alexandria which would enclose her and permit every gesture that confirmed the Alexandrians in their solitude. Her world will be our starting point.

Part II
The Apollonian Quest

The Fairest of Them All: Modes of Vision in *Madame Bovary*

> She had a magic looking-glass and when she stood
> before it and looked at herself she used to say: "Mir-
> ror, mirror, on the wall, who is fairest of us all?" Then
> the glass replied: "Queen, thou'rt fairest of them all."
> —"Snow White"

I

Flaubert forecast Emma Bovary's fate when he invented the encounter between her and the provincial littérateur, Léon Dupuis, which occurs on her first evening in Yonville. Listening to his account of reading, Emma hears for the first time how Romantic imagination elides the distance between art and life. "What is better," he argues, "than to sit by one's fireside in the evening with a book, while the wind beats against the window and the lamp is burning?"

> 'What, indeed?' she said, fixing her large black eyes wide open upon him.
> 'One thinks of nothing,' he continued; 'the hours slip by. Without having to move, we walk through the countries of our imagination, and your thought, blending with the fiction, toys with the details, follows the outline of the adventures. It mingles with the characters, and it seems you are living their lives, that your own heart beats in their breasts.'[1]

Léon's banalities radiate insights for Emma. Here, at last, is someone who responds as she does to the vicarious pleasures of books. But Emma is a more passionate and engaged reader than the clerk who tests her knowledge of *idées reçues*. For her, books encapsulate life itself; people, emotions, even objects are significant only to the degree that they validate the discoveries of her reading, and much of her time is spent recreating her experience to make it conform with the demands of her imagination.

To render this process, Flaubert presents Emma's fantasy life through a series of tableaux in which her imagination is associated with images of mirrors. This imagery always signals a movement toward subjectivity in *Madame Bovary,* and there is a close relationship here with Tzvetan Todorov's perception about the world of the fantastic, where, he argues, "every appearance of a supernatural element is accompanied by the parallel introduction of an element belonging to the realm of sight. It is, in particular, eyeglasses and mirrors that permit penetration into the marvelous universe." These symbols of "indirect, distorted, subverted vision" mediate between reality and the supernatural, reifying the "marvelous universe" for characters and reader alike.[2] However, while Todorov's construct offers an illuminating context for Flaubert's imagery, we need to be aware that the motif of the mirror provides only one element in the structure of a marvelous tale (an element whose function is transitional and therefore generally limited in thematic significance), whereas in *Madame Bovary* it eventually symbolizes Emma's whole subjective life. This is a large claim to make, especially since the initial connection I wish to point out among Todorov's "marvelous universe," Emma's subjectivity, and the mirror motif begins with an examination of the character of the Queen in "Snow White." But the incongruity of this association is superficial, giving way to likeness between novel and fairy tale in both theme and setting.

When the Queen asks her question of the magic mirror, the reader witnesses an act of schizophrenia taking place simultaneously with the unfolding of the dialectic between fantasy and reality. From a psychological perspective, it is not the mirror but her own selfish desires that subvert the Queen's vision and permit her to penetrate the "marvelous universe." While the voice in the mirror originates in the supernatural, what the Queen sees reflected in the mirror is her own subjective conception of herself, which is manifested by projecting an ideal version of herself onto her own image. In other words, the Queen gains access to the subjective equivalent of Todorov's supernatural world by an act of mind so powerful that she can see what she wants to see. Every visual and psychological element in this scene is repeated in the ninth chapter of Part II of *Madame Bovary,* where Emma contemplates her own image after having been seduced by Rodolphe. The tableau of the Queen before her mirror covers Emma like a transparency, and these fused images symbolize Emma's life from the moment she enters the convent until her death. Given this congruence, the "mœurs de province" Flaubert chose to anatomize involve elements one would scarcely attribute, at least at first glance, to the kingdom of the bourgeoisie: magic mirrors, fantastic visions, high adventure in the most ephemeral reaches of the Romantic's imagination.

At the same time, more is at stake here than allusions to the world of fairy tales and the marvelous, for these elements lead directly to what I take to be Flaubert's most devastating irony. Just as there is a dialectic in Emma's consciousness, so is there in the structure of the novel itself. The external events of *Madame Bovary* deal with nuances of boredom exemplified in the lives of those who inhabit the monochromatic countrysides of Tostes and Yonville. Opposed to the banalities of everyday life in these dusty villages is all that Emma sees, and in the congeries of images cast on her imagination we encounter a beautifully contrived paradox: that which is most vital in the novel is most ephemeral, existing only in the distorted world of Emma's visual imagination. More complex than Todorov's, this world resonates with the syllables of Flaubert's *idées reçues,* Aristotle's *endoxon* ("current opinion"),[3] Barthes's codes. For each time Emma sees (or hears) something in the depths of her own subjectivity, "one might say that offstage voices can [also] be heard"—Barthes's cultural codes "whose origin is 'lost' in the vast perspective of the *already-written. . . .*"[4] As I hope the following discussion of modes of vision will show, Emma's universe consists of two equally counterfeit versions of reality: the marvelous, whose elements are derived from her reading, and the endoxal, whose terms are derived from her culture and repeated in the symbols and themes of her reading.

II

Flaubert renders Emma's subjectivity in three visual modes, which I call descriptive, hallucinatory, and autoscopic. The descriptive mode provided Erich Auerbach with the materials for his analysis of Flaubertian realism in *Mimesis;* he begins by citing the following domestic scene:[5]

But it was above all at mealtimes that she could bear it no longer, in that little room on the ground floor, with the smoking stove, the creaking door, the oozing walls, the damp floor-tiles; all the bitterness of life seemed to be served to her on her plate, and, with the steam from the boiled beef, there rose from the depths of her soul other exhalations as it were of disgust. Charles was a slow eater; she would nibble a few hazel-nuts, or else, leaning on her elbow, would amuse herself making marks on the oilcloth with the point of her table-knife.

Auerbach shows how Emma's subjective responses to Charles are indicated by a series of essentially descriptive images, and since his argument is familiar enough not to require lengthy rehearsal, it should be sufficient to reiterate the main points of his conclusion.

The picture above is not presented for itself; it is subordinated to Emma's despair, which has impressed itself more and more heavily on her soul since her marriage. The drabness of the scene "appears to her, and through her to the reader also, as something that is connected with [Charles] . . . yet she is . . . herself part of the picture, she is situated within it" (Auerbach, p. 427). And Auerbach isolates the major characteristic of the descriptive mode when he tells us that Emma "does not simply see, but is herself seen as one seeing, and is thus judged, simply through a plain description of her subjective life, out of her own feelings" (pp. 427–28). In this sense, visual phenomena can become symptoms of subjective states of being.

The scene at the Banneville groves illustrates how this mode functions, even more clearly than Auerbach's example. After asking herself why she married, Emma begins to think of her companions at the convent, imagining them in the theaters and ballrooms of Paris. The contrast is unbearable: "As for her, her life was cold as a garret facing north, and ennui, the silent spider, was weaving its web in the darkness, in every corner of her heart" (p. 32). With her emotional condition thus established, Flaubert goes on to describe the countryside:

Occasionally there came gusts of wind, breezes from the sea rolling in one sweep over the whole plateau of the Caux country, which brought to these fields a salt freshness. The rushes, close to the ground, whistled; the branches of the beech trees trembled in a swift rustling, while their crowns, ceaselessly swaying, kept up a deep murmur. Emma drew her shawl round her shoulders and rose. (P. 32)

The movement of the rushes and branches, the swaying of the crowns of the beech trees, the mournful sound of the wind and the onomatopoetic effect produced in French by the rhymes of "toujours," "leur," and "murmure" present a composite description (with sound effects) of Emma's internal condition, a description, in fact, of the ennui that "was weaving its web" in her soul. Here, as in the Auerbach example, her subjective responses are reported by an omniscient narrator.

In the hallucinatory mode, images of the external world decode subjective images present in the reservoir of Emma's memory, and she frequently perceives images of both sorts simultaneously. It has been suggested that this simultaneity may be related to the hallucinations Flaubert suffered from as a young man,[6] and, in a letter to Taine, Flaubert records their effects in a way that illuminates a good deal about the function of Emma's memory:

Suddenly, like a thunderclap, there is the invasion, or rather the instantaneous irruption of memory, for hallucination, properly speaking, is nothing else but that, to me, at any rate. It is a sickness of the memory, a letting loose of what it hides. It seems as if everything in one's head bursts at once, like a thousand rockets in a fireworks display, and one hasn't the time to watch these inner images rushing furiously past. On other occasions, it begins by a single image which increases in size until it finally covers objective reality, as for example, a spark which flies about and becomes a great flaming fire. In this last case, one may quite easily be thinking of something else at the same time, and this may be almost identical with what we call 'seeing black butterflies'—that is, those round bits of satin that some people see floating in the air when the sky is gray and their eyes are tired.[7]

Or, more simply:

In a hallucination pure and simple, you can easily see an unreal image with one eye, and real objects with the other.

This multiplication of images and the ensuing dysfunction of memory occur during Emma's final retreat from Rodolphe's chateau, when she gazes dumbly at the surrounding countryside:

All the memories and ideas that crowded her head seemed to explode at once like a thousand pieces of fireworks. She saw her father, Lheureux's closet, their room at home, another landscape. . . . Night was falling, crows were flying about.

Suddenly it seemed to her that fiery spheres were exploding in the air like bullets when they strike, and were whirling, whirling, to melt at last upon the snow between the branches of the trees. In the midst of each of them appeared the face of Rodolphe. They multiplied and drew near, they penetrated her. It all disappeared; she recognized the lights of the houses that shone through the fog. (P. 228)

In this highly sensitized condition, Emma cannot distinguish the present from the past, reality from hallucination. Fragmented images impinge on her mind's eye for a millisecond before merging in the vortex where everything is "whirling, whirling" and she is engulfed by the multiple faces of Rodolphe.

Less dramatic situations affect her vision in the same way, as in the following scene from the ball at Vaubyessard:

The atmosphere of the ball was heavy; the lamps were growing dim. Guests were flocking to the billiard-room. A servant got upon a chair and broke the window-panes. At the crash of the glass Madame Bovary turned her head and saw in the garden the faces of peasants pressed against the window looking in at them. Then the memory of the Bertaux came back to her. She saw the farm again, the muddy pond, her father in his apron under the apple-trees, and she saw herself again as formerly, skimming with her finger the cream off the milk-pans in the dairy. (P. 37)

Immersed in the present splendor of the chateau, she sees herself as she used to be, the intensity of the recovered experience so great that it has tactile as well as visual qualities. Here the omniscient narrator has vanished, and it is Emma herself who links external and internal, past and present. But there is more here than simultaneity. This scene, like the previous one, is epiphanic: there is a "showing forth" of the quintessential Emma Bovary as she exists in two places at once, her visual imagination the node of intersecting planes of time. Not only does the encroachment of the past into the present exemplify the power of her imagination, it also epitomizes the tragedy of a life in which it will become increasingly difficulty to distinguish the real from the marvelous, phenomena from dreams, the world of actu-

ality and logical possibility from the world of fantasy and endoxal codes. Emma's problem, as opposed to Flaubert's, is not a
"sickness of the memory" but a sickness of consciousness in
which the ego has been cut loose from its moorings in a stable
psyche and allowed to contemplate itself in the "marvelous universe" of its own reflections: the domain of the autoscopic mode
of vision, where mirrors abound under the sign of Narcissus.

III

At the convent Emma is exposed to the virus of romantic
literature, whose virulence results from the melding of the marvelous plots of fairy tales with identifiable but unspecified glan-
dular longings. Following an exhaustive catalog of images and
codes running through Emma's reading, Flaubert adds that "the
shade of the oil lamp fastened to the wall above Emma's head
lighted up all these pictures of the world, that passed before her
one by one in the silence of the dormitory, and to the distant
noise of some belated carriage still rolling down the Boulevard"
(p. 27). These "pictures of the world," moving in parataxis
through her mind to the rhythm of the "belated carnage" (whose
"distant noise" underscores Emma's sense of mimesis), adum-
brate a crucial structure in her imagination. For the only images
that ever achieve autonomy are of young women, and in the
process of differentiating them from their surroundings, and
from the young men who are sometimes present, Emma reveals
the cause of her perpetual dissatisfaction with her lovers.
    Consider the details of the "tableaux" etched on her memory.
Dreaming over Scott's novels, "she would have liked to live in
some old manor-house, like those long-waisted chatelaines who,
in the shade of pointed arches, spent their days leaning on the
stone, chin in hand, watching a white-plumed knight galloping
on his black horse from the distant fields" (p. 26). Here the focus
of her attention is disclosed in the perspective of the "tableaux."
Compared to the detailed description of the composite
chatelaine occupying the foreground of the scene, the knight is
only an impressionistic blur in the middle distance, a catalyst, as
it were, for *rêverie*. But this fantasy is only the first in a series
that includes a "cult for Mary Stuart and enthusiastic veneration
for illustrious or unhappy women" (p. 26). Emma is equally
fascinated by "English ladies with fair curls, who looked at you

from under their round straw hats with their large clear eyes"
(p. 27), as well as by others "dreaming on sofas with an open
letter, [gazing] at the moon through a slightly open window half
draped by a black curtain" (p. 27). The catalog of heroines is
completed by "the innocent ones, a tear on their cheeks, kissing
doves through the bars of a Gothic cage, or smiling, their heads
on one side . . . plucking the leaves of a marguerite with their
taper fingers, that curved at the tips like peaked shoes" (p. 27).

The convent tableaux prefigure Emma's increasingly dangerous fantasies, which begin to turn up shortly after the ball at
Vaubyessard. As the weeks following her experience there fade
away, "the memory of this ball . . . became an occupation for
Emma" (p. 40). At the center of these memories is an image of
the Viscount who "always cropped up in everything she read.
She made comparisons between him and the fictional characters
in her books. But the circle of which he was the centre gradually
widened round him, and the aureole that he bore, fading from his
form and extending beyond his image, lit up her other dreams"
(p. 41). This light, once shed on "pictures of the world," now
illuminates Paris as it emerges from her imagination like Mal-
larmé's flower absent from the bouquets of this world:

> Paris, more vague than the ocean, glimmered before Emma's
> eyes with a silvery glow. The many lives that stirred amid this
> tumult were, however, divided into parts, classed as distinct
> pictures. Emma perceived only two or three that hid from her
> all the rest, and in themselves represented all humanity. The
> world of ambassadors moved over polished floors in drawing-
> rooms lined with mirrors, round oval tables covered with vel-
> vet and gold-fringed cloths. There were dresses with trains,
> deep mysteries, anguish hidden beneath smiles. Then came
> the society of the duchesses; all were pale; all got up at four
> o'clock; the women, poor angels, wore English point on their
> petticoats; and the men, their talents hidden under a frivolous
> appearance, rode horses to death at pleasure parties, spent the
> summer season at Baden, and ended up, on reaching their
> forties, by marrying heiresses. (P. 42)

A street map; a magazine; novels by Sue, Balzac, and Sand;
memories of her convent reading and of the waltz at Vaubyessard; a green cigar case—this is a reasonably accurate inventory
of the data that nurtured the Parisian *rêverie*. In the paragraph

preceding that fantasia, the Viscount is momentarily the brightest star in Emma's constellation, but his image soon fades; the aureole emanating from him is first diffused and then reconstituted in the dream of Paris that emerges slowly in her imagination. The subject of the *rêverie* is not the Viscount, but rather the aureole he bears, which irradiates details of the larger dream of Paris. And it is important to see that in both examples the Viscount cannot maintain his position at the center of Emma's imaginative circle. Although the fantasy begins with her memory of him, he is absorbed into the mirrored images of the Parisian drawing rooms and the *women who move among them*. Compared with these poor angels, the men Emma imagines remain undifferentiated abstractions. Clearly, the Viscount has become another of the disappearing men, reduced to a charge of light shed on bright images of women.

Vaubyessard "made a gap in her life" (p. 42) by juxtaposing the dreariness of village life with the ambience of chateaux; at the same time, it provided Emma with an experience whereby she could synthesize the disparate images that had crowded her imagination since adolescence, when solitary heroines in stylized attitudes of melancholy longing became her emblem of love. Moreover, it is in the nature of her fascination with these heroines that their significance to her own personality and to the mirror motif becomes apparent. As a girl, Emma perceived an embryonic ideal of herself in these women, which she realizes in her maturity, and, I have tried to show, it is always the avatar of herself that survives in Emma's fantasies. Men function exclusively as catalysts in the process of her self-discovery, vehicles for her journeys toward herself. Consequently, her narcissism goes beyond the self-love normally associated with the word to infatuation with women in general and particularly with women as erotic objects. Emma's attraction to herself thus participates in a larger attraction to her own sex.[8] And it can be argued, I think, that the dialectic formed by the phenomena of the disappearing men and the photographically envisioned women at least partially explains Emma's dissatisfaction with Charles, Rodolphe, and Léon. This aspect of Emma's character is examined below in detail, following a discussion of her response to herself after she has been seduced by Rodolphe. At this point, it should be sufficient to say that narcissism ultimately replaces infidelity as the source of her most intense erotic experience.

IV

The Parisian fantasy marks the end of the first stage of Emma's voyage into the "marvelous universe." Afterward, she is conscious of nothing for days on end but the gap in her life, and during the last weeks she spends in Tostes, ennui settles over her soul as if it were dust raised by carts passing in the street below her window, where she sits for hours waiting for something to happen. Occasionally it does:

> Sometimes in the afternoon outside the window of her room, the head of a man appeared, a swarthy head with black whiskers, smiling slowly, with a broad, gentle smile that showed his white teeth. A waltz began, and on the barrel-organ, in a little drawing-room, dancers the size of a finger, women in pink turbans, Tyrolians in jackets, monkeys in frock-coats, gentlemen in knee breeches, turned and turned between the armchairs, the sofas and the tables, reflected in small pieces of mirror that strips of gold paper held together at the corners. . . . The music issued forth from the box, droning through a curtain of pink taffeta underneath an ornate brass grill. They were airs played in other places at the theatres, sung in drawing-rooms, danced to at night under lighted lustres, echoes of the world that reached even to Emma. End-less sarabands ran through her head, and, like an Oriental dancing-girl on the flowers of a carpet, her thoughts leapt with the notes, swung from dream to dream, from sadness to sadness. When the man had caught some pennies in his cap he drew down an old cover of blue cloth, hitched his organ on to his back, and went off with a heavy tread. She watched him going. (Pp. 46–47)

Adumbrating the transformational qualities of her mirrors, Emma's window gives onto a scene that illustrates how the marvelous and endoxal worlds are fused in her imagination. Set against a mirrored background, the figures in the organ grinder's "little drawing room" are symbolic of that congeries of *idées reçues* apprehended in Emma's society magazines and child-hood books. Moreover, these miniatures move in time to music played in imaginary theaters and drawing rooms, and the melodies she hears become "of the world," audible equivalents of the pictures already examined. The configuration of an ironic pattern emerges here, for the images of the "little drawing room" parody the content of the Parisian *rêverie* just as that scene parodied the "pictures of the world" of the convent, and hereafter Flaubert's ironic rendering of Emma's consciousness depends increasingly on the repetition of such images.

Up to this point in the novel, Emma has passively looked on at the imaginary actions unfolding in her mind. In the next phase of her development, soon after she realizes that she is in love with Léon, she projects herself into this world:

> But the more Emma grew conscious of her love, the more she repressed it, hoping thus to hide and to stifle her true feeling. She would have liked Léon to know, and she imagined circumstances, catastrophes that would make this possible. What restrained her, was, no doubt, idleness and fear, as well as a sense of shame. She thought she had repulsed him too much, that the time was past, that all was lost. Then, pride, the joy of being able to say to herself, "I am virtuous," and to look at herself in the mirror striking resigned poses consoled her a little for the sacrifice she thought she was making. (P. 77)

The images and music of the world apprehended in the "little drawing room" are replaced by her own image and voice as she stands before her mirror. But though she experiences the "joy of being able to say to herself, 'I am virtuous'," she is only repeating the statement of some sloe-eyed heroine of her reading. And it is that remembered utterance, in turn, which triggers the mime of "resigned poses" practiced before the mirror. The source of the phrase and gesture is less important than the remarkable change taking place, for in the mirror, that symbol of distorted vision, Emma sees herself in a "picture of the world." Little wonder that she should feel consoled by what she sees; it is as if she had entered that green world of her youthful reading. As if. The identification with a phantom figure in her reading flickers out quickly, never having quite freed itself from conscious analogy. Not until the advent of Rodolphe will Emma become one of the women she has so longingly gazed at in her imagination.

The fastidious comportment that limited her relationship with Léon to exchanges of cactus plants and definitions from the *Dictionnaire des Idées Reçues* is undermined by Rodolphe at the agricultural fair, finally collapsing before his strange smile and comic-opera clenched teeth. Freeing herself from Charles on the night of her seduction, Emma rushes upstairs to her bedroom:

But when she saw herself in the mirror she wondered at her face. Never had her eyes been so large, so black, nor so deep. Something subtle about her being transfigured her.

She repeated: "I have a lover!" delighting at the idea as if a second puberty had come to her. So at last she was to know those joys of love, that fever of happiness of which she had despaired! She was entering upon a marvelous world where all would be passion, ecstasy, delirium. She felt herself surrounded by an endless rapture. A blue space surrounded her and ordinary existence appeared only intermittently between these heights, dark and far away beneath her.

Then she recalled the heroines of the books that she had read, and the lyric legion of these adulterous women began to sing in her memory with the voice of sisters that charmed her. She became herself, as it were, an actual part of these lyrical imaginings; at long last, as she saw herself among those lovers she had so envied, she fulfilled the love-dream of her youth. (P. 117)

Personae metamorphose with lightning rapidity in these four brief paragraphs, where a by-now-familiar process is once again at work. Emma sees Rodolphe, feels the pressure of his arms, hears the rustling of the leaves. And then self-absorption reveals the real source of her ecstasy. "But," Flaubert writes, "But when she saw herself in the mirror": the simple conjunction signals an act of mind that soon relegates Rodolphe to a linguistic category. From an image he is changed into a word: "lover." As Emma confronts her transfigured image in the mirror, Rodolphe becomes another of the disappearing men, his essence subsumed by Emma's vision of herself. He is more important as a concept than as a person, and "amant," that linguistic talisman of her imagination, easily leads Emma to the endoxal world zoned by its synonyms—"passion, ecstasy, delirium." Rising into the fantastic blue space that these words create (an apotheosis is taking place here), the reality of her illusions is confirmed by a choir of "the heroines of the books that she had read"; and accompanied by "the lyric legion of these adulterous women," Emma moves into the marvelous world of the mirror: "She became herself, as it were, an actual part of these lyrical imaginings; at long last, as she saw herself among those lovers she had so envied, she fulfilled the love-dream of her youth" (p. 117). Like Rodolphe, Emma has been changed into a verbal substance, a character in a novel, the fairest of them all.

While Emma's fulfillment is achieved through linguistic manipulation (first, her culture's, whereby emotions are debased to serve the definitions of Romantic love; second, her own, whereby the eviscerated words are made to correspond to her imaginative life), it is also language that leads to her destruction. Todorov's comments about the function of words is particularly appropriate here. The tautological language of the fantastic, I submit, is only a dialect of Romanticism—Emma's mother tongue—and her fate stems from believing that the words she reads, speaks, or thinks describe palpable realities, whereas in fact they are signifiers with no referable matrix for the signified. Such language becomes literally destructive because it sets up an irresolvable opposition between reality and fantasy.[9]

Thus Emma's narcissism—in which the language of the fantastic is deeply implicated—exacerbates an already difficult situation. Scrambled and fragmentarily articulated as it may be, thought almost always precedes feeling for Emma, and this sequence is central to an examination of her narcissism because she has ideas both about the kinds of emotions appropriate to a given situation (a set of beliefs that amounts to a complicated taxonomy) and about herself experiencing those emotions. Whenever she is in her lover's arms, Emma is most fully aware of herself and what she feels in circumstances recapitulating the data of her reading, but this goes considerably beyond the extrapolation of a personality from the texts of Romantic love: her erotic life is equally borrowed, equally linked to imagination. If we look back over the course of her involvement with Rodolphe and Léon, it is easy enough to see that the passionate sensations she experiences during her visits to La Huchette or the Hotel-de-Boulogne are relatively mild compared to her erotic fantasies about what takes place. This is true, not because Flaubert was prohibited from frank sexual description, but rather because Emma simply feels *more* when she imagines erotic sensations. The emphasis Flaubert placed on the autoscopic nature of Emma's sexuality—a sustained and often devastatingly ironic emphasis—can be illustrated by juxtaposing three scenes that enclose the central mirror epiphany.

After settling into Yonville, Emma confronts Léon's coded sensitivities, against which she is defenseless:

She was in love with Léon, and sought solitude that she might more easily delight in his image. His physical presence troubled the voluptuousness of this meditation. Emma thrilled at the sound of his step; then in his presence the emotion subsided, and afterwards there remained in her only an immense astonishment that ended in sorrow. (P. 77)

Three years later, when she is having an affair with him, she feels compelled to write letters. Although the task seems wearisome at first, something strange begins to happen as she joins word to word:

But while writing to him, it was another man she saw, a phantom fashioned out of her most ardent memories, of her favorite books, her strongest desires. He dwelt in that azure land where silken ladders swung from balconies in the moonlight, beneath a flower-scented breeze. She felt him near her; he was coming and would ravish her entire being in a kiss. Then she would fall back to earth again shattered; for these vague extasies of imaginary love would exhaust her more than the wildest orgies. (P. 211)

In addition to presenting variations of the disappearing-man motif, both examples bring forward into Emma's erotic life the central predilection of her adolescent fantasies. However, more is revealed here than the continuation of an imagery pattern, for two sentences condense the essence of her sexuality:

His physical presence troubled the voluptuousness of this meditation.
Then she would fall back to earth again shattered; for these vague extasies of imaginary love would exhaust her more than the wildest orgies. (P. 211)

Given the ultraromantic nature of her character, how can "vague ectasies of imaginary love" be more satisfying than the actual pleasures of the boudoir? The answer is there in the pendant noun of the first sentence, "meditation," for narcissism is a *contemplative* affliction that cannot be actualized; the self can only be experienced imaginatively. If, like Emma, one has not been able to make the shift from ego- to object-libido, one's fullest erotic sensations must take place in fantasies, because that is where the inward-turning libido has no competition. The homoerotic aspect of Emma's narcissism becomes clear when we realize that her erotic fantasies are always linked to a female avatar born of her reading.

This process is confirmed at the opera, where she gives herself up to the melodies, costumes, scenery, actors, and "all those imaginary things that vibrated in the music as in the atmosphere of another world" (p. 161). These "imaginations" once furnished the images of the "pictures of the world" of the convent; now they are transformed into a *tableau vivant* on the rickety stage of Rouen's opera house, where Emma begins to see herself in Lucie. Primed by the words of the libretto, Emma is overwhelmed by Lagardy's appearance. Unrivaled in the suspension of disbelief, Emma is drawn to Lagardy "by the illusion of his character" as she slips once again into the world of Romantic love:

> If only they had met! He would have loved her, they would have travelled together through all the kingdoms of Europe from capital to capital, sharing in his success and in his hardships, picking up the flowers thrown to him, mending his clothes. Every night, hidden behind the golden lattice of her box, she would have drunk in eagerly the expansions of his soul that would have sung for her alone; from the stage, even as he acted, he would have looked at her. A mad idea took possession of her: he was looking at her right now!

Emma has created a demanding role for herself as Lucie of Yonville, and after the curtain "she fell back in her armchair with palpitations that choked her." These palpitations are the result of experienced sensuality, of passionate emotion; the problem, of course, is that Emma has all along been communing with herself in the image of another woman.

This brings us full circle to Todorov's perception that the fantastic "has no reality outside language," and I think the same can be said about Emma's erotic life. With Rodolphe and Léon she acts out her ideal of herself, but the pleasures available are of herself involved in the pleasures of her reading. In this sense, she reminds one of Roland Barthes, who takes pleasure in a "reported pleasure" by making himself the text's voyeur.[10] But Emma is really a step ahead of Barthes. In page after page of *Madame Bovary*, we see her emotionally engaged in a special kind of voyeurism. Since her imagination has developed in such a way that the women in her texts all become versions of herself, Emma is her own voyeur: the perfect narcissist, meditating on successions of words.

V

Regardless of her efforts, that world of words and mirrors
cannot survive in the world of unpaid bills assumed to buy time
and the furnishings of dreams. Eroded by a series of collisions
with reality, the marvelous, whose perfect expression occurred
when Emma realized the "love-dream of her youth," deliquesces
during her last visit to Rodolphe's chateau.

Although she takes arsenic to avoid any further confrontations
with reality, habits persist even on the deathbed, where Emma
gazes at herself one last time:

> In fact, she looked around her slowly, as one awakening from
> a dream; then in a distinct voice she asked for her mirror, and
> remained bent over it for some time, until big tears fell from
> her eyes. Then she turned away her head with a sigh and fell
> back upon the pillows. (P. 237)

Suddenly Flaubert's scathing irony is vividly before us in the
synecdoche of the dream metaphor. Awakening into life, Emma
requests the mirror that gave form to her dream of life only to
discover that the magic is gone. Like the Queen's in "Snow
White," Emma's mirror now tells the truth, and what she sees at
last is herself—not Rodolphe's mistress, not Léon's, not Lagardy's imaginary lover. The avatar of the "lovers she had so envied" has vanished, and the face looking back at her is no longer
the fairest of them all: it is now her *memento mori*.

The significance of the mirror motif and the destructive power
brought into play by autoscopic vision are reinforced by the
projected ending of an early draft of *Madame Bovary*. Wearing
the Croix de la Legion d'Honneur, Homais was to have walked
up and down in a room full of mirrors, admiring himself. The
ensuing crisis, and the probable reason for Flaubert's canceling
this ending, bear importantly on Emma's final vision. Here is the
text:

> The day he received it (he) couldn't believe it. Mr. X deputy
> had sent him a piece of ribbon—puts it on, looks at himself in
> the mirror. Vertigo.
> Doubt about himself—looks at the drug bottles—doubt about
> his existence (delirium. fantastic effects. the cross repeated in
> the mirrors. torrent lighning flash of red ribbon)—"am I only a
> character in a novel, the fruit of a delirious imagination, the

invention of a mere no-body which I have seen born and who has invented me to foster the belief that I do exist/ Oh, that's not impossible. Look, there are the foetuses (there are my children, there there)."
Then, summing himself up, he finishes with the great dictum of modern rationalism; "Cogito, ergo sum."[11]

Christopher Prendergast, rightly calling Homais "the supreme incarnation of the endoxal," takes this scene as an illustration of the existential "néant" (p. 212). While it is easy enough to see how such an ending would have appealed to the pessimist in Flaubert, to have concluded *Madame Bovary* with Homais's crisis and his relatively easy resolution of that crisis would have deflected, even muted, the carefully wrought irony inhering in the mirror motif. It would also have repeated, with much less force, the insight Emma achieves on her deathbed. While her initial response is to the ravaged features reflected in her mirror, the dream metaphor suggests a discovery that goes beyond Homais's brief moment of doubt. Awakening to reality during the last moments of her life, she discovers the nature of the dream she has lived, "the fruit of a delirious imagination," and the horror of that realization cannot be avoided by uttering a Cartesian dictum whose terms have been responsible for her own misapprehension of the world. Emma is all too aware of the gap between who she is and what she has thought.

That awareness begins with her contemplation of herself in the mirror, and it is completed when she hears the beggar's voice beyond her window as he stridently sings of love and seduction:

"The blind man!" she cried.
And Emma began to laugh, an atrocious, frantic, desperate laugh, thinking she saw the hideous face of the poor wretch loom out of the eternal darkness like a menace. (P. 238)

At the peak of her imaginative powers, what Emma perceived in her mind's eye and in her mirrors were pictures of the world that graphed a culture's myths. As her life flickers out, these pictures are replaced by her own death mask and the image of the beggar's "hideous face" looming out of the eternal darkness. Emma is demystified, and while the world of the mirror paradoxically brought her to the threshold of reality, death spares her the agony of living with her newly acquired knowledge.

Flaubert establishes the model of the narcissistic character

whose ephemeral desires are dramatized in Emma's belated recognition that she had projected her ideals into the mirror which
all along reflected only an absence. The mirror and the void,
clearly equated by Flaubert, thus symbolize the Apollonian's
drift into the "inner world of fantasy." Moreover, Emma's eventual discovery of the imagination's dissimulation and her death
by suicide become common structural and thematic features
binding *Madame Bovary* to *The Awakening, Lord Jim, The
Good Soldier,* and *The Great Gatsby.* The discovery of the lie
becomes even more central in *The Awakening,* and I now want
to trace how Chopin gradually unveils the psychic consequences
of immersion in what Conrad calls the "destructive element" of
the sea dream.

3
The Awakening: A Political Romance

> The food of hope
> Is meditated action; robbed of this
> Her sole support, she languishes and dies.
> —Wordsworth, *The Excursion*

I

Anyone familiar with *The Awakening* knows that it echoes characters and events in *Madame Bovary,* but Chopin's indebtedness to Flaubert stops short of merely imitating the problems Flaubert imagined for his heroine. First of all, while Edna Pontellier and Emma Bovary are both narcissists, Edna becomes aware of political crises related to her position within Creole society that sharply distinguish her from Emma, who responds to French provincial society only as a mirror of her romantic fantasies. Secondly, Edna's existential crisis lasts much longer than Emma's short and brutal confrontation with reality. In addition to her political theme, Chopin carefully and almost leisurely explores the shocks to the romantic consciousness which were briefly glimpsed at the end of *Madame Bovary.*

The similarities and differences in aims become immediately apparent through a comparison of two important passages. Twelve pages into *The Awakening* we encounter the well-known evocation of the sea that becomes a central motif in the novel:

> The voice of the sea is seductive; never ceasing, whispering, clamoring, murmuring, inviting the soul to wander for a spell in abysses of solitude; to lose itself in mazes of inward contemplation.
> The voice of the sea speaks to the soul. The touch of the sea is sensuous, enfolding the body in its soft, close embrace.[1]

These sentences are reminiscent of the exchange of platitudes between Léon Dupuis and Emma Bovary which moves from shared clichés about reading to Léon's avowal of great passion for sunsets and the seashore:

> "Oh, I love the sea!" said Monsieur Léon.
> "And doesn't it seem to you," continued Madame Bovary, "that the mind travels more freely on this limitless expanse, of which the contemplation elevates the soul, gives ideas to the infinite, the ideal?"[2]

The sea symbolizes imagination in both passages, but there is a considerable difference between Emma's superficial response to received ideas, and Edna's romantic but serious exploration of her own soul. Emma's naiveté is nowhere more evident than in this confession to Léon that the sea is a catalyst to the "ideal" world of sentimental Romanticism. In *The Awakening,* however, the emphasis falls on the seductive, isolating effects of "inward contemplation." Whereas Flaubert is interested in exposing the dry rot of Romanticism, Chopin is concerned with a woman whose susceptibility to Romantic codes ultimately gives way to at least a partial understanding of the lie that animates her visions. Edna's knowledge of the deliquescent nature of Romantic ideals also informs her view of personal freedom, and thus takes her story in another direction from Emma's.

That direction leads to an irresolvable conflict between Edna's vision of herself as an independent woman and the social forces of Creole Louisiana near the end of the nineteenth century. Throughout *The Awakening,* Chopin shows how Edna is deceived both by her private vision and by the society she discovers during the summer on Grand Isle. The hopes she begins to entertain about a new life spring from a congeries of sentimental ideals galvanized by Robert Lebrun, a "blagueur" (p. 12) who devotes himself to a different woman each summer. Edna's friend, Adele Ratignolle, sees the danger Robert poses to someone as impressionable as Edna and asks him to "let Mrs. Pontellier alone" (p. 20), which he declines to do, even after Adele tells him that "she is not one of us; she is not like us. She might make the unfortunate blunder of taking you seriously" (p. 21). The deceptiveness Adele recognizes in Robert mirrors the deceptiveness of Creole society which seems to accord women greater latitude than it is willing to grant. That women could smoke cigarettes, listen to men tell risqué stories, and read French novels soon appears as only a veneer covering a solidly conventional society that titillated itself with flourishes of libertinism.[3] For, despite their apparent standing within the Creole world (a standing, it should be noted, gained solely through marriage), women are presented as an oppressed class. Edna's gradual understanding of her oppression becomes part of the conceptual framework of her overall rebellion, and so, along with my analysis of the consequences of Romantic Imagination, I want to show how Chopin shapes her materials through detailed social description and social interpretation.

Because of the social conventions that prescribe behavior in her world, Edna has nowhere to go, succumbing to the promises of Romanticism while living in a society that will not tolerate the terms she sets for her own freedom. Although she manages by sheer force of will to free herself from the oppressive marriage with Léonce, Edna does not experience freedom; instead, she finds herself trapped by her romantic visions and by what Léonce calls *les convenances*. If *The Awakening* were only another examination of narcissism and the romantic predictions of a bourgeois woman, it would simply repeat the material Flaubert renders in his great novel. Chopin is not Flaubert, but within the range of her talent she treats questions about Romanticism, narcissism, and women's independence that are essentially political and thus considerably different from those raised in *Madame Bovary*. Moreover, we care about Edna Pontellier in ways that we cannot care about Emma Bovary because Edna's intimations of an autonomous life force us to consider the problems of freedom and oppression within society, while Emma's whole life revolves around sentimental fatuities. If Edna at times seems predictable and even tiresome, these characteristics are countered by Chopin's subtle rendering of the process of "inward contemplation" that leads Edna to an understanding of an insurmountable social dilemma which can only be escaped in death.

II

For roughly the first half of the novel Chopin subordinates the political implications of Edna's predicament to the solitude and tentative self-exploration that begins to occupy her heroine during the summer idyll on Grand Isle. In the opening scenes Edna's undefined sense of longing is symbolized by the voice of the sea, which encourages the soul "to lose itself in mazes of inward contemplation," so that the relationships between Edna's isolation, her Romantic sensibility, and the social significance of her situation do not emerge with any clarity until the guests at Madame Lebrun's establishment gather for an evening of entertainment. Even then, there is no specific statement to link the motifs together; what Chopin gives us instead is the motif of music, which indirectly leads to images of flight and escape. As Mademoiselle Reisz begins to play the piano, Edna recalls the pleasure she derives from listening to her friend Adele when she

practices. One piece Adele plays Edna calls "Solitude": "When she heard it there came before her imagination the figure of a man standing beside a desolate rock on the seashore. He was naked. His attitude was one of hopeless resignation as he looked toward a distant bird winging its flight away from him" (pp. 26–27). The image of the bird does not assume its full significance as a unifying symbol for another sixty pages when Edna remembers a comment of Mademoiselle Reisz's as she and Alcée sit before the fire in the "pigeon house": "When I left today," she tells him, "she put her arms around me and felt my shoulder blades, to see if my wings were strong, she said. 'The bird that would soar above the level plain of tradition and prejudice must have strong winds. It is a sad spectacle to see the weaklings bruised, exhausted, fluttering back to earth' " (p. 82). As the reader knows, escape from the labyrinth of self or tradition demands a cunning Edna does not possess. This failure is made explicit on the final page of the novel when she returns to *Chênière Caminada:* "A bird with a broken wing was beating the air above, reeling fluttering, circling disabled down, down to the water" (p. 113). Trapped in romantic longings whose objects are always vague and shifting in her mind's eye, and in a culture whose codes of duty and responsibility make escape impossible for even the most reluctant of "mother-women" (p. 10), Edna's fate is clearly foreshadowed in the imagery of defeated flight Chopin weaves into *The Awakening.*

At this point, we need to ask why, in a novel that addresses a woman's fate in society, Chopin chose a male figure to symbolize her heroine's solitude. The reason stems from Chopin's having realized that, on an unconscious level, Edna can only imagine a man in a position suggesting freedom and escape. His failure represents Edna's projection of herself onto the imagined figure. This view is consonant with the rest of the novel where we see that only men are free to act as they like and to go where they want: Robert to Mexico, Léonce to New York, Alcée from bed to bed. Whether it is Grand Isle, *Chênière Caminada,* or New Orleans, men escape, women remain. The New Woman Edna feels emerging from her "fictitious self" (p. 57) demands the prerogatives of men, but in making these demands she can only be destroyed by overreaching in a society that has no place for her.

But there are other reasons beyond the fact that there was little hope for independent women in New Orleans at the turn of the century that must be considered in an account of Edna's failure. Simply put, she cannot see beyond the Romantic prison of imagination. To illustrate her myopia, Chopin introduces Mademoiselle Reisz, whose clarity of mind offers a striking contrast to the essentially abstract nature of Edna's quest. Through music she discovers a kindred spirit in Edna, whose vision of the naked man occurs shortly before the musician plays a Chopin impromptu that arouses Edna's passions and brings her to tears. "Mademoiselle Reisz perceived her agitation . . . She patted her . . . upon the shoulder as she said: 'You are the only one worth playing for. Those others? Bah!' " (p. 27). She realizes that for her young friend music is the correlative of passion just as it is for her, but once their relationship develops Mademoiselle Reisz discovers that Edna's sensitivity does not encompass the discipline or the clarity of vision requisite to either the artist or the rebel. This is made clear one afternoon when Edna explains that she is becoming an artist. The older woman responds harshly, saying that "you have pretensions, Madame," pointing out that "to succeed, the artist must possess the courageous soul . . . that dares and defies" (p. 63).

Mademoiselle Reisz is to Edna what Marlow and Stein are to Lord Jim: a romantic who has found a "way to be" that does not compromise her ideals. Like Marlow and Stein again, she functions as a mentor who recognizes Edna's potentiality for independence while understanding that her impressionable young friend must learn to see more clearly in order to achieve what she wants and avoid disaster.

Once they have begun to meet in New Orleans, the musician's misgivings about Edna's ability to find her way in a new Romantic world are expressed in another kind of music. Edna demands to see a letter Robert has written to Mademoiselle Reisz, hoping that she will find some mention of herself. That she is over-whelmed by Robert and misled by their relationship troubles the older woman, and her sense of impending disaster leads her to weave fragments of Wagner's *Liebestod* into the Chopin piece she has been playing. This double theme of Romantic life and death becomes part of the atmosphere of the city, floating "out upon the night, over the housetops, the crescent of the moon, losing itself in the silence of the upper air" (p. 64). Like Stein's great speech on the destructive element that presents the posi-tive and negative aspects of Romanticism, Mademoiselle Reisz's music symbolizes the antithetical modes of Romance repre-sented by Chopin and Wagner, and her evocation of Tristan and Isolde becomes an important part of *The Awakening*'s imagery of destruction.

Mademoiselle Reisz functions as the only example of a free, independent woman whose hardiness Edna must emulate if she is to succeed and soar above "tradition and prejudice." There is no question that the older woman provides Edna with a more viable model than Adele Ratignolle who is, after all, trapped without even knowing it. Mademoiselle Reisz's apartment be-comes a refuge for Edna and the pianist comes closer than any-one else to making contact and supplying advice that could be helpful as Edna tries to find a place for her new self in the world. Nevertheless, her role in the novel is problematic, for she is an imperfect model whose positive qualities are balanced by abra-siveness and ego-centrism. Chopin calls attention to the musi-cian's idiosyncrasies when she introduces her into the story. Robert has gone to ask her to play for his mother's guests and finds her in one of the cottages: "She was dragging a chair in and out of her room, and at intervals objecting to the crying of a baby, which a nurse in the adjoining cottage was endeavoring to put to sleep. She was a disagreeable little woman, no longer young, who had quarreled with almost every one, owing to a temper which was self-assertive and a disposition to trample upon the rights of others" (p. 26). Later, at Edna's dinner party, "Mademoiselle had only disagreeable things to say of the sym-phony concerts, and insulting remarks to make of all the musi-cians of New Orleans, singly and collectively" (p. 87). While Edna instinctively rebels against the larger social dictates of Creole society, those social graces that express less overwhelm-ing *convenances* are still important to her, so that her amusement at her friend's disdain of conventions does not mean that she intends to imitate her. More subtly, Mademoiselle Reisz fails as a model because at this point Edna's passions, unlike her friend's, cannot be sublimated to music, but need physical expression. Like all her friends, Mademoiselle Reisz is eventually left behind as Edna increasingly dissociates herself from society and moves further into the mazes of solitude.

The musical motif in *The Awakening* provides specific dramatic referents to Edna's emotional states, but her imaginative life belongs to the realm of fantasy. Following her swim in the Gulf, Edna wants to think about her double experience of freedom and the "vision of death" (p. 29) that came to her in the water. Robert suddenly appears and Edna finds herself explaining that she has been overwhelmed by powerful experiences she does not understand: "There must be spirits abroad tonight," she muses, half-seriously. Picking up the cue, Robert invents a Gulf spirit who has searched for "one mortal worthy to hold him company, worthy of being exalted for a few hours into the realms of the semi-celestials" (p. 30). Robert does not understand Edna's experiences, nor does he particularly care to; his interests are in the direction of establishing himself in Edna's imaginative life. Whether by intention or pure chance, his words do enter her consciousness so that the Gulf spirit becomes a symbolic presence for Edna on Grand Isle and later in New Orleans.

In fact, the next section of the novel is given over to an elaboration of the fantastic. In the course of exposing the structure of fiction devoted to the unreal, Tzvetan Todorov cites the following comment by Olga Riemann: "The hero (of a fantastic tale) continually and distinctly feels the contradiction between two worlds, that of the real and that of the fantastic, and is himself amazed by the extraordinary phenomena which surround him."[4] What Edna experiences during the next few days approximates this situation very closely, for Robert's invention of the Gulf spirit and Edna's vigil before the sea that night lead to an awareness of a "contradiction between two worlds," particularly when she wakes up the next morning:

> She slept but a few hours. They were troubled and feverish hours, disturbed with dreams that were intangible, that eluded her, leaving only an impression upon her half-awakened sense of something unattainable. The air was invigorating and

steadied somewhat her faculties. However, she was not seeking refreshment or help from any source, either external or from within. She was blindly following whatever impulse moved her, as if she had placed herself in alien hands for direction, and freed her soul of responsibility. (P. 33)

Like a princess in a fairy-tale, Edna awakens to an enchanted world where the old rules of reality no longer seem valid.

The immediate result of her new perspective is to propose taking a boat trip to *Chênière Caminada* with Robert, and from the moment of their departure to the island the day contains experiences suggesting that reality had been altered. For example, as they sail toward the island, "Edna felt as if she were being borne away from some anchorage which held her fast, whose chains had been loosening—had snapped the night before when the mystic spirit was abroad, leaving her free to drift whithersoever she chose to set her sails" (p. 35). Soon after they reach the island Edna takes a nap. When she awakens, she tells Robert that "the whole island seems changed. A new race of beings must have sprung up. . . ." (p. 38). Later that afternoon she and Robert listen to one of Madame Antonie's stories about the Baratarian pirates. As she speaks, "Edna could hear the whispering voices of dead men and the clink of muffled gold" (p. 39). The fantasy continues during the return trip to Grand Isle, for Edna believes that "misty spirit forms were prowling in the shadows and among the reeds, and upon the water phantom ships [were] speeding to cover" (pp. 39–40). Edna recreates the atmosphere of these imaginary encounters at the dinner party she gives for her father when she tells the story "of a woman who paddled away with her lover one night in a pirogue and never came back. They were lost amid the Baratarian Islands, and no one ever heard of them or found a trace of them from that day to this" (p. 70). It should be clear that the day Edna and Robert spend on *Chênière Caminada* is filled with examples of "extraordinary phenomena."

The fantastic is implied in Chopin's early evocation of the sea, just as it is in Edna's visions of the unbinding of chains, pirate ships, and the lovers who disappear somewhere in the Baratarian Islands, freed forever from the mundane world of responsibility. Taken together, these events establish the atmosphere of Edna's mind, the mood of her thought. In this regard, it is important to see that *The Awakening* does not force the reader "to hesitate between a natural and a supernatural explanation of the events described";[5] only Edna hesitates between the fanastic and the real. The reader becomes increasingly aware of the ironic presentation of events, as well as the distance opening between Edna and reality.

Edna cannot actualize the self that increasingly absorbs her attention because that imagined self has no substance. Even when she is most deeply immersed in her newly discovered world, none of her visions of her self, or of a future, achieve clarity. In this respect, there is a distinction between Edna and Emma Bovary that should be explored. Emma constructs extremely detailed imaginary worlds for herself and Léon, Rodolphe, and Largardy from the raw materials of sentimental literature, images of Parisian social life, and the drama that unfolds before her on the stage of the Rouen Opera House. But her world begins and ends in that matrix of images, which to her are "pictures of the world." While Robert, in the guise of demon lover, appears in several of Edna's visions, she does not create detailed alternatives to the dreary life she has shared with Léonce. The reason should be clear enough: Edna's awakening corresponds with the attentions she receives from Robert who reifies the "realms of romance" anesthetized by Léonce, but her ultimate desire is for freedom to do as she likes, not, like Emma's, to find the man of her dreams. Thus, the journey into the Baratarian Islands she imagines with a demon lover is less important than her perception that she is "free to drift whithersoever she chose to set her sails."

III

The motifs of music and fantasy that I have discussed so far shape *The Awakening*'s themes of marriage, sexuality, and liberation. For the moment, I want to consider these themes separately in the order I have just mentioned, since that order corresponds to the direction of Edna's growth. Later, I will discuss them as a synthesis, a single perspective on the conditions of Edna's life, and by extension, that of women in Creole society.

All of these themes are announced in the first scene of the novel. Edna and Robert have just returned from a walk on the beach when Léonce remarks on Edna's tan, looking at her as "at a valuable piece of personal property which has suffered some damage" (p. 4). At the same time, Edna surveys her hand "critically," remembers her rings given over to Léonce for safekeeping, and takes them back. The conflict between freedom and oppression, the problem of narcissism, and Edna's retreat from and return to the symbols of marriage are neatly set out in three sentences. But there is more here, for marriage already appears to be incompatible with Edna's solipsistic character. From this muted beginning, marriage becomes the great fact of the novel, inescapable and monolithic, repeatedly described as oppressive, the source of ennui, and the means by which women are brought to suffer the pain of childbirth, the "torture" of nature as Edna perceives it while watching over Adele Ratignolle's *accouchement*.

We encounter a complex manifestation of Edna's feelings about marriage later that night after Léonce has returned from billiards at Klein's Hotel. She and Léonce have had a disagreement about the care of the children and Edna begins to cry, overcome by vague feelings that cancel any memory of her husband's former "kindness": "An indescribable oppression, which seemed to generate in some unfamiliar part of her consciousness, filled her whole being with a vague anguish. It was like a shadow, like a mist passing across her soul's summer day. It was strange and unfamiliar; it was a mood" (p. 8). This unspecified malaise is an inseparable part of marriage, producing a mood like a "shadow" or a "mist," phenomena that can obscure the outline of things, perhaps even obscure the self. These images soon become part of *The Awakening*'s symbolic design, for by suggesting that marriage obscures the essential self, they establish quite early one of Chopin's central political concerns. They allow us to see how Edna is oppressed by the facts of marriage and by her temperament in much the same way that the scene at the Banneville grove, where the wind coaxes a murmuring sound from the trees, symbolized Emma's ennui and disillusionment over her marriage to Charles.

The suggestion of obscurity and isolation that emerges from Edna's reverie reappears when Chopin writes that, "Mrs. Pontellier was not a mother-woman . . . one who idolized their children, worshipped their husbands, and esteemed it a holy privilege to efface themselves as individuals and grow wings as ministering angels" (p. 10). Adele Ratignolle is the type of such selfless creatures: "There are no words to describe her save the old ones that have served so often to picture the bygone heroine of romance and the fair lady of our dreams" (p. 10). What does Chopin mean to suggest by saying that there are no words to describe such women? Primarily, I would argue, that this epitome of the "mother-woman" is an anachronism, even though the beaches at Grand Isle are covered with them and they exemplify society's vision of woman's function. By saying that there are only the old words to describe Adele, Chopin subtly links her to the received ideas of woman's role in society. The "mother-woman" is a fiction. The old words have created a woman who fulfills "our" expectation and these words, associated with romance and dream, have created the self-image in which women like Adele bask. The point is that the essential self of both kinds of women is obscured, first by the institution of marriage, which separates the inner from the outer self, and second by the myths of womanhood that equate effacement of self, even the abjuring of self, with ideal and natural behavior. Thus both the romantic woman and the woman who mirrors the romantic clichés of a society's myths are blighted by the very terms of marriage.

But one of the novel's most interesting themes becomes apparent when we realize that, despite her rebelliousness, the associations Edna brings to marriage as a young woman can never be fully escaped. This is the case despite Léonce's lack of anything like the vigor of her youthful romantic fantasies that culminated in her infatuation with a "great tragedian" whose picture she kept and sometimes kissed. In fact, her entrapment is partly the result of the blandness she experiences with Léonce:

> Her marriage to Léonce Pontellier was purely an accident, in this respect resembling many other marriages which masquerade as decrees of Fate. It was in the midst of her secret great passion that she met him. He fell in love, as men are in the habit of doing, and pressed his suit with an earnestness and an ardor which left nothing to be desired. He pleased her, his absolute devotion flattered her. She fancied there was a sympathy of thought and taste between them in which fantasy she was mistaken. (P. 19)

Edna then comes to see her marriage, with its initial vague resemblance to her adolescent longings, as a step into the "world of reality," the act of a mature woman who will leave behind forever the "realm of romance and dreams." It is not long before she finds herself forced to confront realities that are clearly antithetical to her modest expectations: "She grew fond of her husband, realizing with some unaccountable satisfaction that no trace of passion or excessive and fictitious warmth colored her affection, thereby threatening its dissolution" (pp. 19–20). So marriage for Edna devolves to fondness, and the absence of passionate emotion seems to guarantee stability.

The stultifying effects of the relationship with Léonce—the price Edna and all other wives pay for stability—are quickly developed. When she visits Adele in New Orleans, "the little glimpse of domestic harmony which had been offered her, gave her no regret, no longing. It was not a condition of life which fitted her, and she could see in it but an appalling and hopeless ennui" (p. 56). In response to Léonce's entreaties for her to attend her sister's wedding, she says that "a wedding is one of the most lamentable spectacles on earth" (p. 6). Later, her awareness of having become a possession increasingly grates on Edna's sense of her individuality, and she gives her opinion of men who treat her as an object near the end of the novel during a conversation with Robert. "You have been a very, very foolish boy," she says,

> wasting your time dreaming of impossible things when you speak of Mr. Pontellier setting me free! I am no longer one of Mr. Pontellier's possessions to dispose of or not. I give myself where I choose. If he were to say, 'Here, Robert, take her and be happy, she is yours,' I should laugh at you both. (Pp. 106–7)

Earlier, when Edna first began to express her independence by ignoring the custom of her Tuesday at homes, Léonce responded by saying, "I should think you'd understand by this time that people don't do such things; we've got to observe *les convenances*" (p. 51). Léonce's comment cuts to the heart of what Edna rebels against; for her, marriage has come to seem like only one more convention within the myriad social forms that have become oppressive to her. Although she feels that marriage is "not a condition of life which fitted her," that she is no longer a possession, the facts of her life argue against her interpretation of it. Margaret Culley stresses Edna's delight in her independence as an element of the novel's tragedy. Referring to her comment about no longer being a possession of any man's, Culley says that "we glimpse the ecstasy of the discovery of the power of the self and the refusal to abjure it."[6] But there is a considerable distance between what Edna says and does that makes Culley's assessment more optimistic than the situation warrants. Surely the "delight [Edna] takes in her solitary self"[7] measures the distance between her imagination and reality in a painfully ironic way. Regardless of what she thinks, the shadow cast on Edna's soul by the convention of marriage and society cannot be escaped. Her decision to take her own life acknowledges the impossibility of returning to marriage, or of finding satisfaction in her solitude. It is the logical culmination of despair engendered by the loss of stability and her awareness of never being able to find a substitute for it in her affair with Alcée, or anyone else.

IV

Edna is deceived by the promises of sex just as she is misled by the conventions of marriage, but even though she delights in the adulterous pleasures discovered with Alcée, *The Awakening* is not an erotic novel. Lazar Ziff sees the true significance of her sexuality when he writes that Edna "was an American woman, raised in the Protestant mistrust of the senses and in the detestation of sexual desire as the root of evil. As a result, the hidden act came for her to be equivalent to the hidden and true self, once her nature awakened in the open surroundings of Creole Louisiana."[8] Ziff's observation alludes to the "shadow" Jung characterized as "a moral problem that challenges the whole ego personality, for no one can become conscious of the shadow without considerable moral effort. To become conscious of it involves recognizing the dark aspects of the personality as present and real. This act is the essential condition for any kind of self-knowledge."[9] Ironically, Edna's discovery of the "dark aspects" of her "true self" leads to increased self-knowledge, which isolates her from human contact, rather than providing a means by which she could experience emotional and physical gratification.

Such reflexiveness is clearly illustrated in the affair with Arobin. Edna has agreed to go to the races with Alcée and Mrs. Highcamp and later, when he takes her home, we are told that she "wanted something to happen—something, anything; she did not know what" (p. 75). Like Rodolphe when he first meets

Emma, Alcée senses an easy conquest. All he has to do is fulfill
her expectations:

> His manner invited easy confidence. . . . They laughed and
> talked; and before it was time to go he was telling her how
> different life might have been if he had known her years be-
> fore. With ingenuous frankness he spoke of what a wicked, ill-
> disciplined boy he had been, and impulsively drew up his cuff
> to exhibit on his wrist the scar of a saber cut which he had
> received in a duel outside of Paris when he was nineteen.
> (P. 76)

This apocryphal story of Alcée's past as a hero out of the pages
of Dumas provides the opportunity for an even bolder gesture:
"He stood close to her, and the effrontery of his eyes repelled
the old, vanishing self in her, yet drew all her awakening sen-
suousness" (p. 76). Here Alcée's melodramatic persona appeals
to Edna for the same reason she was drawn to the cavalry officer
and the tragedian—he embodies the "realm of romance" left
behind with her marriage and reawakened by Robert.

What follows is as inevitable as Rodolphe's success with
Emma, for what Edna wants is an opportunity to express the
"animalism" that "strove impatiently within her" (p. 78). A
mutual seduction follows "the first kiss of her life to which her
nature had really responded" (p. 83). However, despite this expression of freedom, which was clearly inevitable, when Arobin
leaves later that night "there was an overwhelming feeling of
irresponsibility. There was the shock of the unexpected and the
unaccustomed." There was also something more important:

> Above all, there was understanding. She felt as if a mist had
> been lifted from her eyes, enabling her to look upon and com-
> prehend the significance of life, that monster made up of
> beauty and brutality. But among the conflicting sensations
> which assailed her, there was neither shame nor remorse.
> (P. 83)

The mist "lifted from her eyes" is the same mist Chopin refers to
in the passage dealing with the "vague anguish" Edna discovers
in marriage. What Edna understands here is that she has been
liberated from the kind of life for which she is "not suited," from
marriage and from the shadow marriage cast on her sexuality. At
the same time, this scene reveals another important aspect of her

character. Edna always greets each new experience hyperbolically and she is constantly duped by fresh promises. Her conviction that she can now "comprehend the significance of life" is only another example, since her understanding fades with the waning of her enthusiasm about her passional self. She has learned nothing that could help her escape from the solitude steadily encroaching on her inner life.

The affair with Alcée becomes part of an emerging pattern of longing and restlessness which recalls the shadows and mists of her earliest sense of oppression. At the farewell party she gives to her old life on Esplanade Street such unfocused yearning is obvious:

> . . . As she sat there amid her guests, she felt the old ennui overtaking her; the hopelessness which so often assailed her, which came upon her like an obsession, like something extraneous, independent of volition. It was something which announced itself; a chill breath that seemed to issue from some vast cavern wherein discords wailed. There came over her the acute longing which always summoned into her spiritual vision the presence of the beloved one, overpowering her at once with a sense of the unattainable. (P. 88)

The sense of ennui returns us to the bedroom of her cottage on Grand Isle where she wept without knowing why, and felt a "vague anguish" whose source was inexplicable. The only substantial difference between the passage above and Edna's earlier encounters with hopelessness is the vision of the "beloved one" who is obviously "unattainable." Clearly, her vision has been enlarged while the conditions of her life remain as they were on the night the novel opens.

Thus every detail in *The Awakening* contributes to a growing impression that Edna's beginning is her end. Ten pages into the novel, Chopin writes that "Mrs. Pontellier was beginning to realize her position in the universe as a human being, and to recognize her relations as an individual to the world within and about her" (pp. 14–15). Yet, a sentence later, in a paragraph introducing the first reference to the sensuous voice of the sea, the narrator warns that "The beginning of things, of a world especially, is necessarily vague, tangled, chaotic, and exceedingly disturbing. How few of us ever emerge from such beginnings! How many souls perish in the tumult!" The voice of the sea, as well as the Gulf spirit, hold out to Edna a promise that cannot be fulfilled. When the voice is heard once again on the last page it echoes the earlier promise of the sea, but concludes on the word "solitude," and the invitation to Edna's soul to "lose itself in mazes of inward contemplation" is replaced by the image of the "bird with the broken wing." Moreover, between these images of the sea framing the novel we see other motifs and themes also turning away from the promises they held out for Edna to their beginnings: the positive suggestiveness of Chopin's impromptu is transposed to Wagner's evocation of the dying Isolde; the fantastic worlds of *Chênière Caminada* and Grand Isle become the house on Esplanade Street; the sexual passion with Alcée deliquesces into loneliness; and the promise of Robert's attention on Grand Isle turns into his farewell letter.

It is Robert's letter that finally shatters Edna's illusions of escape. After sitting up all night thinking about it, her dilemma finally becomes clear:

> She had said over and over to herself: 'To-day it is Arobin; tomorrow it will be some one else. It makes no difference to me, it doesn't matter about Léonce Pontellier—but Raoul and Etienne!' . . . . There was no human being whom she wanted near her except Robert; and she even realized that the day would come when he, too, and the thought of him would melt out of her existence, leaving her alone. The children appeared before her like antagonists who had overcome her; who had overpowered and sought to drag her into the soul's slavery for the rest of her days. But she knew a way to elude them. (P. 113)

Edna now understands that Alcée, Robert, and her own sexual awakening belong to a metaphor for the unattainable. Her life has no direction, her world no form, and the emptiness she has come to feel is Chopin's comment on the "realms of romance."

But this is not the end. Edna's void is suddenly filled with a vision of her children, which not only takes her back to her beginning, but also becomes the sign of her "soul's slavery." Regardless of her casual attention to them, and her attempts to break away from marriage, they have always been there. Once, Edna said to Adele Ratignolle that "I would give up the unessential; I would give my money, I would give my life for my children; but I wouldn't give myself" (p. 48). That was when their antagonism was veiled. During her vigil, Edna has come to realize that it is Raoul and Etienne, not Léonce, who bind her to the ennui of a life that does not fit her. And so it is a double vision Edna experiences; she understands the mendacity of her "spiritual vision" and also that the "soul's slavery" her children would drag her back to is too great a price to pay now that she has tasted freedom, however confusedly. The agony she feels has a moral basis because she realizes that continuing to live as she must in a world circumscribed by *les convenances* could only destroy her children, and that realization adds considerably to her stature.

Defeated by the lies of romance and the facts of *les convenances,* Edna's return to the seashore at *Chênière Caminada* is accompanied not by thoughts or Robert or Alcée, but by the overwhelming pressure of Léonce, Raoul, and Etienne. As she swims out to sea, her mind is filled with sounds from her youth, above all the clang of the cavalry officer's spurs. We are left, as Edna dies, to meditate on that sound with intimations of a world that vanished as she reached out to grasp it.

Chopin's novel is prophetic of concerns that Virginia Woolf, Dorothy Richardson, and other women novelists would explore in the next quarter-century; were it not for her blindness to alternatives at the end, her virtual isolation, Edna might have grown up to keep company with Mrs. Dalloway and Mrs. Ramsey, and to achieve a sense of identity similar to theirs. Though my argument in this book depends on (among other things) the persistence of a fictional critique of Romantic Idealism that extends well into our own time, it is important to see that Kate Chopin's treatment is idiosyncratic and focused on its debilitating effects not only on a single character but also on all women caught in the rigidities of a social system like that of Creole Louisiana. And this leads to an interesting irony that emerges from the conjunction of the two previous studies of female characters and the chapter that follows on *Lord Jim.* The "realms of romance" explored by Chopin and Flaubert are unquestionably destructive, and both novelists show that romance was the preeminent form of thought, the matrix of identity, available to women in the nineteenth century. Emma and Edna, because of their narcissism, are not free to choose another mode of thought, but it should be kept in mind that Jim and the other male characters at least have available to them other means of

achieving identity or establishing personality. No novel considered here is so bleak as Chopin's in this regard, for she shows
us that the illusions of romance were the dead end of identity for
nineteenth-century women. As we will see in the next chapter, it
is just the potential, the freedom to disabuse himself of similar
illusions, that makes Conrad's Jim such a problematic case.

4

"So Fine As He Can Never Be": *Lord Jim* and the Problem of Imagination

"Words, as is well-known, are the great foes of reality."

—Joseph Conrad, *Under Western Eyes*

I

Conrad takes us more deeply into the irrational workings of the Romantic Imagination than either Chopin or Flaubert. This can be accounted for partly because of Conrad's impressionistic techniques, which allowed him to render the actual functions of imagination more completely and realistically than his predecessors, and partly because of the angle of vision he chose, for in Marlow's frustrated attempts to unravel the principles of Jim's thought Conrad is simply closer to the compulsive demands of the ego. I will consider *Lord Jim* as the first of three novels narrated by a Jamesian observer. Flaubert's patient omniscience and Chopin's sometimes preachy avowals of significance directed towards their protagonist's misapprehensions of reality give way to an equally rich but more problematic irony as the quirks of Jim's, Edward's, and Gatsby's minds are revealed through another consciousness. What is revealed most notably is Jim's position as the exemplar of Apollonian idealism. He is at once associated with the light and idealism of Apollo and with the naiveté Nietzsche sees as essential for overcoming "the somber contemplation of reality." The result is a gain in energy from Chopin, not only in the portrayal of character but also in the persuasiveness of ideas. Once Edna reaches her impasse Chopin seems to lose her own imaginative energy, but Conrad's is stimulated by the moral complexity of a situation which Chopin's limited talent could not fully encompass. Through its in-

voluted narrative, *Lord Jim* intensifies the atmosphere of both
Flaubert and Chopin. We can begin to gauge that intensity by
briefly examining Conrad's views on the imagination and its
functions.

In Chapter 36 of *Lord Jim* a "privileged man," who alone of
Marlow's listeners has maintained an interest in Jim's fate, receives a packet containing an aborted letter of Jim's as well as a
narrative and cover letter written by Marlow:

> The story of the last events you will find in the few pages
> enclosed here. You must admit that it is romantic beyond the
> wildest dreams of his boyhood, and yet there is to my mind a
> sort of profound and terrifying logic to it, as if it were our
> imagination alone that set loose upon us the might of an over-
> whelming destiny. The imprudence of our thoughts recoils
> upon our heads; who toys with the sword shall perish by the
> sword. This astounding adventure, of which the most astound-
> ing part is that it is true, comes on as an unavoidable conse-
> quence. Something of the sort had to happen.[1]

There are three key words here—"romantic," "imagination,"
"destiny"—whose order follows what Conrad calls "terrifying
logic." By moving backwards along this causal chain, we find
that the seed of Jim's destruction lies in his reading, and more
minutely still in the images of himself and of the world created
from his adolescent encounters with Romantic texts. Conrad's
exploration of naive Romanticism in *Lord Jim* focuses predomi-
nantly on the consequences of undisciplined imagination, and
we will see how the structure of Jim's solipsistic consciousness
reflects the problematic relationship of reading and imagination
to destiny.

Before analyzing the connections between Marlow's comments and the major themes of *Lord Jim,* I want to discuss three
passages from *Nostromo, Lord Jim,* and *Under Western Eyes* in
order to show that the responsible use of the imagination is
central to Conrad's work both as a determinant of character and
as a theme. In raising the question of how imagination can distort reality, these passages provide a context for my analysis of
Lord Jim by suggesting that Conrad's interest in the shaping
force of imagination is equal to his more well-known concerns
with the relationship of the individual to society and the moral
consequences entailed in certain irreversible acts.

I would like to begin with a scene from the last pages of

Chapter 26 of *Nostromo* which Conrad devotes to Decoud's
sensations while alone on an island in the Golpho Placido. Until
this time Decoud's ironic persona has shielded him from himself,
but as the only human on the Great Isabel he encounters circumstances that strip him of this protection. Decoud is now dominated by solitude that "becomes very swiftly a state of soul in
which the affectations of irony and scepticism have no place."[2]
As he grows increasingly aware of his isolation, he "caught himself entertaining a doubt of his own individuality. It had merged
into the world of cloud and water, of natural forces and forms of
nature." The brilliance of the last half of this chapter, and its
relevance to the problem of imagination, lies in Conrad's rendering of Decoud's character. Decoud's self-image and the way
he appears to others cannot be separated from the language he
has used to create that image both in Sulaco and in Europe; but,
as Conrad points out, Decoud's language is exclusively ironic,
and irony cannot function in solitude. Decoud is unable to see
beyond the temporary nature of his situation; all he can imagine
is that he has lost his identity, that his ego has spilled over into
the undifferentiated natural world, and he is soon overwhelmed
by a self-created void that is directly responsible for his suicide.

Decoud's fantasy parallels two scenarios of disaster and disgrace that forever alter the lives of Jim and Razumov. Here is
what Jim imagines as his shipmates struggle to escape the *Patna:*

> Nothing in the world moved before his eyes, and he could
> depict to himself without hindrance the sudden swing upwards
> of the dark skyline, the sudden tilt up of the vast plain of the
> sea, the swift still rise, the brutal fling, the grasp of the abyss,
> the struggle without hope, the starlight closing over the head
> for ever like the vault of a tomb—the revolt of his young life
> . . . the black end . . . . (P. 59)

"And you must remember," Marlow adds, "he was the finished
artist in that peculiar way, he was a gifted poor devil with the
faculty of swift and forestalling vision." The same faculty that
leads to Jim's vision of disaster and thus to his destiny also
prompts Razumov's fantasy of the wreck of his life as he listens
horrified to Haldin's confession of De P——'s assassination:

> Razumov saw himself shut up in a fortress, worried,
> badgered, perhaps ill-used. He saw himself deported by an
> administrative order, his life broken, ruined and robbed of all

hope. He saw himself—at best—leading a miserable existence
under police supervision, in some small provincial town . . . .
He saw his youth pass away from him in misery and half-
starvation—his strength give way, his mind become an abject
thing. He saw himself creeping, broken down and shabby,
about the streets—lying unattended in some filthy hole of a
room, or on the sordid bed of a Government hospital.[3]

There are two strikingly common features that bind these
scenes together. First of all, Decoud's suicide, Jim's disgrace,
and Razumov's entrapment by the autocracy occur because
each responds to an imagined crisis as if it were real. Secondly,
each character is vulnerable because of his sensitivity to a particular kind of language. There is no question that Decoud's ego-
ideal has been shaped by the ironic language of scepticism, and
he is driven to suicide when he imagines himself abandoned in a
wordless world. Images conjured up from the bleak official language of Russian autocracy are so horribly vivid that Razumov
informs on Haldin in order to avoid the imagined consequences
of being labelled a conspirator. And the language of Jim's imagined disaster is superimposed on the rusted plates and crowded
decks of the *Patna*. As we will see, *Lord Jim* illuminates a theme
that occupied Conrad in *Nostromo* and *Under Western Eyes* as
well as in *Heart of Darkness* and some of his lesser works. The
"terrifying logic" that Marlow remarks to the "privileged man"
defines the history of an *halluciné,* a "finished artist" inspired by
tales of adventure whose remembered words are responsible for
Jim's life and his destruction.

II

The source of Jim's "swift and forestalling vision" can be
traced to his youth when a "course of light holiday literature"
convinced him that he had a vocation for the sea. Sent to a
"training-ship for officers of the mercantile marine," Jim's
youthful fantasies are reified "on the lower deck [where] in the
babel of two hundred voices he would forget himself and be-
forehand live in his mind the sea-life of light literature. He saw
himself saving people from sinking ships, cutting away masts in
a hurricane . . . always an example of devotion to duty, and as
unflinching as a hero in a book" (p. 5). Jim finds models for these

reveries in the pages of novels like Marryat's *Mr. Midshipman Easy,* Hope's *The Prisoner of Zenda,* and Stevenson's *Treasure Island,*[4] and he believes that imitation will result in the realization of his ego-ideal and acceptance on his own terms by a grateful society.

Now Conrad makes it clear that Jim's eventual destruction results from the unresolvable tension that arises between Jim's fantasies and the social world, and this tension provides one of the major ironies in the novel which begins, we remember, with a line Conrad culled from Novalis: "My conviction gains infinitely, the moment another soul will believe it." It is an intriguing sentence, but it yields more energy than clarity, since the assertion in the first phrase vanishes in the second where the speaker's "conviction" becomes startlingly equivocal. As a means of evoking the problematic of Jim's identity Conrad could not have done better. Convinced that he is the embodiment of heroic virtues, Jim vainly tries to close the distance between his ego-ideal and a sceptical world which refuses to believe in it. There are Conradians who will argue that Marlow shares Jim's idea, but I am inclined to believe that it is more a matter of Marlow wanting to believe in Jim than sharing his conviction. Jim moves in and out of the light of day just as Stein does and I think there is ample evidence in the novel to suggest that Marlow is sceptical about both of them.

To be more specific, Conrad attributes Jim's distorted view of himself to literature. We have already seen some of the transpositional qualities of Jim's imagination that allow him to recreate within himself his literary experiences.[5] The peculiarly naive quality of Jim's intellect makes it easy for him to absorb the attractive qualities of the texts of adventure he reads and then create an identity that he holds in his mind until his death. My point is that the distortion of reality in *Lord Jim* occurs at the interface of Jim's Romantic imagination and the literary text. The merger of the Romantic text with Jim's ego-ideal displaces the fictional hero from his position within the text and creates a fantasy in which Jim is the central figure. Jim then responds to himself exactly as he does to his literary models, but he never understands that his life cannot be confined to selfless heroic action—which is what defines his models and makes them attractive in the first place. In other words, Jim cannot see that his humanity forever separates him from the model's world, and the fundamental cause of his tragedy is found in his inability to distinguish between the ideal, closed world of literature and the problematic, open, and even irrational elements that define reality.

The major scenes of *Lord Jim* are built on the paradigm I have just described. We can see it at work on the night of the *Patna*'s accident when a clear sky encourages Jim's sense of "unbounded safety and peace":

> Jim would glance at the compass, would glance around the unattainable horizon, would stretch himself in the very excess of well-being . . . . At such times his thoughts would be full of valorous deeds: he loved these dreams and the success of his imaginary achievements. They were the best parts of life, its secret truth, its hidden reality. They had a gorgeous virility, the charm of vagueness, they passed before him with an heroic tread; they carried his soul away with them and made it drunk with the divine philtre of an unbounded confidence in itself. There was nothing he could not face. (P. 13)

The sea as surrogate text enables Jim's *rêverie* which is soon disturbed by the captain and the second engineer who are squabbling over the latter's having drunk too much brandy. Jim is "faintly amused" by the confrontation, and even though he is still in touch with "hidden reality," he compares his shipmates to himself. "The quality of these men did not matter," he thinks, "he rubbed shoulders with them, but they could not touch him; he shared the air they breathed, but he was different" (p. 16). Jim's attention to the tasks of the watch lags, and even though his eyes are the eyes of the ship, they are turned inward in a meditative gaze as he investigates his "achievements." He idly wonders if the captain would attack the engineer, but then he was "too sure of himself—too sure of himself to . . . The line dividing his meditation from a surreptitious doze on his feet was thinner than a thread in a spider's web." And within minutes disaster strikes.

By neglecting his duty for the "shape of his dream" (p. 106), Jim violates a basic principle of seamanship which leaves the *Patna* virtually blind as it makes its way at night toward the Red Sea. Like the captain in "The Secret Sharer," who is so distracted by Leggatt that he almost loses his ship as he comes too close to shore, Jim ignores the details of the craft, the all-important attention to the surface of things. In both cases, communal responsibility is ignored and the conflict between the world of imagination and the welfare of society is dramatically evident. The problem here is of course not new to literature, and Jim is remarkably like the young sailor in *Moby Dick* "given to unseasonable meditativeness . . . who offers to ship with the Phaedon instead of Bowditch in his head,"[6] only to discover that his identity "comes back in horror" when he slips his hold while high aloft. But Conrad makes the situation even more complex. Jim's absorption in the texts of Romance plunges him into the humiliation of the trial where he is briefly forced to acknowledge the complex world outside his fantasies. That acknowledgement is as superficial as it is brief, for Jim never sees himself as part of social reality. One of Conrad's most telling observations emphasizes Jim's obsession with his disgrace and his inability to recognize his guilt which would have established a link with the social world. Conrad's point is that in the realm of "imaginary achievements" Jim is aware only of a breach of faith with his ego-ideal, not with the community of mankind.

III

My aim so far has been to show how the act of reading and the content of Jim's texts combine to produce an irresolvable problem of imagination. In coming to focus now on the Patusan section of the novel, I want to deal with the way Conrad develops this theme through Stein, the talismanic ring, and the symbols of the moon and the Eastern bride. While Stein's comments about the Romantic introduce specific images of instability and destruction, the ring, the moon, and the shadowy figure of the Eastern bride warn that Jim's success in Patusan is not to be seen as proof that he has fused reality with his extraordinary ideals—quite the contrary. They signal ambiguity and deception and they function as increasingly ironic points of reference for the reader.

The second section of *Lord Jim* begins with Marlow's assertion that Stein was "an eminently suitable person to receive my confidences about Jim's difficulties" (p. 123). Stein is a polymath whom Marlow reveres, and, as Ian Watt has recently argued, his attractiveness as a counselor is tied to his ability to embody "both the adventurous and idealising aspects" of Romanticism, to see the virtues and pitfalls of an imagination encoded like Jim's.[7] Conscious of this expertise, Marlow listens in a vast room surrounded by glass cases and dark boxes housing collections of butterflies and beetles as Stein formulates the phenomenology of Romantic Idealism:

> A man that is born falls into a dream like a man who falls into the sea. If he tries to climb out into the air as inexperienced people endeavor to do, he drowns, *nicht war? . . .* No! I tell you! The way is to the destructive element submit yourself, and with the exertions of your hands and feet in the water make the deep, deep sea keep you up. (P. 130)

The first thing to notice about this passage is the instability of such idealism; the Romantic's convictions ("exertions") only postpone disaster. And we cannot avoid being struck by Stein's unmistakable pessimism in his insistence on the untenable, dream-like nature of Jim's Apollonian desire, a desire whose trajectory has been traced through Novalis to the heart of the German Romantic Movement, whose limitations Conrad understands.[8] While there has been considerable disagreement over how we should take the terms of the metaphor (Ian Watt shows that opinion changes every decade), the context of this study suggests that the "destructive element" of the sea must be equated with Romantic imagination from which there can be no escape. Thus Stein's argument that Jim can only survive temporarily within the dream reinforces the themes of the novel already discussed. Moreover, Stein's view of the dream guides our responses to the events that will take place in Patusan. Located in the very center of the novel, Stein's metaphor functions like Virginia Woolf's lighthouse; it is the one constant in a book filled with mists, fogs, misapprehensions.

Before further exploring the interrelation of Romanticism, reading, and imitation in *Lord Jim,* I want to point out that this famous passage provides a means for us to discriminate between what may at first appear to be identical responses to Romantic imagination in Flaubert, Chopin, and Conrad. Flaubert's portrait of Emma Bovary, as well as his autopsy of provincial attitudes endemic to the bourgeoisie, emphasize the ironies of naive Romanticism and the spiritual poverty of a culture's cliches. I have shown that Chopin's novel also takes into account the effects of received ideas within a society, while at the same time revealing the problematic situation of women whose only mode of identity is rigidly defined by traditional attitudes about the female psyche. Flaubert confronts the void in Emma's vision of the blind man, and something like this occurs in *The Awakening* when Edna swims out to her death, but the thematic concerns underlying these scenes are developed much more completely in *Lord Jim*. The philosophical concerns associated with Emma's and Edna's beliefs are muted when compared to Stein's prescription and many other comments in Conrad's novel. Presenting as complete a social world as either Flaubert or Chopin, Conrad offers us in addition a detailed philosophical study of the consequences of Romantic Idealism in the life of a well-intentioned but naive young man. The absence Stein envisions is thus fraught with more implications about the destructiveness of Romanticism than anything we are likely to find in the previously discussed novels. There is little that is mysterious or problematic in Emma's *rêveries* or Edna's vision of the Baratarian isles, but there is in Conrad, and it is a mark of his genius that he can present Jim's apparently simple-minded desires in such a way that Romanticism becomes a deeply disturbing philosophical problem which leads us to the speculations about the nature of human understanding that *Lord Jim* continues to provoke.

Now that these distinctions have been made, I want to return to the question of reading and imitation. Stein is implicated in the transformations of reading because Jim responds to him and what he tells Jim of himself exactly as he has in the past to the words and images of a tale of adventure. That Jim simultaneously fictionalizes Stein and creates an identity for himself based partly on the older man and partly on his earlier reading becomes obvious on the evening of his departure for Patusan. Returning to Marlow after spending the previous night with Stein, Jim "was voluble like a youngster on the eve of a long holiday with the prospect of delightful scrapes, and such an attitude of mind in a grown man and in this connection had in it something phenomenal, a little mad, dangerous, unsafe" (p. 143). Jim's exhilaration is divided between the attraction of Stein's personality and the state of things in Patusan. As he points out to Marlow, that was where the old Bavarian experienced countless adventures, where he became the "War-comrade" of Doramin, where he "had to make a dash for dear life out of the country. . . ." And in the midst of his excitement, Jim "exhibited with glee a silver ring" (p. 142) which will bear increasingly ironic significations. "The ring was a sort of credential" that would identify him to Doramin as a friend of Stein's.

" 'It's like something you read of in books,' he threw in apprecia-
tively." Jim's appreciation is particularly evident because what
Stein told him about life in Patusan mirrored the content of his
reading, a world seemingly lost after the trial and during his
purgatorial existence as a water-clerk. Stein's tales of adventures rekindle Jim's faith and achieve unimpeachable authenticity through the talismantic ring, an artifact of Jim's heretofore
dreamed-of world. Thus the fantasy Jim created for himself out
of his literary experience is actualized by the older man's
generosity.

The relationship between Patusan and the world of Jim's
imagination is reinforced by a number of images that suggest
distance and separation from the world "out there," which in this
context means both the physical world of Eastern ports and,
more generally, reality itself. Marlow emphasizes this binding of
Patusan with Jim's fantasies when he points out that "had Stein
arranged to send him to a star of the fifth magnitude the change
could not have been greater. He left his earthly failings behind
him and what sort of reputation he had, and there was a totally
new set of conditions for his imaginative faculty to work upon.
Entirely new, entirely remarkable. And he got hold of them in a
remarkable way" (p. 133). The interstellar metaphor will reappear in Marlow's meditation about the moon, but his initial
thoughts about the geography of Jim's opportunity focus on the
compatability of sheer distance and Jim's imagination. The idea
of such compatability leads directly to another of Marlow's observations that sheds new light on the problem of reading and the
creation of fictive worlds: "But do you notice how, three hundred miles beyond the end of telegraph cables and mail-boat
lines, the haggard utilitarian lies of our civilization wither and
die, to be replaced by pure exercises of imagination, that have
the futility, often the charm, and sometimes the deep hidden
truthfulness of works of Art?" (p. 172). The connections between Jim's "imaginative faculty," an environment conducive to
"pure exercises of imagination," and Patusan could not be
clearer, nor could the suggestion that that which enables such
connections also makes them problematic. Having left behind
the "haggard utilitarian lies of our civilization," Jim finds himself
in a situation where the exigencies of reality make no demands.
The opportunities afforded by Patusan allow Jim to create a
work of art in which he is the only character, but in this creative
act Jim becomes lost in the labyrinth of self that Stein describes

in his famous prescription. The tragedy of solipsism then is not so much that the individual is separated from social reality (though this is serious in itself) as that he becomes literally lost in himself, incapable of understanding that the link between himself and society has been broken.

Marlow's visit to Jim provides an excellent example of this myopia. Eager to show his friend how he has got on, Jim takes Marlow to a meeting presided over by the immense and powerful Doramin: " 'They are like people in a book, aren't they?' he said triumphantly. 'And Dain Waris—their son—is the best friend (barring you) I ever had. What Mr. Stein would call a good "War-comrade" ' " (p. 159). Jim has every reason to speak "triumphantly" about the collapsed distinctions between life and art, for it is as if he were living Stein's former life in Patusan. In addition, his experiences up to this time mirror the violence, assassination plots, and even the love affairs gleaned from his reading. But if we look closely at this passage we see that Jim's relationship to Doramin and Dain Waris is analogical; they are real to him because they are like "people in a book," and Jim is real to himself because he is like Stein and the composite hero of his reading. In fulfilling roles that allow Jim to feel the potency of his ego-ideal, Doramin and Dain Waris lose their humanity while Jim believes that he is asserting his own.

Although Jim appears to have "achieved success" in Patusan through his victory over Sherif Ali's forces and his subjugation of Rajah Allang, his past is brought forward both in the Stein fantasies and in the symbols of the moon and the Eastern bride. Each figure reinforces previous distinctions between the real and the imagined, the complex world of human interaction and the simplified, one-dimensional world of Romantic *rêverie*. This is apparent in Marlow's first lengthy description of the interior of Patusan which leads the eye upwards to the moon, as if to emphasize the dominant feature of Jim's new world. Rising behind a deeply-fissured hill, the moon "floated away above the summits, as if escaping from a yawning grave in gentle triumph" (p. 135). Later, Marlow senses a distinctly different and ominous quality in what he sees. The moon is still "like an ascending spirit out of a grave," but the simile of escape and triumph is not repeated; instead he remarks that the moon's "sheen descended, cold and pale, like the ghost of dead sunlight" (p. 150). Here the eroded vitality of the moon leads to Marlow's perception of "dead sunlight" from which he draws the contrasting images of reality and illusion that form the dialectic of the following passage:

> There is something haunting in the light of the moon; it has all the dispassionateness of a disembodied soul, and something of its inconceivable mystery. It is to our sunshine which—say what you like—is all we have to live by, what the echo is to the sound: misleading and confusing whether the note be mocking or sad. It robs all forms of matter—which, after all, is our domain—of their substance, and gives a sinister reality to shadows alone. (P. 150)

Jim's fantasies, exemplified in his responses to Stein's tales and his remarks to Marlow about the literariness of the encounter with Doramin and his followers, distort and vitiate the substance of the experiences by robbing them of their "matter." In this way the moon symbolizes the undisciplined imagination that promotes Jim's "swift and forestalling vision," since its "misleading and confusing" light, like Jim's imagination, eviscerates the real.

What, finally, is the source of the moon's deceptive light? I would argue that it is the world of "light literature" whose impossible tales of Romance and high adventure catalyzed Jim's imagination. Consequently the symbolism of the moon extends to the very atmosphere of the novel. The numerous images of mists, fogs, clouds, and other ephemera with which Jim is associated in Marlow's mind are also manifestations of the moon, and the shifting relationships between these images become part of the overall impressionist narration. For example, the change in Marlow's attention from the moon's strength to its weakness and deceptive qualities repeats the basic movement of his interview with Stein: "The light had destroyed the assurance which had inspired him in the distant shadows" (p. 131). This dialectic also occurs in the thematic contrasts between reality and fiction, identity and ego-ideal, awareness and naiveté that contribute to the sharp ironic juxtapositions of the narrative. Thus the moon guides our response to the development of Jim's "overwhelming destiny" by keeping before us, in one form or another, a symbol of his instability and unworldliness.

The moon's deceptive light also illuminates the Eastern bride in whom Conrad found a remarkable metaphor for the imaginative world created by the conjunction of Jim's ego-ideal and his Romantic texts. We remember that Jim enters the world of Patusan in a dugout, "and his opportunity sat veiled by his side like an Eastern bride waiting to be uncovered by the hand of the master" (p. 149). On a superficial level Jim's arrival in Patusan and the unveiling of the bride can be seen as the culmination of his longings as well as the end of his solipsistic isolation. This is the first meaning we are likely to associate with the metaphor and it is consistent with the view that *Lord Jim* is a novel of atonement in which Jim eventually exonerates himself. But such a reading misses Conrad's irony: the Eastern bride represents Jim's "opportunity;" she is an embodiment of his ego-ideal and as such emphasizes his solipsism and his inability to respond to anything outside of himself. The metaphor functions as an ironic sign of Jim's isolation from the social world, and his fidelity to the veiled image of his ego-ideal prefigures his destruction in the third and final section of the novel.

IV

The agent of Jim's destruction is Gentleman Brown, and Marlow's narrative of Jim's "astounding adventure" begins with an interesting description of this strange figure:

Till I discovered the fellow my information was incomplete, but most unexpectedly I did come upon him a few hours before he gave up his arrogant ghost. Fortunately, he was willing and able to talk between the choking fits of asthma, and his racked body writhed with malicious exultation at the bare thought of Jim. He exulted thus at the idea that he had 'paid out the stuck-up beggar after all.' He gloated over his action. I had to bear the sunken glare of his fierce, crow-footed eyes if I wanted to know; and so I bore it, reflecting how much certain forms of evil are akin to madness, derived from intense egoism, inflamed by resistance, tearing the soul to pieces, and giving factitious vigour to the body. (P. 209)

The details of this sketch help to explain why Jim's response to Brown is so strong. In their confrontation across the muddy creek, Brown simultaneously expresses maliciousness, the anger so apparent in the "sunken glare" of his eyes, and more generally that form of evil Marlow believes is "akin to madness." The misanthropy evident in these characteristics has its source in stock figures of evil: Jim has seen Brown's likes before in books, and he is simply overcome by the real thing. Obviously, Conrad was less interested in developing Brown's character than he was in Jim's response to the old pirate, and I would argue that he exists as a foil to Jim's imagination. In responding as he does, Jim repeats the process of identification that allowed him to assume Stein's personality (or at least what he thought were Stein's heroic qualities), and a large part of Brown's influence can be traced to the fact that he becomes as vital a presence in Jim's imagined world as Stein had been.

But this is only one of the literary associations responsible for the irony in the last section of *Lord Jim*. The other stems from Brown's "satanic gift of finding out the best and the weakest spot in his victims" (p. 234). Brown taunts Jim, asking him if his own past is unblemished, and as their conversation proceeds, "there ran through the rough talk a vein of common experience; a sickening suggestion of common guilt, of secret knowledge that was like a bond of their minds and of their hearts" (p. 235). Brown's words act as a text for Jim's imagination to work upon, and from these words Jim creates a vivid sense of shared guilt. Confused by his growing identification with Brown, Jim cannot understand that his "breach of faith" and Brown's anthology of crime are categorically different, that Brown's whole past is the natural expression of a deranged mind. As a consequence of this identification, Jim is paralyzed by visions of complicity, unable to do battle, and in despair because of the workings of the "imaginative faculty" that once allowed him to see Patusan as a living book.

Jim's sensitivity to real or imagined criticism is also at issue here. The "cur" incident at the trial and the chance references to the *Patna* by seamen at various ports illustrate Jim's ingrained habit of seeing himself as the center of the world's attention. To take offense where none is offered is as natural as breathing to him, and it is the other side of the coin of the exalted fantasies of heroism he entertains. This egoism—or megalomania—must be considered as an element in his identification with Brown. What happens in the confrontation with Brown is that the ego-ideal informing Jim's heroic fantasies, his belief in the humiliation that would follow upon the discovery of his identity in various Eastern ports, and his exploits in Patusan—all of which place him at the very center of the world—are rearranged by Brown's accusations. Just as the pattern of a kaleidoscope changes when the instrument is rotated, Jim comes to see himself as nothing less than an arch-criminal after Brown's words "'get in and shake his twopenny soul around and inside out and upside down.'" (p. 234). And once Jim's "romantic conscience" (p. 201) is activated by his identification with Brown, he conjures up images of disgrace "out there" that destroy his confidence in himself and at least temporarily in the text he has created for his life.

Gustaf Morf sees a considerably different set of psychological determinants at work when he argues that Jim refuses to fight because his complete identification with Brown produces an "unconscious wish . . . to see Brown (i.e., himself) go off free and powerful."[9] But if this were the case, Jim would not have endured the humiliation of the trial, and such an interpretation simplifies the complexity of Jim's reaction to Brown. While there is no question that Jim perceives a relationship through his imagined complicity in Brown's evil, his refusal to confront Brown is not an unconscious means of evading guilt but rather a dramatic recognition of guilt that he directs towards all that exists "out there"—the trial board, Marlow, and, still further back, his family and his youthful, untarnished vision of himself. Jim cannot act on the level of violent, physical battle because he is paralyzed by the identification we have been exploring, but he does act imaginatively out of a confused but deeply-felt conviction that he is somehow atoning for a "breach of faith" that he has tragically conflated with Brown's crimes.

Many of the tensions of the Patusan section are resolved by Jim's announcement to the Bugis community of his decision to let Brown and his men go. The full significance of the Eastern bride remains to be revealed, but the implications of the symbol of the moon and of Jim's literary reaction to Patusan are clarified in the confrontation with Brown which illustrates the "profound and terrifying logic" of Marlow's earlier observation that imagination can "set loose upon us the might of an overwhelming destiny."

There is no need to rehearse the disastrous events leading up to Jim's appearance before Doramin where he is determined that "the dark powers should not rob him twice of his peace" (p. 248). But we should remember that as Jim prepares to cross the river to Doramin's compound, he responds to Jewel's frantic question about whether he will defend himself with a phrase he always reserves for dramatic moments: "'Nothing can touch me,' he said in a last flicker of superb egoism" (p. 251). Nothing can touch him because, in giving himself up to certain death, Jim disdains the "dark powers" of his fate that have brought a second disgrace upon him; as he sees it, the manner of his death will transcend the Brown fiasco and cancel his past. And what he foresees is true. At the moment he takes Doramin's shot, "they say that the white man sent right and left at all those faces a proud and unflinching glance" (p. 253). This pride and his "superb egoism" are brought into focus during the last moments of Jim's life: "Not in the wildest days of his boyish visions could he have seen the alluring shape of such an extraordinary success! For it may very well be that in the short moment of his last proud and unflinching glance, he had beheld the face of that opportunity which, like an Eastern bride, has come veiled to his side" (p. 253). Unveiled, it disclosed Jim as one of those "impeccable men who never fall out of the ranks" (p. 239), and his last gesture of pride confirms Jim's view of his own death as an act of remarkable heroism that places him ineluctably among those ranks. "We can see him," Marlow says, "an obscure conqueror of fame, tearing himself out of the arms of a jealous love at the sign, at the call of his exalted egoism. He goes away from a living woman to celebrate his pitiless wedding with a shadowy ideal of conduct." And so what we have witnessed in this melodramatic scene is a celebration of self, a consummation with the ego-ideal whose "alluring shape" no narcissist can resist.

V

In *Lord Jim* Conrad's philosophical position is set against what in 1900 was still a relatively new and profoundly disturbing problem: the isolating effect of consciousness. Acknowledging in his correspondence as well as his fiction his tendency to see isolation as the condition of modern man, and admitting probably more often than he would have liked that life is like a dream, Conrad showed how exclusive attention to the self and the severing of one's ties with the social world inevitably lead to disaster. He has been called a pessimist who was convinced that humanity had no choice but to accept the impersonal forces of the universe,[10] but he nevertheless managed to forge a philosophy which, if not conducive to happiness, at least made survival and even satisfaction possible. The basis of this philosophy is his "conviction that the world, the temporal world, rests on a few very simple ideas. . . . It rests notably, among others, on the idea of Fidelity"[11] to what one can perceive of reality, to one's place in the community of mankind, and to the craftsmanship of whatever profession one has chosen. Conrad's "conviction" is clearly manifested in Marlow and those other sailors who are acutely conscious of their relationship to each other, their ships, and the sea.

While the theme of isolation appears throughout Conrad's work, he emphasizes personal responsibility in a way that we do not feel in many other modern novels, and it is just this advocacy that makes him a special case. If the human condition in the twentieth century is often summarized in the image of a solitary individual wandering the streets of Dublin or the beaches of Algiers, Conrad places at least part of the responsibility for this isolation on the misuse of imagination. Solipsism is the modern condition for many of the novelists represented in this study, but in *Lord Jim* it is also symptomatic of disrespect for the limited but rich possibilities of life.

5
"A Queer and Fantastic World": Romance and Society in *The Good Soldier*

> I suppose that Impressionism exists to render those queer effects of real life that are like so many views seen through bright glass—through glass so bright that whilst you perceive through it a landscape or a backyard, you are aware that, on its surface, it reflects a face of a person behind you. For the whole of life is really like that; we are almost always in one place with our minds somewhere quite other.
> —Ford Madox Ford, "On Impressionism"

I

In *The Good Soldier* Ford shows us two worlds simultaneously coming apart at the seams: the "four-square coterie"[1] of the Dowells and Ashburnhams and the society of Edwardian England on the eve of the First World War. The disintegration of these worlds is manifested in the conflict between the bourgeois, dogma-ridden Irish Catholic, Leonora, and her aristocratic Anglican husband, Edward. But the theme of disintegration is also present in the materials of Romance associated with Edward's background and his habitual reading of sentimental literature. Ford's achievement rests not only on the "intricate tangle of references and cross-references" (p. xx) that constitutes the remarkable impressionistic structure of the novel, but also on his ironic deployment of historical motifs that inform Edward's imagination and define the central vision of *The Good Soldier*.

A medieval ideology guides Edward's attitudes towards himself and everyone with whom he comes in contact. In his study of the English novel Arnold Kettle discusses those elements of feudalism and its literature that exert an irresistible influence on

98

Edward's imagination. "Feudalism," argues Kettle, "the society of the Middle Ages, had as its principal characteristic a peculiar rigidity of human relationships and ideas which sprang inevitably from the social structure. . . . Their whole interest, their very existence as the kind of people they were, demanded the preservation . . . of the *status quo.*"[2] Rigidity within this context means stasis, attitudes frozen in time, unamenable to other pursuasions. *The Good Soldier* consistently dramatizes the consequences of stasis or rigidity as it is reflected in Edward's imagination. But even more important to the argument of this book is the fact that Ford's novel develops a dialectic between Edward's fantasies and the irretrievability of the past, reflecting the deadweight of gone worlds. This obviously encourages comparisons to the novels I have previously discussed. Notice first that, despite his dedication to "the world of impossible achievements," Jim's fantasies are organized around a desire to live in the world "out there," that is, the present. Much the same can be said of Chopin's Edna Pontellier—in fact, we see an interesting tension in *The Awakening* between the timelessness of Romance, which Edna initially succumbs to, and her subsequent efforts to come to grips with the present. But Edward's thought always leads him backwards in time to the medieval world Ford also idealized, and such regressiveness shows him to be as ignorant of the demands of contingent reality as Emma Bovary.

Edward's passions cannot be separated from his aristocratic, feudal view of the nature of relationships between men and women. In this he is also like Emma Bovary, for his actions play havoc with established social mores and threaten the basic order of society. But Edward resembles Emma in another, more important way: he dehumanizes his women just as Emma dehumanizes her men by making them projections of his reading so that we are always conscious of a distance between a woman and the person Edward imagines her to be. Such imaginative projection could succeed during the flowering of courtly love because those associated with the courts believed in the same fictions—the ladies and knights were rigidly typecast, seeing themselves mirrored in their roles, seeing only the roles of those surrounding them. But a society of personae can survive only so long as everyone believes in personification—when only Edward takes seriously the tenets of courtly love and the feudal concept of social order, then we have a conflict identical to that which lies at the center of *Madame Bovary,* a conflict between a personal fiction and social reality, which can only result in the destruction of the individual because the perpetuation of his fictions is inimical to the welfare of society. The social order of the Middle Ages and Edwardian England was complex and multi-layered, but the Romantic personal fiction is simple and denies by definition any and all ties beyond the "community of the elect." What we have here finally is a dialectical opposition between stasis and kinesis, past and present, history and the contemporary, evolving social moment. A large part of Edward's attraction to the static world of feudalism lies in the fact that it does not change, that it presents a world in which all variables are known—and this confirms the distinctions I have been making between the simplified world of Romance, where life functions according to something like a plot, and reality, where chance replaces the predictable.

The conflict engendered by this dialectic occupies much of the third chapter of Part III of *The Good Soldier,* where John Dowell explains the basic difference between Edward and Leonora:

> You see, Edward was really a very simply soul—very simple. He imagined that no man can satisfactorily accomplish his life's work without loyal and whole-hearted co-operation of the woman he lives with. And he was beginning to perceive dimly that, whereas his own traditions were entirely collective, his wife was a sheer individualist. His own theory—the feudal theory of an overlord doing his best for his dependents, the dependents meanwhile doing their best for the overlord—this theory was entirely foreign to Leonora's nature. She came of a family of small Irish landlords—that hostile garrison in a plundered country. And she was thinking unceasingly of the children she wished to have. (P. 146)

The first of their many differences occurs when Edward speaks of his "desire to build a Roman Catholic chapel at Branshaw" (p. 142) for Leonora. "Real trouble between them" began at this point, for Edward was "truly grieved at his wife's want of sentiment—at her refusal to receive that amount of public homage from him. She appeared to him to be wanting in imagination—to be cold and hard" (p. 142). From that moment Edward reacts against what he considers to be the mundane economic responsibility Leonora increasingly insists on, dimly perceiving in each of her objections a threat to his imagined world. At the same time, Leonora's original passion for Edward becomes confused by frustration, for in Edward's extravagance she sees her own security, and that of any children she might have, threatened by impecunious tenants and Edward's troops.

These differences in class ideologies are not confined to Edward's relationship with Leonora. While his sentimental "heart" leads Edward into his various affairs, his conduct in those affairs generally reflects the traditional attitudes and privileges of his class. For example, Edward can "console" the Kilsyte girl *because* she is a member of the working class, and, while it seems only natural for him to offer her the benefits of his comforts, the girl does not feel the same way: "All of her life, by her mother, by other girls, by school-teachers, by the whole tradition of her class she had been warned against gentlemen. She was being kissed by a gentleman. She screamed . . . " (p. 150). Similar class attitudes can be traced in Edward's relationships with La Dolciquita, Maisie Maiden, and even in the platonic entanglement with Nancy (Mrs. Basil and Florence are ladies of the court) where we see distorted, but perceptible, signs of the feudal doctrine of *droit de seigneur.*

In what follows I hope to show that Edward's passions are undeniably authentic and moving, but that his search for an ideal woman can only lead to disaster because of his heritage, whose simplified paradigm of life is further skewed by his Romantic imagination. Edward is incapable of distinguishing between the ideal, closed, static world of history and Romantic literature and the problematic, open, unpredictable elements of reality. This naiveté leads to devastating consequences for Ford's "Beati Immaculati."

II

The first three chapters unfold against this complex social background, and by the time we reach the end of the third chapter we have encountered the major elements that define the strange *ménage* that centers on a man who is being flayed alive by his own emotions and his wife's jealousy. Chapters 1 and 2 introduce the themes of romance and social disintegration in allusions to the troubadour Peire Vidal and to the French revolution. In the third chapter we are taken back nine years to the German spa Bad Nauheim, where "the whole round table [was] begun" (p. 33). This time shift introduces a second, more ironic, evaluation of what Dowell characterizes as the "minuet of the Hessian bathing places" (p. 16). There are striking images contrasting the platonic minuet with the "mad house" of human emotions, as well as seemingly incongrous anecdotes dealing with Leonora's failed attempt at sex with Rodney Bayham in the dark recesses of a carriage and with the idefatigable energy of Vidal who sought the favors of a chatelaine in the Provençal countryside. These stories of arrested and frustrated passion are given in the memoirs of John Dowell, who has recorded his impressions of a life spent "wander[ing] upon the face of public resorts" (p. 21), a life which led him, years later, to the country house where Edward Ashburnham was suffering from the final passion of his life: "That poor devil beside me was in an agony. Absolute, hopeless, dumb agony such as surpasses the mind of man to imagine" (p. 20).

The imagery of these initial chapters is remarkably rich and varied; it is also characteristically violent. Ford proceeds, by way of abrupt juxtapositions, from ordered but superficial forms to the chaotic reality underlying them. Nowhere in the novel is this method more apparent than in Dowell's opening evaluations of his experiences at Bad Nauheim. After sketching in the social background of the Ashburnhams and of himself and his wife, Dowell's attention shifts to images of disintegration—"the sack of a city or the falling to pieces of a people" (p. 5), decay— "Someone has said that the death of a mouse from cancer is the whole sack of Rome by the Goths, and I swear to you that the breaking up of our little four-square coterie was such another unthinkable event" (p. 5), and disbelief—"Permanence? Stability! I can't believe it's gone" (p. 6). His incredulity over the fate of their coterie continues in a speech organized around an image of a highly sophisticated society that reflects the typical elements of the closed world of Romance:

> I can't believe that that long, tranquil life, which was just stepping a minuet, vanished in four crashing days at the end of nine years and six weeks. Upon my word, yes, our intimacy was like a minuet, simply because on every possible occasion and in every possible circumstance we knew where to go, where to sit, which table we unanimously should choose; and we could rise and go, all four together, without a signal from any one of us, always to the music of the Kur orchestra, always in the temperate sunshine, or, if it rained, in discreet shelters. No, indeed, it can't be gone. You can't kill a minuet

de la cour. You may shut up the music-book, close the harp-
sichord; in the cupboard and presses the rats may destroy the
while satin favours. The mob may sack Versailles; the Trianon
may fall, but surely the minuet—the minuet itself is dancing
itself away into the furthest stars, even as our minuet of the
Hessian bathing places must be stepping itself still. Isn't there
any Nirvana pervaded by the faint thrilling of instruments that
have fallen into the dust of wormwood but that yet had frail,
tremulous, and everlasting souls? (Pp. 6–7)

But in the time it takes for the rhythm of that last sentence to
settle into his consciousness, Dowell sees the contradiction of
his experience:

No, by God, it is false! It wasn't a minuet that we stepped; it
was a prison—a prison full of screaming hysterics, tied down
so that they might not outsound the rolling of our carriage
wheels as we went along the shaded avenues of the Taunus
Wald. (P. 7)

Despite the intensity of their desires, Ford's characters discover, each in his own way, that it is not in the measured form of
the minuet, but rather in the violent prison "full of screaming
hysterics" that the meaning of their lives is reflected.

In his evocation of the minuet, Dowell wistfully hopes for an
order that transcends the mutability of time, a kind of romantic
synchronicity capable of surviving social anarchy and guaran-
teeing permanence. By taking the minuet as a symbol of social
perfection, Dowell's attitude merges with Edward's, for the
highly structured musical form mirrors the "peculiar rigidity of
human relationships" within Edward's historical vision of society. One could also argue that the music of the "Hessian bathing
places," as well as the songs of the troubadours with which we
associate Edward through Peire Vidal, are both meant to evoke
a shock-proof world. Unlike Edward, however, Dowell comes
to understand that there is a discrepancy between his desire and
reality, admitting in his conclusion that the harmony of the
minuet only masks the dissonance of human experience. While
Edward never discriminates between the dancer and the dance,
Dowell learns that the elegant but static form must inevitably be
left behind in the diachronic world of change, disorder, and nihilism.

The figure of the minuet striving towards nirvana thus complements Conrad's metaphor of the destructive element; in fact, its trajectory passes through *Lord Jim* to corresponding figures of the sea in *The Awakening* and *Madame Bovary*. The equivalence of the terms in Ford's and Conrad's novels can be stated as follows: the minuet is to the sea as nirvana is to Romantic Idealism, and the prison, or death by drowning, signifies the reality principle. In relation to Stein's metaphor, Dowell's prison image can be seen to complete Stein's final comment that the dream must be followed until the end, where, in the case of *The Good Soldier,* are revealed the disorder of reality, the falseness of the minuet's promise, the disintegration of social and personal stability. By placing this passage at the beginning of his novel, Ford achieved an extremely economical means of coloring every action and statement by his four major characters. Of fundamental importance here is that each of the four novels discussed so far offers central images of Romanticism which are remarkably close in terminology and implication.

The violence that lies beyond the "shaded avenues of the Taunus Wald" is transposed to another setting when Dowell introduces the "lamentable history of Peire Vidal" (p. 13) during his recollection of a trip into Provence:

> Two years ago Florence and I motored from Biarritz to Las Tours, which is in the Black Mountains. In the middle of a tortuous valley there rises up an immense pinnacle and on the pinnacle are four castles—Las Tours, the Towers. And the immense mistral blew down that valley which was the way from France into Provence so that the silver-grey olive leaves appeared like hair flying in the wind, and the tufts of rosemary crept into the iron rocks that they might not be torn up by the roots. (P. 13)

The essence of *The Good Soldier* is symbolized in these images of discord and stress, and, by reminding us that "hair flying in the wind" is the "classical image of grief,"[3] John Meixner emphasizes the central emotion of the novel. There is no question that the violence of the mistral is in perfect accord with the violent passions that drive Vidal in his attempts to win the favours of La Louve, and the two paragraphs Ford gives over to Vidal's antics a few pages later describe, in comic terms, the same kind of agonies as Edward suffers in each of his affairs, but especially in his unrequited passion for Nancy Rufford.

Vidal is the fool of love, a direct link to the Provençal courts and feudalism, but we miss his significance if we see him merely as a symbol of the ethics of passion that once flourished in Provence. There is a disjunction between Vidal's antics which, comic as they are, were an acceptable part of the courtly social world and Edward's, which are socially out of place because they are out of time. Ezra Pound's poem about Vidal—"O Age gone lax! O stunted followers,/ That mask at passions and desire desires"—[4] chastizes modern man for sublimating his emotions, but it also registers a difference between Vidal's age and Edward's. Vidal's love is heroic because it expresses a very limited, but nevertheless real, social attitude toward love; Edward's represents the degenerate ideal of love that has come down to him through Romantic literature. The source of Edward's fantasies can be found in the self-consciousness of his narcissism; the source of Vidal's in the will of a stratum of medieval society. Thus the juxtaposition of Edward and Vidal reveals a tension between Vidal's twelfth century Provence and Edward's modern India and Europe. But the main point to emphasize here is that their ideals of love cannot be separated from Romantic egocentrism that forces roles to displace personality. So the irony often mentioned in Edward's resemblance to Vidal is really more deeply rooted in the novel's thematic texture than has been noticed, particularly in the disturbing questions Dowell raises at the end of his narrative about the conflict between passion and society and the fantasies men entertain about themselves.

A closer look at the literary sources of Edward's fantasies takes us into territory previously explored by Flaubert and Conrad. Just as the source of Emma's romantic notions was her convent reading and Jim's his double apprenticeship to tales of adventure and the sea, Edward's adolescent fantasies were confirmed by the sentimental literature he read even when he was a military cadet:

At Sandhurst . . . he was keen on soldiering, keen on mathematics, on land-surveying, on politics, and, by a queer warp of his mind, on literature. Even when he was twenty-two he would pass hours reading one of Scott's novels or the Chronicles of Froissart. (P. 137)

And he was especially attracted to

novels in which typewriter girls married marquises and gover-

nesses earls. And in his books, as a rule, the course of true
love ran as smooth as buttered honey. And he was fond of
poetry, of a certain type—and he could even read a perfectly
sad love story. I have seen his eyes filled with tears at reading
of a hopeless parting. (P. 27)

Edward's sentimental vulnerability is balanced by his wife's de-
cidedly unromantic views of love and marriage. Within a few
years Leonora's attitudes become antithetical to all that is assumed in her husband's "sentimental view of the cosmos"
(p. 27). She has come to see "life as a perpetual sex-battle"
(p. 186) between unfaithful husbands and faithful suffering
wives, a position Dowell attributes to the absence of a literary
sensibility:

> Man, for her, was a sort of brute who must have his divaga-
> tions, his moments of excess, his night out, his, let us say,
> rutting seasons. She had read few novels, so that the idea of a
> pure and constant love succeeding the sound of wedding bells
> had never been very much presented to her. (P. 186)

The comic irony of Edward's reading, of course, is that it has
produced a dedication to those "divagations" which offend the
ethics of popular romantic fiction while confirming those of adulterous courtly-love liaisons.

It is sentimental literature, along with radically different class
ideologies, that separates Leonora and her husband. Edward
tries for a while to draw Leonora into his fictive world, but she
cannot enter because she does not have the requisite imaginative
sensibility, and Edward begins to look for others who can satisfy
his literary desires—as well as his physical ones. Opposed to
Edward's optimistic belief that his divagations reflect a superre-
ality is Leonora's religious tradition, which counsels resignation
in the face of such indulgences. This is comically but painfully
apparent when Leonora seeks advice about Edward's adventure
with the Spanish dancer from the Mother Superior of her old
convent. "Men are like that," the nun says. "By the blessing of
God it will all come right in the end" (p. 186). What we have here
is a difference between optimistic, passionate expectation and
pessimistic, resigned acceptance of fate; and the dramatic consequences of these differences are obvious in *The Good Soldier*.
Leonora cannot be drawn into Edward's imaginative world because it denies all that she has learned about reality. For her,

Edward is not ennobled by his sentimental views; he is only made to appear more irresponsible, more prone to "moments of excess."

But what drives Leonora away attracts Mrs. Basil, Maisie Maidan, and Nancy (La Dolciquita and Florence are special cases—the first responds to Edward only as a business liaison, the second as a sexual object). "What did they all see in him?" Dowell wonders. "Suddenly, as if by a flash of inspiration," he knew: "All good soldiers are sentimentalists—all good soldiers of that type. Their profession, for one thing, is full of the big words—'courage,' 'loyalty,' 'honor,' 'constancy'" (p. 27). Dowell then sketches in what Edward at times "blurted out" concerning "the sentimental view of the cosmos that was his," at the center of which were received ideas about the redemptive effects of a woman on a man and the virtues of fidelity. "So you see," Dowell concludes, "he would have plenty to gurgle about to a woman—with that and his sound common sense about martingales and his—still sentimental—experiences as a county magistrate; and with his intense, optimistic belief that the woman he was making love to at the moment was the one he was destined, at last, to be eternally constant to . . . (pp. 27–28). As I suggested earlier, Edward's sentimentality is never far away from narcissism, and the women he finds irresistible are largely attractive because they see him as he sees himself. Maisie Maidan was star-struck, "perpetually asking her boy husband why he could not dress, ride, shoot, play polo, or even recite sentimental poems, like their Major" (p. 181). For Nancy Rufford, Edward was the "Cid; he was Lohengrin, he was the Chevalier Bayard" (p. 226). Such affirmations of his ego-ideal beguile Edward with the force of magic one associates with fairy tales, and it is unquestionably a fantasy world Edward hopes to enter with all of his women (even with Leonora when they are first married)—a fantasy world characterized by the absence of pain that issues from moments of insight, accidents of character, or social demands that complicate reality—a world frozen in time where feelings respond to the dictates of a medieval code.

III

The violent, tragic effects of Edward's beliefs are dramatized in the last half of *The Good Soldier* where Ford develops the bizarre triangle formed by Leonora, Edward, and Nancy. Nancy has grown up with Edward and, as we have seen, worshipped him: "He was for her, in everything that she said . . . the model of humanity, the hero, the athlete, the father of his country, the lawgiver" (p. 112). While she was a child, Edward accepted these accolades as a grateful and happy guardian, but, when he suddenly senses that she has become a woman, he develops a passion for her that exceeds anything he experienced with his former mistresses or his wife. The effects of Edward's newly discovered passion are devastating for both Nancy and Leonora. His unspoken but clearly felt demands literally push Leonora over the edge, causing her mind to "waver," and the instability we sense in Nancy from the moment she is introduced is tragically heightened by the confusion of feelings she develops towards this man. By attempting to force Leonora and Nancy into the field of his imagination, Edward deprives both of them of their own ground, for his solipsistic concerns serve to cut them off from all connections with the security of their private worlds and traditions. While the result of this appropriation is muted until they all return to Branshaw Teleragh, Leonora's suffering begins at Nauheim.

The ground is cut from under Leonora on the night Edward discovers his passion for Nancy and speaks to her of the great sentimental verities. Leonora "had guessed what had happened under the trees near the Casino" (p. 123), and, from that moment of intuition until Edward's death, is consumed by jealousy and frightening visions of chaos encroaching on what she believed was an ordered world. But Leonora does not know that Edward never intended to tell Nancy more than he did that night, nor to do anything more than worship her in his sentimental way. "He was very careful to assure me that at that time there was no physical motive about his declaration," Dowell writes. "It did not appear to him to be a matter of a dark night and a propinquity and so on. No, it was simply of her effect on the moral side of his life that he appears to have talked" (p. 112). Leonora's ignorance of this indulgence in innocent admiration leads her to keep a strict vigil, never allowing Edward and Nancy to be alone together except in crowded places in broad daylight. Her suspicions are justified because during this time Edward had begun to show the tell-tale signs of unrequited love—that is, a disjunction between his imagination and reality—with which Leonora was familiar from his previous infatuations. It is only a matter of time before her suspicions are confirmed that it is Nancy, and not memories of the now dead Florence, who is the source of the latest, and what proves to be the last, of Edward's passionate afflictions.

The events of the last three weeks at Nauheim are extraordinarily dramatic; time seems to have been suspended in this elegant spa where we are aware only of profound emotions slowly intersecting each other in a dream-like world. Leonora watches Edward "as a fierce cat watches an unconscious pigeon in the road way" (p. 130), Edward remains silent and drinks late into the night, and Nancy is sent to bed at ten and performs a "nightly orison" with Leonora for Florence. While Nancy remains ignorant of the conflict between her guardians, Leonora is consumed by the agony of jealousy, and beneath his somnambulistic torpor Edward is being torn to "rags and tatters" (p. 116) by his feelings for the girl. All of this emotion is masked by superficial conversation that can best be illustrated by a comment Ford once made about Henry James: "His characters will talk about the rain, about the opera, about the moral aspects of the selling of Old Masters to the New Republic, and those conversations will convey to your mind that the quiet talkers are living in an atmosphere of horror, of bankruptcy, of passion as hopeless as the Dies Irae!"[5] The unvoiced suffering Ford points to dominates the Ashburnhams at Nauheim, and one scene in particular conveys these Jamesian qualities. On the last night of their stay, Leonora relents in her vigilance and allows Edward to take Nancy on a final visit to the Casino. Later that night,

> Leonora could hear Edward going about his room, but, owing to the girl's chatter, she could not tell whether he went out again or not. And then, much later, because she thought that if he were drinking again something must be done to stop it, she opened for the first time, and very softly, the never-opened door between their rooms. She wanted to see if he had gone out again. Edward was kneeling beside his bed with his head hidden in the counterpane. His arms, outstretched, held out before him a little image of the blessed virgin—a tawdry, scarlet and Prussian-blue affair that the girl had given him on her first return from the convent. His shoulders heaved convulsively three times, and heavy sobs came from him before she could close the door. He was not a Catholic; but that was the way it took him. (Pp. 133–134)

Edward's pain prefigures the emotional disaster that lies in wait for all of them at Branshaw Teleragh, for from this moment the

"Beati Immaculati" will move under the "shadow of an eternal wrath . . . drifting down life, like fireships afloat on a lagoon and causing miseries, heartaches, agony of the mind, and death" (p. 164).

Readers are inclined to see Leonora as the source of these miseries and Edward as a heroic figure who gives all for love, but Ford's treatment of Leonora is considerably more sympathetic than it may first appear to be. Up to this point Leonora has been presented as a woman who is cold and unresponsive and whose vision has been delimited by the rigorous Catholicism inherited from her Irish background. Once the *ménage* arrives at Branshaw, Leonora's distress forces her into acts that she would very likely have avoided had she the strength and insight of normal health. Dowell tells us that "with the slackening of her vigilance, came the slackening of her entire mind. This is perhaps the most miserable part of the entire story, for it is miserable to see a clear intelligence waver; and Leonora wavered" (p. 134). With the relaxation of tension following her conviction that Edward will not seduce Nancy comes a vulnerability to all the emotions she has repressed over the years. The destructive, violent acts that follow upon this vulnerability are the result of an intense concentration of contradictory and unresolvable emotions of maternal love for Nancy, jealousy of her as the final passion of Edward's life, disgust for Edward's weakness in giving in to this passion, and pity and respect for his decision to leave Nancy alone. The crisis Leonora helps to precipitate at Branshaw is largely the result of neurosis and hysteria in a woman who for years has been driven closer and closer to the breaking point by her husband's extraordinarily insensitive and irresponsible behavior.

An uneasy silence pervades Branshaw for a while as the days are filled with Leonora's absorption in her migraines and Edward's in his silences and drink. But this hiatus in what Dowell characterizes as a "duel with invisible weapons" (p. 123) ends when Nancy's innocence is shaken by her recognition of a "profound difference" between her guardians because of Edward's gift of a horse to a young man whose family has long been in the service of the Ashburnhams. In this act Nancy sees a further example of Edward's heroic generosity, but in response to her praise of Edward Leonora bursts out: "I wish to God that he was your husband and not mine. We shall be ruined, we shall be ruined. Am I *never* to have a chance?" (p. 208). Nancy's enthusiasm could not have come at a worse moment since that day Leonora had been occupied with feelings of hatred and jealousy for both Nancy and Edward. Just before Nancy had spoken to her, Leonora had heard them return to the house:

> At that moment Leonora hated Edward with a hatred that was like hell, and she would have liked to bring her riding-whip down across the girl's face. . . . Yes, Leonora wished to bring her riding-whip down in Nancy's young face. She imagined the pleasure she would feel when the lash fell across those queer features, the pleasure she would feel at drawing the handle at the same moment toward her, so as to cut deep into the flesh and to leave a lasting wheal. (P. 210)

Leonora's jealousy of Edward is redirected to Nancy who has innocently brought before Leonora one more time her husband's financial irresponsibility. In the gift of the horse is concentrated all of Leonora's frustrations, and the sexual jealousy that lies at the center of her feelings simply blots out all perspective and leads to a series of actions that are among the most painful and most psychologically accurate graphs of human emotions in modern literature. Ford presents a double challenge to his reader here: to understand why Leonora feels as she does, and to understand that the rational world has been left forever in the past for all three of these sufferers. It is partly this explosion of feeling and its consequences that Dowell had in mind earlier when he described the underlying reality of the "four-square coterie" as a place filled with "screaming hysterics."

And this is when Dowell arrives to find Edward in "hopeless, dumb agony such as surpasses the mind of man to imagine." What he finds continues the tension between appearance and reality, the superficial talk in perfect accord with the Ashburnham's British decorum that masks the sense of the Dies Irae. But it is only a mask and Dowell learns that "what had happened was just hell":

> Leonora had spoken to Nancy; Nancy had spoken to Edward; Edward had spoken to Leonora—and they had talked and talked. And talked. You have to imagine horrible pictures of gloom and half lights, and emotions running through silent nights—through whole nights. You have to imagine my beautiful Nancy appearing suddenly to Edward, rising up at the foot of his bed, with her long hair falling, like a split cone of

shadow, in the glimmer of a night-light that burned beside him. You have to imagine her, a silent, no doubt agonized figure, like a spectre, suddenly offering herself to him—to save his reason! And you have to imagine his frantic refusal—and talk. And talk! My God! (P. 201)

Their words "flayed the skin off him" (p. 239). In Leonora's accusations and Nancy's offering of herself to save his life, "they were like a couple of Sioux who had got hold of an Apache and had him well tied to a stake. I tell you there was no end to the tortures they inflicted upon him" (p. 239).

The type of this confrontation is Dowell's story of Vidal, with Leonora acting the role of La Louve's husband who "remonstrated seriously with her" (p. 18) when she rejected the troubadour's love. But in the passion of his life Edward is steadfastly virtuous, suffering "like one of the ancient Greek damned" (p. 252). "Drunk or sober," Dowell writes, Edward "stuck to what was demanded by convention and by the traditions of his house" (p. 238), avoiding one of the oldest taboos of mankind, for what is often glossed over is the blatantly incestuous nature of his passion for Nancy. In resisting her innocent offer of herself to save his reason, Edward upholds the feudal-romantic tradition that Leonora's hysterical reaction almost succeeded in destroying. At the same time, we need to remember that it was Edward's view of himself as a composite lord of the manor and courtly lover that precipitated the situation with Nancy, while Leonora's years of suffering are responsible for her hysteria and the revenge she attempts. There are no easy answers here, no measuring out of unmitigated guilt or virtue. As Hugh Kenner has said, Ford is "in an impasse of sympathy for all sides."[6]

It is inevitable that Edward commits suicide because the absence of any acknowledged suffering in Nancy's telegram violates his imagined world. It is also inevitable that Nancy is driven into incurable madness when she learns of Edward's death—despite what she had learned about him from Leonora, he was still the symbol of order in a world that had come crashing down around her. In light of these tragic events, as well as Leonora's having found peace with Rodney Bayham and Dowell's new role as Nancy's nurse whom he enshrines in the silent rooms of Branshaw, Dowell's final evaluation of their communal experience is especially disturbing. "It is," he says, "a queer and fantastic world":

Is there then any terrestrial paradise where, amidst the whispering of the olive-leaves, people can be with whom they like and have what they like and take their ease in shadows and in coolness? Or are all men's lives like the lives of us good people—like the lives of the Ashburnhams, of the Dowells, of the Ruffords—broken, tumultuous, agonized, and unromantic lives, periods punctuated by screams, by imbecilities, by deaths, by agonies. Who the devil knows? (P. 238)

Dowell has learned much since he first sat down to order his impressions of the "coterie," and these questions reverberate ironically against his earlier naive evocation of the inviolable minuet. That naiveté is faintly perceptible in his answers to these questions, particularly in the bitterness we sense against the parameters society imposes on idiosyncratic desires and behavior. "Yes," he muses, "society must go on" (p. 254). "Edward was the normal man, but there was too much of the sentimentalist about him and society does not need too many sentimentalists. Nancy was a splendid creature but she had about her a touch of madness. Society does not need individuals with touches of madness about them" (p. 238). And these speculations conclude with his notion that "Edward and Nancy found themselves steam-rolled out and Leonora survives, the perfectly normal type, married to a man who is rather like a rabbit" (p. 238). Edward's Romantic imagination posited "a community of the elect, a circle of solidarity . . . set apart from the common herd," but Dowell has learned that the romantic's inability to see himself and others as individuals enmeshed in the common life of humanity threatens the integrity of both the individual and the social order.

IV

There is much of Ford himself in Edward Ashburnham, and perhaps the most telling observation about this congruence is Ezra Pound's: "That Ford was almost an *halluciné* few of his intimates can doubt. He felt until it paralyzed his efficient action, he saw distinctly the Venus immortal crossing the tram tracks."[7] But, while Ford may have personally mourned the loss of "courtesie" and the plot that Romance gave to one's passional life, he was deeply aware of the destructive qualities inherent in Edward's view of history. Edward's attempt to actualize his

idiosyncratic vision fails, Ford argues, because the love it manifests only masks solipsism and devalues the loved one since it
forces each of Edward's women into his imaginative world
where they become fictional projections of his fantasies. The
direct result of this tension between desire and reality is that
values in *The Good Soldier* remained mired in the realm of possibility, because Edward's romanticism lacks any consciously apprehended principles. Like Emma Bovary, Edward reductively
interpolates Romanticism, for his sentimental, unexamined feelings are imposed on the complex ideals of this movement, distorting it in his narcissistic expropriation of its tenets to his own
ends. Such distortion suggests a nihilistic view of human experience only if we do not see that the values of the novel are not
negated, only suspended, and that the alienation of the "Beati
Immaculati" carries with it the condition necessary for escape.
That condition involves movement away from solipsism to integration, from the "rigidity of human relationships" as Edward
conceived of them to a new perspective where individuals can be
seen as themselves as well as members of the social order. The
division we sense in *The Good Soldier* between Edward's fantasies about social purpose and what he helplessly *does* to those
nearest him is resolved in *Parade's End,* where Ford reimagines
an English country gentleman whose idealism and medieval
code of conduct spring from compassion rather than from a
sense of inherited duty, where Christopher Tietjen's love for
Valentine Wannop and his often repeated motto—"I stand for
monogamy and chastity"—[8] graph the distance between a man of
honor and an engaging but sentimental and corrupting *puer eter-
nus*. Having regressed to the ideals of feudalism and the courts
of love, Edward is stranded in a static world out of time. This
isolation is also true of Fitzgerald's mercurial Gatsby who, like
Edward, seeks the past with a Romantic divining rod.

6
F. Scott Fitzgerald's "Universe of Ineffable Gaudiness"

> "Isabelle," he cried, half involuntarily, and held out
> his arms. As in the story-books, she ran into them, and
> on that half-minute, as their lips first touched, rested
> the high point of vanity, the crest of his young egotism.
> —F. Scott Fitzgerald, *This Side of Paradise*

I

The following interpretation of *The Great Gatsby* is the most controversial in this book. It will not please Fitzgerald enthusiasts, and there is a distinct possibility that even those readers with reservations similar to mine will begin to feel defensive. But evidence that the novel misfires, that Fitzgerald's own romantic attitudes seriously compromise what he was trying to say in his best work, justifies the critical position I have taken here, which extends ideas familiar from my earlier discussions.

The problem I am interested in exploring is set out in the novel's epigraph:

> Then wear the gold hat, if that will move her;
> 　If you can bounce high, bounce for her too,
> Till she cry "Lover, gold-hatted, high-bouncing lover,
> 　I must have you!"

Like Gatsby, Fitzgerald wore the gold hat, convinced that the demon lover Zelda symbolized would be overwhelmed by his "unutterable vision."[1] This congruence makes *The Great Gatsby* a special case because Fitzgerald's own "heightened sensitivity to the promises of life" (p. 2) presents difficulties not encountered in *Madame Bovary, The Awakening, Lord Jim* or *The*

Good Soldier. Along with Nick and Gatsby, he was victimized by romantic visions to such an extent that his inability to distinguish between real and imagined experience, to keep his own views suppressed or at least disguised, brings into "life" a problematic situation confined until now to fictive worlds. The trace of Fitzgerald's own "romantic readiness" dominates *The Great Gatsby.* To understand how it damages the novel, it will be necessary to review what Fitzgerald was attempting to do and then to explore how his personality interfered with those intentions.

We know that between 1920 and 1925 Fitzgerald was searching for a means to improve his narrative technique, which, combined with his subject matter, had led to the less-than-critical success of *This Side of Paradise* and *The Beautiful and Damned.* In James, Conrad, and Ford, among others, he found examples of narration and scenic presentation that eventually made their way into his book.[2] The most obvious influences were *Heart of Darkness, Lord Jim,* and *The Good Soldier,* all substantial examples of impressionist fiction whose tenets Ford codified in his 1924 book on Conrad and in an earlier 1913 essay titled "On Impressionism":

> One is an Impressionist because one tries to produce an illusion of reality . . . or rather the business of Impressionism is to produce that illusion. . . . The Impressionist author is sedulous to avoid letting his personality appear in the course of his book. . . . You attempt to involve the reader amongst the personages of the story. . . . You do this by presentation and by presentation and again by presentation. The moment you depart from presentation . . . at that very moment your reader's illusion that he is present at an affair in real life . . . will depart.[3]

The apparent objectivity of impressionism, which located the point of view in narrators or centers of consciousness like Marlow, John Dowell, and Lambert Strether and allowed events to unfold in *their* minds, seemed to answer at least one of the problems Fitzgerald encountered in his earlier novels—he had been too much present. Like Conrad and Ford, he was "a subjective visionary committed to the ideal of objectivity,"[4] and he was confident that, with the invention of Nick Carraway, he had found a means of focusing his materials and removing himself from the fray. In the 1934 Modern Library Edition of *The Great*

Gatsby we see Fitzgerald confidently attesting to his success: "I think it is an honest book, that is to say, that one used none of one's virtuosity to get an effect, and, to boast again, one soft-pedalled the emotional side to avoid the tears leaking from the socket of the left eye, or the large false face peering around the corner of a character's head."[5]

Fitzgerald's confidence registers more hope than fact. While he succeeded in appropriating the techniques of his predecessors and as a consequence produced a novel considerably more subtle than his earlier efforts, *Gatsby* still suffers from the imperfectly disguised authorial voice that mars *This Side of Paradise* and *The Beautiful and Damned*. As in a palimpsest, the working title of his first novel, *The Romantic Egoist*, appears just beneath the surface of *Gatsby*. Amory has been written over with Nick and Jay, while the damnation of his earlier beautiful people is reworked in his portrait of West Egg Society. In the case of *The Great Gatsby*, technique cannot anesthetize the romantic demiurge, which led Fitzgerald to repeat the visions of the earlier novels and to peer constantly around the corner of his characters' heads. "Style is the man"—and so in the case of *The Great Gatsby* is narrator, protagonist, and theme.

Arthur Mizener neatly defines the two sides of Fitzgerald's character that are compressed in *Gatsby:*

> Partly he was an enthusiastic, romantic young man. Partly he was what he called himself in the 'General Plan' for *Tender is the Night*, 'a spoiled priest.' This division shows itself in nearly every aspect of his life. The romantic young man was full of confidence about his own ability and the world's friendliness, the spoiled priest distrusted both himself and the world.[6]

The antithetical qualities of distrust and enthusiasm—read objectivity and Romanticism—dominate the narrative voice of *Gatsby*. On the one hand, there is an archness that appears in the novel's first sentence—"In my younger and more vulnerable years my father gave me some advice that I've been turning over in my mind ever since"—and sporadically reappears in phrases that evoke dour Middle Western uprightness. For example, when Nick recalls his as yet unbroken commitment to a girl back in St. Paul, he can say without flinching that "every one suspects himself of at least one of the cardinal virtues, and this is mine: I

am one of the few honest people that I have ever known" (p. 60).
On the other hand, Nick can break into Romantic lyricism at a
moment's notice. Consider his description of Gatsby's emotions
after visiting Daisy's house in Louisville when he returned from
the war: "The track curved and now it was going away from the
sun, which, as it sank lower, seemed to spread itself in benedic-
tion over the vanishing city where she had drawn her breath"
(p. 153).The young man who confidently traces his roots back to
the Dukes of Buccleuch and up through the Civil War to a solid
bourgeois "wholesale hardware business" over which his father
presides seems like an unlikely source of such evocative, if sentimental, prose. The lyrical voice obviously issues from Fitzgerald, who was compelled to peer around Nick's head because
he was overpowered by the gravitational pull of his subject. Not
only does *The Great Gatsby* reveal itself as a palimpsest—the
latest of Fitzgerald's attempts to come to grips with Romance—
but its redactive nature also manifests itself in two contradictory
narrative voices: Nick Carraway's, pragmatic Midwesterner,
and Nick Carraway's, ventriloquist's dummy for Scott Fitzgerald, irrepressible Romantic visionary.

II

"You must get to know the values," says the Count in *The Sun
Also Rises*. An attempt to know them in *The Great Gatsby* discloses two sets, one belonging to St. Paul, Minnesota, the other
to Plato. Although there seems to be nothing in common between staunch bourgeois morality and Gatsby's fantasies, Fitzgerald thought he had found a common ground in the
philosophical position he creates for Nick near the end of the
book. The apocalyptic events surrounding Gatsby's death have
caused Nick such great emotional stress that he retreats to the
past, where he experiences relief in memories "of coming back
West from prep school and later from college at Christmas
time." In Chicago's Union Station, images of expensive girls and
the promise of limitless parties crowd his mind. When the train
left it seemed headed toward a beatific vision, all of its adolescent passengers "unutterably aware of [their] identity with this
country for one strange hour, before we melted indistinguishably
into it again." And the memory becomes a gestalt allowing Nick
to understand the significance of his summer in West Egg.

"That's my Middle West," he continues, "not the wheat or the prairies or the lost Swede towns, but the thrilling returning trains of my youth. . . ." (p. 176). The simplicity of Nick's vision with its self-congratulatory coda suggesting that he and the others were deficient in guile and opportunism fixes the ethical norm of the novel not only in Middle Western ideology, but specifically in Nick's undergraduate revelation. The corrupt and corrupting East, repository of the "heap of broken images"[7] that once constituted the American Dream, is set against an idealized past which has for armature Nick's naive sensibility. The problem here is not so much with the sentimentality of Nick's vision as with the inadequacy of what it is intended to represent—an acceptable world view. Once we perceive that Nick's regression to the sensations of adolescence cannot accommodate a more complex and mature vision of human experience, *The Great Gatsby* verges on nihilism. Sympathetic as one may be to what Nick remembers as valid and valuable, its sentimentality ironically turns upon itself and reveals an emptiness which until now has been linked to fictional characters, but which in *The Great Gatsby* eventually emerges as Fitzgerald's own considered philosophical position.

What, precisely, does Nick retreat from? What is the source of corruption? We find out in the paragraph immediately following Nick's revelation. "Even when the East excited me most," he recalls, "it had always for me a quality of distortion" (p. 177). Following the famous El Greco image, he concludes that "after Gatsby's death the East was haunted for me like that, distorted beyond my eyes' power of correction. So when the blue smoke of brittle leaves was in the air and the wind blew the wet laundry stiff on the line I decided to come back home" (p. 178).

If Nick's dream is all that is attended to, then it seems as if he chooses to retreat from a world that is too rich and dramatic in human frailty and degradation for his tastes. But there is more involved. As he says on page 2 when he prepares to tell his story of the East from the safety of his ancestral halls: "I wanted the world to be in uniform and at a sort of moral attention forever." In other words, after his brief encounter with the diversity of the human heart, Nick needs to return to the predictable way of life that assures stability and guarantees a relationship between experience and his conviction of what that experience should and should not encompass. Reality for Nick and Fitzgerald lies at the juncture of Romantic Idealism and the staunch, faintly Puritan world of Middle Western burghers. "The foul dust [that] floated in the wake of [Gatsby's] dreams" (p. 2), that is, unmediated reality, distorts Union Station where the human heart responds in predetermined ways, where platonic conceptions of the permissable range of human interaction and feeling replace the threatening potentialities of the East. For Nick the present evokes the distortion of El Greco's *View of Toledo:* Gatsby's squalid connections with Wolfsheim, Daisy's and Tom's marriage, Tom's affair with Myrtle, the architecture of East Egg and New York. The past is lyrical, safe, ideal: Gatsby's creation of himself, his love for Daisy, Nick's memories of his youth. In this dialectic that values memory over thought and forms over spontaneity, we are reminded of the convictions of Edward Ashburnham, who was drawn to the static conditions of feudalism because there all action and feeling were neatly prescribed. Ford demonstrated the inadequacy of such atavism, but Fitzgerald turns it into a *raison d'être:* "Can't repeat the past? . . . Why of course you can!" (p. 111).

In this insistence on the reality of the ideal, *The Great Gatsby* parts company with the preceding novels. Flaubert, Chopin, Conrad, and Ford leave no doubt that the void looms behind the romantic fantasies of their characters, and each presents an antidote to imagination in the ironic perspectives of their narratives which evaluate both characters and events. Edna's "unattainable vision" and the world she constructs around it have no more substance than similar fantasies experienced by Emma or Gatsby, but the ironic perspective of Chopin's novel clearly illuminates the reality of the Creole society that oppresses Edna and illuminates as well Edna's right to live as an autonomous person. Similarly, Jim's "imaginary achievements" are unarguably insubstantial, especially when this array of heroic acts is juxtaposed to the un–self-conscious heroism of the French lieutenant, but Marlow's exploration of the ambiguous nature of honor and fidelity provides a subtle and complex alternative to Jim's fantasies, an alternative that has a place in "reality." Edward is absolutely blinded by his "sentimental view of the world," yet Dowell's assessment of the past leads to a realistic understanding of the tragedy in which he was involved and to at least a glimpse into the mysteries of the "human heart." But in *The Great Gatsby* the only alternative to "the colossal vitality of [Gatsby's] illusion" (p. 97) is another vision of the same order: Nick's simplistic, adolescent ethos.

The conclusion is inescapable—the endoxal discourse criticized by Flaubert, Chopin, Conrad, and Ford constitutes "reality" for Fitzgerald and provides him with a history as well as a set of principles for Gatsby. When Gatsby's ideals give way to Nick's at the end of the novel, Fitzgerald's alternative springs from a code that may now be recognized as Middle Western Virtue and, by advocating an ethos based on Nick's sentimental philosophy, Fitzgerald reverses the thrust of irony we have seen in the preceding texts. While Flaubert and the others deconstruct the "realm of romance" to reveal what Auerbach calls "true reality,"[8] Fitzgerald had another agenda in mind. He began by attempting to present a stock character out of magazine Romance as an exemplar of a culture's history; but, when Gatsby's vacuousness became apparent, Fitzgerald attempted to rescue his novel from its slide into negation by propping it up with sentimental values he associated with St. Paul. Thus the "reality" Fitzgerald would persuade us to accept lies back in Minnesota and is symbolized by the Union Station, the memories of wealthy girls and of the "yellow cars of the Chicago, Milwaukee & St. Paul railroad looking cheerful as Christmas itself" (p. 177). His fidelity to that sentimental world never falters.

III

The Great Gatsby begins and ends in Nick's consciousness, which has been enlivened by his exposure to Gatsby. At the beginning of their relationship Nick is convinced that his neighbor is merely the ostentatious "proprietor of an elaborate roadhouse" (p. 64), but by the end of the summer he can tell Gatsby, "You're worth the whole damn bunch together" (p. 154). Nick's rectitude, his ethical sensibility formed by the mores of the Middle West, makes it impossible for him to dream Gatsby's dream, but he comes to admire the Romantic ideals that are revealed during the summer[9] and, as we have already seen, expresses a muted version of them in his retreat home.

What Nick sees is not at all clear . He evokes Gatsby's magic in terms of seismographic sensitivity which expresses itself in "an extraordinary gift for hope, a romantic readiness such as I have never found in any other person and which it is not likely I shall ever find again" (p. 2). Much has been written about that readiness and the nature of Gatsby's dreams, and those critics

who are sympathetic to Fitzgerald more often than not attempt
to justify the novel by adopting Nick's position. Regardless of
his peccadilloes, Gatsby, we are told, reflects the last light of
American Romanticism. He is an heroic figure, a kind of last
Mohican of Romance who also embodies the American Dream.
Such a view ignores the argument developed in the first part of
this chapter—that is, that Fitzgerald was considerably more interested in justifying his own Romantic connection (as he had
done in his previous novels) than he was in a sustained exploration of the political, economic, and spiritual history of America.
It is my contention that neither Gatsby, with his "romantic readiness," nor American spiritual history were adequately conceived and that neither convincingly manifests the wide range of
significations that have been assumed to bear.

A brief survey of Gatsby's past will begin to confirm this
notion. As James Gatz, he is interesting and full of promise; an
Algeresque world lay before him much as Paradise did for the
innocent Adam.[10] In the young hustler who was trying to make
his living on the shores of Lake Superior, Fitzgerald found a
character and a situation that could have been exploited in any
number of ways. For example, it would have been interesting to
know what happened to Gatsby after he was taken over by Dan
Cody, fitted out with clothes to match the splendor of Cody's
fabulous yacht, and schooled in dubious arts. In fact, in order for
Gatsby to emerge from the two-dimensional world of unspecific
symbol, it is crucial for us to know how his mind worked at this
juncture of his life, just as it is necessary to have some idea of his
thoughts when he met Wolfsheim, and later still when Daisy
reentered his life. But we are left with only questions. How *did*
Gatsby respond to Cody? How *did* he deal with the faded ethics
of Wolfsheim? What lay behind the "fantastic conceits" of his
imagination? There are no answers; instead, we have Gatsby's
amorphous vision filtered through Nick's impressions.

Fitzgerald acknowledged these problems in letters to John
Peale Bishop and Edmund Wilson. To the first he wrote: "You
are right about Gatsby being blurred and patchy. I never at any
time saw him clearly myself—for he started as one man I knew
and then changed into myself—the amalgam was never complete
in my mind."[11] His comments to Wilson are equally revealing:

The worst fault in it, I think is a BIG FAULT: I gave no
account (and had no feeling about or knowledge of) the emo-

tional relations between Gatsby and Daisy from the time of their reunion to the catastrophe. However the lack is so astutely concealed by the retrospect of Gatsby's past and by blankets of excellent prose that no one had noticed it—though everyone has felt the lack and called it by another name.[12]

Having been mistreated by critics who read his first two realistic novels, Fitzgerald decided that *Gatsby* would not be realistic, but that decision only led to a hero who stands as symbol on one page and as an incompletely conceived *homme moyen sensuel* on another. Whereas Emma, Edna, Jim, and Edward are rendered as discrete individuals first and then as victims of irrepressible Romantic imaginations, Gatsby never escapes from the miasma of Fitzgerald's own conception of Romance, or, to follow the lead of the Bishop letter, from his conception of himself. The others, especially Ford, shared his Romantic inclinations, but Fitzgerald could not go beyond his own awareness of Romance to a critical and objective understanding of what it held out in the way of promise, or of how it could threaten or even make possible the life of a character in something resembling the modern world.

"For he started as one man I knew and then changed into myself." That self was subjected to painfully open scrutiny in a February 1936 essay entitled "The Crack Up." Here is Fitzgerald writing about himself when he was writing *Gatsby:*

> As the twenties passed, with my own twenties marching a little ahead of them, my two juvenile regrets—at not being big enough (or good enough) to play football in college, and at not getting overseas during the war—resolved themselves into childish waking dreams of imaginary heroism that were good enough to go to sleep on in restless nights.[13]

And here is Gatsby before Cody entered his life, Gatsby who during the day dug clams and fished for salmon, but whose heart at night was "in a constant, turbulent riot" while "a universe of ineffable gaudiness spun itself out in his brain" (p. 99). Then Cody, veteran of Yukon mining fields and Montana copper deals, catalyzed these conceits, for, as James Gatz rowed out to warn Cody of the danger he faced with the tides, he became Jay Gatsby, devoted to "his Father's business, the service of a vast, vulgar, and meretricious beauty" (p. 99).

This amalgam discloses the two basic flaws of the novel—its

less-than-clear philosophical position and Gatsby's insubstantiality. Assuming that the "meretricious beauty Gatsby is called
to serve reflects the melding of wealth and power known as the
American Dream, where does that leave us? To argue, as Marius
Bewley has done, that Gatsby's "blurred and patchy" qualities
substantiate his "impersonal significance"[14] is not very helpful,
for Bewley's interpretation (and others of the same general per-
suasion) can ultimately end up only as defenses of an abstrac-
tion—a "likable, romantic hero" characterized by his "goodness
and faith in life."[15] Far more damning, however, is the conclusion Fitzgerald provides to Gatsby's spiritual birth, for beneath
the "blankets of excellent prose" we find a seventeen-year-old
boy's "conception" to which Fitzgerald was also "faithful to the
end."

There are echoes here of Stein's memorable speech on the
destructive element—in fact, the coincidence of Gatsby's birth
occurring as he rows out on Lake Superior is a little disquieting.
Unlike Gatsby's, Jim's struggle to keep himself afloat in his
imaginative world is waged by a complex personality. Even
more to the point, with Jim we are in touch with the human
significance of an overpowering imagination. This leads to an
important distinction between Fitzgerald's protagonist and all
the others we have seen so far, even Emma Bovary. I am thinking of the passage in *Lord Jim* where Marlow senses the
hopelessness of Jim ever being able to function in the world "out
there." Brooding over his banishment to Patusan, Marlow sym-
pathizes with Jim's sense of loss and that sympathy leads him to
assert that "in virtue of his feeling he mattered."[16] It is Jim's
subjectivity that joins him to Marlow and, by extension, to all
Conrad's sailors; that is one of the reasons Marlow constantly
refers to Jim as "one of us." Such a comment would sound
ludicrous if it were applied to Gatsby, who may matter
philosophically, but whose character consists of ideals rather
than a set of emotions in which we see our own reflected.

IV

It is because Fitzgerald never got beyond what Gatsby symbolized that he could give no account of "the emotional relations
between Gatsby and Daisy from the time of their reunion to the
catastrophe." They are both stereotypes whose relationship is

developed along strictly formulaic lines. First of all, Daisy is a rich girl deceived into believing that Gatsby occupies the "same stratum as herself" (p. 149). Then there is an ironic reversal. Having seduced Daisy "because he had no real right to touch her hand," Gatsby "found that he had committed himself to the following of a grail" (p. 149). Fortuitously, the Chapel Perilous turns out to be a Louisville sidewalk along which Gatsby and Daisy strolled one moonlit night. There Gatsby is confronted with another test. Although he has found the girl of his dreams, he is aware that the moment is propitious to embark upon another quest that would lead him into the stars where he could "gulp down the incomparable milk of wonder" (p. 112).

Then the music of the spheres becomes audible to him in the accents of a Southern Belle—Daisy has brought the Gods to earth. This summary describes the essence of their relationship and also the essence of Fitzgerald's problem. What could he have invented for them to say to each other that had not already appeared in the pages of *The Saturday Evening Post?* That in itself is an insurmountable difficulty, but it is compounded by the fact that Fitzgerald's conception of what happens between men and women was fixed in undergraduate enthusiasm and self-love. Thus the "BIG FAULT" of *The Great Gatsby* is congenital: there is no way to describe "emotional relations" between stereotypes.

Only once in the course of the novel does Gatsby emerge from this miasma—in the scene at the Plaza Hotel when his past suddenly confronts him in a few curt phrases of Tom Buchanan's. Frightened that Daisy seems to be drifting toward her lover, Tom decides that the moment has come to play his trump card. Responding to Gatsby's irrational insistence that Daisy renounce him and her marriage, Tom counterattacks: "You're one of that bunch that hangs around with Meyer Wolfsheim" (p. 134). And suddenly Gatsby's mystery vanishes: "He and this Wolfsheim bought up a lot of sidestreet drug-stores here and in Chicago and sold grain alcohol over the counter.[11] In the silence that follows, Nick notices that Daisy is "terrified." When he turns to Gatsby, he sees a "fantastic" expression, something that had never before appeared on his friend's face. What happens here is that Fitzgerald briefly discovers the human dimensions of his character, and he succeeds admirably in presenting the fear and humiliation Gatsby feels as his lies are exposed.

Gatsby's response is simple and believable. Fitzgerald allows

him to gain control of his expression as he tries to convince
Daisy that what she has just heard is wrong. It is a pathetic
scene: " . . . he began to talk excitedly to Daisy, denying everything, defending his name against accusations that had not been
made. But with every word she was drawing futher and further
into herself. . . ." (p. 135). Up until this moment in his life Gatsby
has conceived of himself and his relationship to Daisy in a
metalanguage whose charm has succeeded in beguiling both of
them. With the encroachment of reality in Tom's accusations,
we see the fraudulence of that language, the insubstantiality of
Gatsby's "fantastic conceits." Once Tom realizes that he has
gained control, he sends them back to West Egg as if he were
banishing children from an enchanted world where "anything
can happen" (p. 69): "Go on," Tom says to Daisy. "I think he
realizes that his presumptuous little flirtation is over":

> They were gone, without a word, snapped out, made acciden-
> tal, isolated, like ghosts, even from our pity. (P. 136)

Gatsby's existence, and Daisy's within the syntax of his conceits, evaporate at the moment his words lose their power. The
broken dream is coterminous with the language which formed
Gatsby's world, language which, as Todorov observes, "permits
the description of a fantastic universe, one that has no reality
outside language; the description and what is described are not
of a different nature."[17]
	The wake of Gatsby's nightmare cuts through the valley of
ashes. Myrtle Wilson soon lies dead in the road; Tom and Daisy
are reduced to collaborators in an alibi for her carelessness;
Gatsby will be murdered as he floats in his abandoned pool;
George Wilson will relieve his own agony in suicide; Nick will
break off with Jordan and flee the East. This is unadorned reality, the El Greco world of Nick's vision. The emptiness of the
present dominates the final pages of *The Great Gatsby* as Nick
evokes the wonder he imagines Dutch sailors experienced when
they looked out on the "fresh, green breast of the new world"
(p. 182). His dreams, Gatsby's, Myrtle's, and all the others'
have turned to ashes in Nick's pessimistic assessment that
man's fate is to be caught up in something like the riptide of
history:" So we beat on, boats against the current, borne back
ceaselessly into the past!"

V

The problematic nature of *The Great Gatsby* results from Fitzgerald's inability to envision clearly what he wanted to say about Gatsby, Daisy, and Nick, but even more fundamentally it results from the task he set himself—to portray the history of a country through his perceptions of its characteristics during the Jazz Age. We can accept Fitzgerald's interpretation of American history and the individuals who made it only at the risk of simplifying man and history, for the sense of Eastern life he presents lacks the fullness of insight that would allow it to become an adequate projection of American experience in either specific or symbolic terms.

In this sense, T. S. Eliot can help put *The Great Gatsby* in perspective. In "The Waste Land" we encounter a complex, tragic vision, the product of an extraordinarily subtle mind steeped in world literature and world history, and we can respond to Eliot's judgements with a confidence that cannot be brought to Fitzgerald's. This distinction can be focused by referring to a comment in Eliot's essay "Ulysses, Order, and Myth," where he addresses the uses of history in modern literature. There he suggests that many others will follow Joyce "in manipulating a continuous parallel between contemporaneity and antiquity. . . . It is simply a way of controlling, of ordering, of giving a shape and a significance to the immense panorama of futility and anarchy which is contemporary history. . . . It is, I seriously believe, a step toward making the modern world possible in art."[18] Whereas Eliot and Joyce could dramatize the "panorama" of history by making it reveal archetypes that informed the modern world, Fitzgerald dramatized a received idea of history and attempted to show its contemporary significance in the fatuities of the Jazz Age and in the hollowness of stereotyped characters. *Ulysses* and "The Waste Land" open up human experience in time so that the worlds of Homer and of the Upanishads communicate with contemporary human experience. *The Great Gatsby* finally has no substance outside of Fitzgerald's consciousness, ultimately turning back upon itself and its Romantic terminology rather than opening a discourse with a mature and critical world. Fitzgerald could only accept human experience as it appeared through the bright windows of "the thrilling returning trains of his youth."

Given the context of this book, such reservations about *The Great Gatsby* are unavoidable. Fitzgerald's failure to distance himself from Gatsby and Nick, as well as his own admissions concerning the unstable line between life and art, have forced a discussion that makes him seem like a fictional character rather than a novelist. And his problem is more than a little similar to that of the characters I have examined. Seduced by the "realms of romance," he could only offer his own deeply felt but defensive vision of an idealized Middle Western adolescence against the crumbling values he consciously or unconsciously apprehended in the world he was creating for Gatsby. The emptiness of the Apollonian vision, the truth of Nietzsche's perception that it encapsulates an illusion within an illusion, is thus more troublesome here than in the earlier chapters because of what is at stake—the struggle of a "gifted artist" with a profound existential problem. His solution, like Emma's, Edna's, Jim's, and Edward's, was to opt for the illusion through Gatsby and Nick. In the concluding chapter of this section I show how the two dilemmas faced by both Fitzgerald and his characters— solipsism and Romantic Idealism—lead Durrell even further into the labyrinth of self. Unlike his predecessors, Durrell finds a way out by approaching reality from the perspectives of Wordsworth's Romantic doctrine of experience and his deep conviction of the necessity for a harmonious relationship with nature.

Narcissism and Selflessness in *The Alexandria Quartet*

Gone—ah, gone—untouched, unreachable! . . .
A broken bundle of mirrors . . .!

—Ezra Pound, "Near Perigord"

I

Durrell's Alexandrian epic penetrates the fragile surface of naive Romantic Idealism as it is manifested in narcissistic characters to reveal the nihilism Fitzgerald took such pains to avoid confronting in his novel. There is the same sense of discovery in Darley's initial relation with Justine that we find in Gatsby's with Daisy, but the thematic movement of the *Quartet* is toward an understanding of how such idealization fails. In *The Great Gatsby* the persona is all-important; it is the source of vitality and praised throughout. In the *Quartet* Durrell takes up where Fitzgerald left off, presenting example after example of the void which is disguised by the mask of an expropriated persona. In the *Quartet* Durrell's novelist-narrator Darley becomes increasingly engaged in a search for significant human feeling and experience devoid of masks and repitions. The direction of his mind is always towards a coherent sense of self and of the self's relation to both past and present. The disparity between Darley's gradual acceptance of things as they are and the refusal to give up the dream which characterizes Gatsby makes the *Quartet* far more ironic and psychologically interesting than *The Great Gatsby*. Fitzgerald has unconsciously portrayed the labyrinth, but Durrell's interest is in illuminating its mazes in order to understand how we achieve an identity free of masks and how this in turn makes possible mature self-knowledge and relation to others. That the gestures made out of these discoveries are tentative suggests that Durrell was deeply aware of the problematic nature of modern man's sense of identity and his ability to shun the insistent demands of the ego-libido.

The nature of the problem Durrell explores is clearly set out near the end of *Clea* where Capodistria, one of Alexandria's connoisseurs of sensuality who has recently taken refuge from his body in the study of hermetic arts, writes to Balthazar about certain events concerning "ten homunculi" created by his mentor, a mysterious Austrian baron. Preserved in "huge glass canisters," a series of misadventures befall these creatures, one of whom represents a king "who managed to escape from his bottle during the night:"

> he was found sitting upon the bottle containing the Queen, scratching with his nails to get the seal away. He was beside himself, and very agile, though weakening desperately from his exposure to the air. Nevertheless he led us quite a chase among the bottles—which we were afraid of overturning. It was really extraordinary how nimble he was, and had he not become increasingly faint from being out of his native element I doubt whether we could have caught him.[1]

The adventure of the homunculus king illuminates the emotional history of Alexandria whose inhabitants also frantically search for fulfillment—and in doing so suffer psychic as well as physical wounds. Trapped in the prison of self and mistaking his sense of isolation for self-knowledge, the modern Alexandrian systematically destroys his ability to love. Such, at any rate, in conjunction with a criticism of the received ideas of Romantic values unmatched in contemporary literature, is what I take to be central to Durrell's enterprise. This theme is embodied in a variety of separate motifs but principally in the fictions each of the Alexandrians creates for themselves and those nearest them. Page after page of the *Quartet* posits the distance that exists between persona and person, disclosing the seemingly unbridgeable gap between the characters and the objects of their desires. In this sense, the *Quartet* can be read as a moving criticism of the isolation and despair of the modern world. But to end one's inquiry there would be to miss the complex achievement of Durrell's art. The purpose of this chapter is to demonstrate how the nihilism of Alexandrian life is transcended through the restoration of personal and social values that reverse, for at least a few of the characters, the drift toward the void of solipsism.

Darley explains the dilemma he and the others face near the beginning of *Clea*. Trapped in his own fictions, he slowly and painfully learns how to deconstruct them so that when he returns from self-imposed exile he can say, "I saw now that my own Justine had indeed been an illusionist's creation, raised upon the faulty armature of misinterpreted words, actions, gestures. Truly there was no blame here; the real culprit was my love which had invented an image on which to feed. Nor was there any question of dishonesty, for the picture was coloured after the necessities of the love which invented it" (p. 55 C).

The "love which had invented an image on which to feed" was in turn invented by Darley's fiction of himself—the Romantic artist, complete with faintly discernible Pre-Raphaelite trappings. Blinded by the predetermined attitudes inherent in his role, Darley indulges in sentimental rhetoric—"At the time when I met Justine I was almost a happy man" (p. 17 J)—that reveals his completely unconscious absorption in his persona. A few pages later his fiction-making propensity becomes even clearer as he recalls a speech made to Justine: "It can come to nothing, this love-affair between a poor schoolteacher and an Alexandrian society woman. How bitter it would be to have it all end in a conventional scandal which would leave us alone together and give you the task of deciding how to dispose of me" (p. 26 J). Darley's creation of hackneyed romantic roles for himself and Justine opens a perspective on the theme of narcissism that dominates *Justine*. Throughout that text Darley describes an hermetically-sealed world in which he experiences premeditated emotional states induced by the catalyst of Justine or Melissa. Like Darley, Clea, Justine, Balthazar, Mountolive, and Pursewarden are also turned inward upon themselves, consumed by their own sensations. At one time or another, all the Alexandrians mirror the stark world of Descartes, their self-indulgent fantasies corollaries of *cogito ergo sum*.

This conjunction of Cartesian myopia and Romantic fantasy increases the withering effects of self-consciousness which separate the individual from life. Geoffrey Hartman has argued that self-awareness leads to the essential paradox of Romanticism, for as awareness of self grows, so too does one's isolation. Dramatized in the theme of the Solitary (Faust, Wandering Jew, Ancient Mariner), the paradox dominates characters who are "separated from life in the midst of life . . . doomed to live a middle or purgatorial existence which is neither life nor death," and burdened by "a self which religion or death or a return to the state of nature might dissolve."² While the effect of self-consciousness is the same for the Alexandrians, Darley's problem, and that of the others, is compounded by the fact that his consciousness belongs to a fantasy self. The Alexandrians are doubly separated from life—first by the isolation imposed by consciousness, second by the personas they assume. Some, most notably Justine, will remain trapped in this labyrinth, but others, particularly Darley and Clea, will escape from these fictive worlds. But escape does not assure self-realization. Throughout the *Quartet* Durrell is preoccupied with unity of self and unity of self with the world at large. Escape from self, from the "austere mindless primitive face of Aphrodite" (p. 109 J), can only be achieved through a process that involves the healing experience of nature.

In this context, Durrell's work can be illuminated by Robert Langbaum's observations about Wordsworth's belief in the continuity between place and self. "Place, in Wordsworth," writes Langbaum, "is the spatial projection of psyche. . . . We can understand the relation in Wordsworth between the themes of memory and growing up, once we have understood that for Wordsworth you advance by traveling back again to the beginning, by reassessing your life, by binding your days together anew."³ Aided by Balthazar's Interlinear, Darley's perception of his relation to the natural world allows him to reassess his life, reorder the misconceptions he entertained about himself and his friends and, in reclaiming himself from his destructive Romantic fantasies, turn the energy once expended in the interior world of solipsism into a fruitful alliance with nature, self, and other. Thus the larger narrative movement from the sterility of *Justine* to the continuity of *Clea* involves a movement from isolation to connection, a movement from a world in which experience is a meaningless fragment of an equally meaningless whole, to a world in which patterns of continuity have emerged that can restore vitality and participate in the restoration of ethical and spiritual values.

II

Durrell's investigation of modern love ends with the promise of Darley's and Clea's love, but it begins in a remarkably Freudian world of mirrors and self-delusion, the domain of Justine

Hosnani. "I remember her sitting before the multiple mirrors at the dressmaker's," Darley recalls, "being fitted for a sharkskin costume, and saying: 'Look! five different pictures of the same subject. Now if I wrote I would try for a multi-dimensional effect in character, a sort of prism-sightedness. Why should not people show more than one profile at a time?'" (p. 27 J). The book of mirrors[4] begins with these images and even Durrell's heavy-handed advertising of his narrative technique cannot blunt their importance. This is the first of numerous scenes where Durrell explores the consequences of narcissism which, notwithstanding Leon Edel's consignment of Durrell's evocation of Freud to "window-dressing,"[5] correspond point by point to Freud's assessment of the debilitating nature of this neurosis.

In his essay, "On Narcissism," Freud writes of the megalomania characteristic of people like Justine who seem to have "withdrawn their libido from persons and things in the outer world." He then makes two observations that are particularly important to Durrell's themes:

> [Narcissistic] women love only themselves with an intensity comparable to that of the man's love for them. Nor does their need lie in the direction of loving, but of being loved; and that man finds favour with them who fulfills this condition. . . .
>
> It seems very evident that one person's narcissism has a great attraction for those others who have renounced part of their own narcissism and are seeking after object-love; the charm of a child is to a great extent in his narcissism, his self-sufficiency and inaccessibility. . . .[6]

As is evident in Arnauti's comments about Justine in his book, *Moeurs,* many of her needs were fulfilled by the simple fact that he loved her, and in her subsequent relationships with both men and women the same dynamic is apparent. Moreover, her attractiveness responds precisely to Freud's second observation, for Arnauti, Nessim, and Darley find her dual qualities of self-sufficiency and inaccessibility irresistible. Arnauti speaks for the others when he says "I was bewitched by the illusion that I could really come to know her" (p. 68 J). While Freud's view of narcissism pervades each of these examples, his comment about the charm of children is particularly illuminating as a gloss on the mirror motif and Justine. It also returns us to my comments in Chapter 1 about Lacan, who argues that the child's discovery of itself in a mirror represents a potent fantasy of unity. Justine's

rejection of reality closely follows Lacan's paradigm. The fragmented, only partially controllable image of the self perceived
without the aid of a mirror, like the child's self in reality, has
been replaced by a complete image that suggests a self-sufficient
world.[7]

One of Justine's diary entries, in which she writes about falling in love, dramatically exemplifies Freud's theory of narcissism:

> Around this event, dazed and preoccupied, the lover moves
> examining his or her own experience; her gratitude alone,
> stretching away towards a mistaken donor, creates the illusion
> that she communicates with her fellow, but this is false. The
> loved object is simply one that has shared an experience at the
> same moment of time, narcissistically; and the desire to be
> near the beloved object is at first not due to the idea of posses-
> sing it, but simply to let the two experiences compare them-
> selves, like reflections in different mirrors. (Pp. 49–50 J)

What is most disturbing in this passage is the distance Justine
describes between herself and her lover. It is clearly her own
experience she finds fascinating so that, for her, lovers function
as catalysts for the primary experience of loving one's self, a
notion substantiated in the pages of *Moeurs* when Arnauti observes that "it was as if somehow her world lacked a dimension,
and love had become turned inward into a kind of idolatry"
(p. 68 J). If Durrell's interest in narcissism did not go beyond this
dramatization of Freudian theories, we would have still learned
a good deal, but Freud is examining a phenomenon he assumes
to be unconscious and that is not the case with Justine. Her
narcissism has *consciously* developed into a nihilistic pseudo-
philosophy. To be unaware of narcissism makes the individual
clinically interesting, but to be aware of it and to believe that
nothing can be done adds a philosophical dimension to a psychological problem. This entrapment of Justine's self and the centripetal motion it imparts to her emotions form half of an
emerging paradigm of modern love that is balanced by Melissa's
"charity," which ultimately animates Darley and Clea. In addition, the basic narrative rhythm of the *Quartet* is illustrated in
this paradigm of centripetal to centrifugal motion, whose terms
express the interior space of narcissism and the exterior space of
relation.

Arnauti's perception of the absence of a "dimension" in Justine provides more than a note about her character, for this flaw is shared by all the Alexandrians. It is the node of Balthazar's meditiation on sexual vacuity:

Sex has left the body and entered the imagination now . . . And then, as far as Alexandria is concerned, you can understand why this is really a city of incest—I mean that here the cult of Serapis was founded. For this etiolation of the heart and reins in love-making must make one turn inwards upon one's sister. The lover mirrors himself like Narcissus in his own family; there is no exit from the predicament. (Pp. 96–97 J)

Justine's self-consciousness exemplifies solitary self-love, while narcissism as it is manifested in incest is illuminated by Ludwig and Liza Pursewarden. Following Pursewarden's suicide, Darley and Liza burn his passionate letters to her. As she sits before the fire, Liza recalls a quotation her brother held up as justification of his love for her:

"In african burial rites it is the sister who brings the dead king back to life. In Egypt as well as Peru the king, who was considered as God, took his sister to wife. But the motive was ritual and not sexual, for they symbolized the moon and the sun in their conjunction. The king marries his sister because he, as God the star, wandering on earth, is immortal and may therefore not propagate himself in the children of a strange woman, any more than he is allowed to die a natural death." That is why he was pleased to come there to Egypt, because he felt, he said, an interior poetic link with Osiris and Isis, with Ptolemy and Arisinoe—the race of the sun and the moon. (P. 191 C)

These passages describe the plight of all Durrell's characters. Their images, especially Balthazar's of love's "etiolation," evoke the ephemeral system of mirrors over which Justine presides. Taken together, they represent Durrell's metaphysics of narcissism, and nowhere is the bleakness and destructiveness of such a metaphysics more clearly displayed than in Justine's affair with Clea.

When the affair began, Justine was married to Arnauti and their poverty forced her to model. Clea encounters her one day as she is posing, and, taken by her beauty, arranges for her to sit

for a portrait. But Justine's beauty is only the conscious motiva-
tion for Clea; what attracts her is Justine as Woman. Darley
writes of the "sudden self-consuming experience" as "compara-
ble in its tension and ardour to those ridiculous passions which
school-girls have so often for their mistresses" (p. 53 B), and it is
just this admiration, slightly heightened by unconscious
homoerotic curiosity, that makes the affair inevitable.

Justine had been speaking to Clea about the loss of her child,
and the kiss that interrupted the painting is as much a gesture of
consolation as it is an unexpected prompting from Clea's nas-
cent libido. For Clea, there was no expectation of the kiss being
answered, but this gesture of affection, even of tentative sexuality, is fraught with more tensions than she could possibly be
aware of. "The gesture itself," Darley suggests, "was simply a
clumsy attempt to appropriate the mystery of true experience,
true suffering—as by touching a holy man the supplicant hopes
for a transference of the grace he lacks." Drawn to the mirrored
image of Justine she is creating before her, and to the Justine
beyond the canvas at the center of a newly unfolding reality,
"Clea's own body simply struggled to disengage itself from the
wrappings of its innocence as a baby or a statue struggles for life
under the fingers or forceps of its author" (p. 52 B).

And so they become lovers through the portrait, in the mirrors
of each other's bodies. Clea is consumed by the experience even
though she does not understand what it means, but Justine, true
to the self-absorption so clearly evident throughout the *Quartet,*
seeks nothing but her own sexual pleasure:

> . . . everything that Clea felt was at this time meaningless to
> her. As a prostitute may be unaware that her client is a poet
> who will immortalize her in a sonnet she will never read, so
> Justine in pursuing these deeper sexual pleasures was un-
> aware that they would mark Clea for years: enfeeble her in her
> power of giving undivided love—what she was most designed
> to give by temperament. (P. 56 B)

The tension of the affair recalls Freud's comments about narcissism, for as Justine communes only with her self which she sees
reflected in Clea's body, Clea's passion takes her out of herself
toward Justine and eventually towards her identity as a woman.
Self-knowledge develops with the pain Clea feels, and the affair
"performed one valuable service for her, proving that relation-

ships like these did not answer the needs of her nature. Just as a man knows inside himself from the first hour that he has married the wrong woman but that there is nothing to be done about it. She knew she was a woman at last and belonged to men—and this gave her misery a fugitive relief" (p. 55 B). While Clea's heterosexuality was indeed enfeebled by this experience, it is enabled through it as she develops away from self-communion towards the forgetfulness of self she can ultimately experience with Amaril and Darley. The relationship demonstrates how narcissism can end either in the stasis of self-communion or in the desire to pass through the boundaries of self after self-love has been explored and found insufficient.

These differences can be illustrated by looking at several parallels between Justine's self-absorption and Emma Bovary's. When Justine writes that "the loved object is simply one that has shared an experience at the same moment of time, narcissistically," she articulates a habit of response that led to the disappearance of male images in Emma's imagination once they had performed the function of catalyst. Charles, Léon, Rodolphe, Nessim, Pursewarden, and Darley thus share a common function: as Lover they enable self-love in the two-dimensional world of the narcissist's imagination. But there is an important distinction that must be made between Justine and Emma: whereas Justine has consciously forged a philosophical position out of her commitment to herself, Emma remains ignorant of how her own self-love and auto-eroticism channeled her deepest feelings into an altogether different area of significance. In this respect, the conscious, sensuous exploration of self we find in Justine is most closely aligned with Edna Pontellier's tentative experiments with the physical and emotional sensations of self-love, while Emma's naiveté can be seen to reappear in Jim, Edward, and Gatsby. In the relationship between Justine and Clea these two modes of narcissism are critically juxtaposed. Justine is fated to remain in the prison of her own consciousness, but Clea's "power of giving" will slowly develop because of her ability to understand that vitality exists in relation with another. The terms by which she is able to free herself of self-absorption are thus identical to those in the question Catherine asks in *Wuthering Heights:* "What were the use of my creation if I were entirely contained here?"—a question which Clea and Darley, alone of all the characters I have examined so far, are capable of asking and answering.

III

Central as it is to Durrell's strategies in the *Quartet,* narcissism is only one of the themes that grows out of his investigation of the Romantic Imagination. Fictions superimposed on other people are equally revealing of the malaise of self-consciousness, especially when they involve a mediator. Clea recognizes this problem in a discussion with Darley long before they become lovers: "There is something about love—I will not say defective for the defect lies in ourselves: but something we have mistaken about its nature. For example, the love you now feel for Justine is not a different love for a different object but the same love you feel for Melissa trying to work itself out through the medium of Justine" (pp. 129–30 J). Her theory illuminates the confusion Darley feels on returning home the day he begins his affair with Justine:

> As I opened the door of my room I could still see the imprint of Justine's foot in the wet sand. Melissa was reading, and looking up at me she said with characteristic calm foreknowledge: 'Something has happened—what is it?' I could not tell her since I did not myself know. I took her face in my hands and examined it silently, with a care and attention, with a sadness and hunger I don't remember feeling before. She said: 'It is not me you are seeing, it is someone else.' But in truth I was seeing Melissa for the first time. In some paradoxical way it was Justine who was not permitting me to see Melissa as she really was—and to recognize my love for her. (P. 49 J)

The paradox here is that Darley's libido is attempting to dissociate itself from his ego and make contact with the doubled figure of Justine/Melissa, but, despite the tenderness he feels for Melissa, he has not found in her those qualities that could encourage a complete liberation from the narcissistic world of ego-libido. At the same time, progress is evident, for Darley is entering a transitional stage whose relational qualities can be clearly distinguished from the stasis we have just observed in Justine. Sensitized by his recent passionate experience with Justine, the "hunger" he feels for Melissa is really for an emotional fulfillment he cannot yet fully experience. He is still immersed in his own consciousness, even though his subconscious is forcing the realization that the world of the self is no longer sufficient.

More frequently, the mediation theme focuses on the world of stasis. In the following scene, Narouz's brutal self-sufficiency is violated by his passionate fantasy about Clea. His imagination activated through a visit to one of Alexandria's mystics with whom he has just experienced remarkable visions, Narouz wanders through the back alleys of the Arab district where he hears "the voice of the woman he loved but it came from a hideous form" of an old prostitute. Narouz transforms the woman into a mediator with his money:

> He loosened his clothing and pressed this great doll of flesh down upon the dirty bed, coaxing from her body with his powerful hands the imagined responses he might have coaxed perhaps from another and better-loved form. 'Speak, my mother,' he whispered hoarsely, 'speak while I do it. Speak.' Expressing from this great white caterpillar-form one rare and marvelous image, rare perhaps as an Emperor moth, the beauty of Clea. Oh but how horrible and beautiful to be there at last, squeezed out like an old paint-tube among the weeping ruins of intestate desires: himself, his own inner man, thrown finally back into the isolation of a personal dream, transitory as childhood, and not less heartbreaking: Clea! (Pp. 166–167 B)

Such desires as overwhelm Narouz in his loneliness and isolation measure the despair which lies just below the surface of the fictive worlds created by the Alexandrians. The mediating image always effloresces on the verge of realization.

But it is again to Justine, the *Quartet's* most able fabulist, that we must turn for the definitive version of interior states. Nessim's proposal of marriage fascinates her because of the intrigue and danger life with him implies:

> This was a Faustian compact he was offering her. There was something else more surprising, for the first time she felt desire stir within her, in the loins of that discarded, preempted body which she regarded only as a pleasure-seeker, a mirror-reference to reality. There came over her an unexpected lust to sleep with him—no, with his plans, his dreams, his obsessions, his money, his death! (P. 201 M)

Like an embittered parody of a Beckett character, Justine is always conscious of the Cartesian duality of mind and body, and her "discarded, pre-empted body which she regarded only as a pleasure-seeker, a mirror-reference to reality" documents Balthazar's earlier perception that "sex has left the body and entered the imagination now," for that is precisely what takes place in this passage. And later, disillusioned by the failure of these fantasies, she explains to Darley that while she and Nessim were "conspirators, joined by our work and its dangers, I could feel truly passionate about him. . . . When he does not act, Nessim is nothing; he is completely flavourless, not in touch with himself at any point. Then he has no real self to interest a woman, to grip her" (p. 58 C). Just as she can love only her created image of herself, Justine can respond only to the man she imagines Nessim to be. Her own fantasy functions as a mediator between herself and her husband, but she is also capable of seeing someone other than the person before her eyes. Disabusing Darley of any fantasies he may retain about their relationship, she tells him that "every word I then addressed to you was spoken mentally to him, to Pursewarden! In your bed it was he I embraced and subjugated in my mind. And yet again, in another dimension, everything I felt and did then was really for Nessim" (p. 60 C). Yet, as Durrell consistently reminds us, the imagination is inadequate to such transformations, and its vehicles of mirrors and mediation lead only to stasis.

As we have already seen, narcissism forces a complete split between subject and object. A mediator is interposed between the subject and the object in the hope of bridging the distance between them, but this is impossible because, even though desire seems to be directed outward, the object has no properties of its own, it is still a fantasy—Narouz's of Clea, Justine's of Pursewarden and Nessim, Darley's of Justine.

In *Clea* this dualism is transcended through the relation of subject to object in a way that specifically recalls the Wordsworthian touchstone of continuity. Framed by events that take place on Darley's island, *Clea* opens with Darley's preparations for his return to Alexandria:

> Somewhere along the road I had recovered my peace of mind. This handful of blue days before saying farewell—I treasured them, luxuriating in their simplicity; fires of olive-wood blazing in the old hearth whose painting of Justine would be the last item packed, jumping and gleaming on the battered table and chair, on the blue enamel bowl of early cyclamen (P. 13 C).

At the end, waiting for the time to ripen with Clea, Darley is more specific about what he has gained. "The life is hard, but good":

> What pleasure to actually sweat over a task, actually use one's hands! And while we are harvesting steel to raise, membrane by membrane, this delicate mysterious ex-voto to the sky— why the vines are ripening too with their reminder that long after man has stopped his neurotic fiddling with the death-bringing tools with which he expresses his fear of life, the old dark gods are there, underground, buried in the moist humus of the Chthonian world. . . . They are forever sited in the human wish. (P. 274 C)

Just as the dilemma of solipsism in the *Quartet* is related to the crisis of self-consciousness in Romantic literature, so Durrell's solution suggests another link to Romantic thought, specifically to the pantheistic naturalism of Wordsworth's "Tintern Abbey," "Intimations of Immortality," and "The Prelude." The scenes that frame *Clea* thus show how Darley discovers continuity in his own life through his connection with the sustaining forces above and below the soil.

Durrell dramatizes Darley's transcendence of self in the first three chapters of *Clea.* Aware now of a task that lies before him, Darley realizes that he can no longer stay away from Alexandria: "the city which I now knew I hated held out something different for me—a new evaluation of the experience which had marked me. I must return to it once more in order to be able to leave it forever, to shed it" (p. 14 C). And it is to Justine that he must go first, because to shed her is to shed the destructive fantasies that had grown up around her. The sundering occurs on many levels in Darley's consciousness, not the least of which is appropriately sensual and specifically synaesthetic. Shortly before he arrives at her house, Justine spills on herself the perfume that represents her mysteriousness, power, and deception. When he arrives, Darley is overwhelmed by the scent which once enchanted him: "Its cloying richness half sickened me" (p. 56 C). While his physical revulsion comes from the scent of *Jamais de la Vie,* it also expresses his awareness of the falsity of Alexandria, his own past life, and Justine. The perfume's cloying effect is implicitly compared to the clean odor of cyclamen that infused his room when Darley was preparing to leave the island. Assaulted by the mind and the senses, Darley listens to Justine speak of her life since he left in a voice whose harshness is no longer capable of sustaining the fiction he once so ardently believed.

Her words reveal still further the bleakness of the interior life. Of her present condition she explains that "this unhappiness is not just ennui, spleen. There is also a desire to swallow the world. I have been experimenting with drugs of late, the sleep-givers" (p. 57 C). Twelve pages later Balthazar repeats the phrase as he tells Darley about his passion for a young Greek, which ended badly: "It was as if I wanted to swallow the world, to drain the sore of love until it healed." We can gain a clear idea of the significance of this repeated metaphor by listening to its inventor, Nietzsche's "madman" of *The Joyful Wisdom:*

> "Where is God gone?" he called out. "I mean to tell you! *We have killed him,*—you and I! We are all his murderers! But how have we done it? How were we able to drink up the sea? Who gave us the sponge to wipe away the whole horizon? What did we do when we loosened this earth from its sun? Whither does it now move? Whither do we move? Away from all suns? Do we not dash on unceasingly? Backwards, sideways, forewards, in all directions? Is there still an above and below? Do we not stray, as through infinite nothingness? Does not empty space breathe upon us? Has it not become colder? Does not night come on continually, darker and darker? Shall we not have to light lanterns in the morning? Do we not hear the noise of the grave-diggers who are burying God? Do we not smell the divine putrefaction?—for even Gods putrefy! God is dead! God remains dead! And we have killed him."[8]

J. Hillis Miller argues that this passage defines the nihilism that results from the development of self-consciousness in the nineteenth century. "Man has killed God," he writes, "by separating his subjectivity from everything but itself. The ego has put everything in doubt, and has defined all outside itself as the object of its power. . . . When everything exists only as reflected in the ego, then man has drunk up the sea."[9] Through Nietzsche we discover another dimension in Conrad's "destructive element," Chopin's "voice of the sea," Ford's minuet, and Fitzgerald's platonic conception. With varying degrees of precision these metaphors represent the Romantic Imagination, but, aided by Nietzsche, Durrell increases the torque of the irony associated with them. Nietzsche and Durrell, along with Lacan in his observations about children and mirrors, make clear that narcissism goes beyond mere fascination with the self to a desire to incorporate everything external within the self in a will to power that denies objectivity and the otherness of others. In swallowing the world the narcissist immerses himself in the destructive element of anarchic imagination. But though his acts are aimed at destroying the subject-object balance of the world, his failure, which is exemplified in Justine, reverses the process begun in the mirror: the world remains unscathed while he is destroyed. If we return to the examples from the *Quartet* which gave rise to these observations, we can now see that Justine and Balthazar represent the old, destructive life of Alexandria where nothing exists outside the ego. Thus their metaphor of swallowing the world, and Nietzsche's of drinking up the sea, encapsulate the themes of interiority developed in the first three volumes of the *Quartet*. It is precisely this nihilism of self-consciousness that Darley renounces when, at the end of the third chapter of *Clea,* he says that "some huge iron door had closed forever in his heart" separating [him] irrevocably from Justine and the dark world of the ego.

After this renunciation rebirth can occur, and the next section opens onto the bright exterior world of "spring sunlight" in which Darley "felt like the Adam of the mediaeval legends: the world-compounded body of a man whose flesh was soil, whose bones were stones, whose blood water, whose hair was grass, whose eyesight sunlight, whose breath was wind, and whose thoughts were clouds. And weightless now, as if after some long wasting illness, I found myself turned adrift again to float upon the shallows of Mareotis with its old tide-marks of appetites and desires refunded into the history of the place . . ." (p. 63 C). Recovered from the psychic illness that distorted his inner vision, anagogically sensitive to the natural world, Darley is led once again to Clea. As their relationship achieves its belated flowering, each is aware of a new freedom from self-consciousness. Of his own perception, Darley says that it was "as if the cup of language had silently overflowed into . . . eloquent kisses which replaced words like the rewards of silence itself, perfecting thought and gesture" (p. 95 C). The paradox of silence expressing more than language is not lost on Darley, for he has begun to understand that the language he once wrote and spoke shielded him from the real world of emotion by its rhetoric and premeditated Romantic conceits. In this state of self-forgetfulness he ceases forever to see himself and others as the raw material of fiction.

"So we lingered," he continues, "so we might have stayed, like rapt figures in some forgotten painting, unhurriedly savouring the happiness given to those who set out to enjoy each other without reservations or self-contempts, without the premeditated costumes of selfishness—the invented limitations of human love" (pp. 95–96 C). Darley's perception of the importance of spontaneity, of approaching experience directly, continues to open until he realizes what it is that has impeded all of the Alexandrians, including himself, from entering into the world of relation. What he is now aware of with Clea is the result of "improvisations upon reality itself, and for once devoid of the bitter impulses of the will. We have sailed into this calm water completely without premeditation, all canvas crowded on; and for the first time it felt natural to be where I was, drifting into sleep with her calm body lying beside me" (p. 97 C). Reservations are inseparable from self-contempt and contempt for others. Darley has implicitly associated such reservations with all the relationships he has seen in Alexandria which have consistently demonstrated that to relate to another involves surrendering part of one's self and becoming vulnerable in a way that Justine, Pursewarden, Balthazar, Mountolive, and even Darley himself early on find impossible. Vulnerability is the key to his perception, and in this context it means to loosen one's hold on one's self, which creates a direct threat to the ego. A good deal of the cynicism expressed by Justine, Pursewarden, and Darley grows out of their awareness of what vulnerability involves and of the self-contempt each feels in the face of such a realization. More specifically, Darley now knows that love can only be achieved through banishing the "bitter impulses of the will" which creates fictions and in doing so delimits loving to the old subject-object duality that has left its "tide-marks of appetites and desires" on the history of Alexandria.

Book I of *Clea* thus functions as a transition from the world of "appetites and desires" to the world of relation where the demands of the ego are subsumed by a steadily expanding perception of wholeness. It concludes with a holistic vision prefiguring the final pages of the *Quartet*. Meditating on Clea's naked body as she waits for the sunrise, Darley "caught the sweet voice of the blind *muezzin* from the mosque reciting the *Ebed*—a voice hanging like a hair in the palm-cooled upper airs of Alexandria. 'I praise the perfection of God, the Forever existing; the perfection of God, the desired, the Existing, the Single, the Supreme; the Perfection of God, the One, the sole' . . . (p. 99 C). And Darley goes on to observe that "the buoyancy of a new freedom possessed me like a draught from what the Cabal once called 'The fountain of All Existing Things,' . . . I knew that Clea would share everything with me, withholding nothing. . . . " This "buoyancy of a new freedom" associated with the Cabal's node of existence, and the *muezzin*'s evocation of perfection and order, coalesce in Darley's expanding awareness of an order that binds together the seen and unseen and patterns the individual life within the larger pattern of the universe itself.

IV

The middle chapters of *Clea* are rich in events which collectively point to the denouement. While subplots are brought to their conclusions in the union of Mountolive and Liza, the deaths of Sveva and Narouz, and the winding down of the war that has brooded over the city like some "fearful prehistoric bird" (p. 24 C), the growth of the relationship between Darley and Clea dominates these other events as the theme of a fugue dominates its variations. The terrible accident that results in Clea's losing her painting hand may be the most dramatic single event in the whole of the *Quartet,* but, while it seems to announce a tragedy as abrupt and absurd as Sveva's being killed as she and Pombal sail in the bay, it also symbolically severs Clea's last attachment to the past and represents for her the equivalent of Darley's iron door which shut on his past with Justine. An aspect of their individual growth is manifested in their increasing awareness that their life together involves a process toward an ultimate union that still lies somewhere in the future, and Darley characterizes this mutual awareness in a remembered phrase of Pursewarden's": "The richest love is that which submits to the arbitration of time" (p. 257 C). Accepting the necessity of such arbitration, Darley arranges to return for a time to his island as a laborer on the site of a new communications station.

His departure coincides with the celebration of Scobie's irrepressible spirit at the Mulid of El Scob, and, during the religious procession he observes with Balthazar that night, he witnesses a remarkable event:

> the chanters moved forward to recite the holy texts [and] six Mevlevi dervishes suddenly took the center of the stage, expanding in a slow fan of movement until they had formed a semi-circle. They wore brilliant white robes reaching to their green slippered feet and tall brown hats shaped like huge *bombes glacées*. Calmly, beautifully, they begin to whir, these 'tops spun by God,' while the music of the flutes haunted them with their piercing quibbles. As they gathered momentum their arms, which at first they hugged fast to their shoulders, unfolded as if by centrifugal force and stretched out to full reach, the right palm turned upward to heaven, the left downward to the ground. So, with heads and tall rounded hats tilted slightly, like the axis of the earth, they stayed there miraculously spinning, their feet hardly seeming to touch the floor, in this wonderful parody of the heavenly bodies in their perpetual motion. (P. 269 C)

The holistic view of the world expressed in the *muezzin's* prayer that opens the final section of *Clea* and represents for Darley the beginning of a new life is completed by the whirling dervishes, in whose centrifugal force is symbolized both balance and harmony in the universe and the breaking of the membrane of self that separates men from the continuum of the "heavenly bodies." And the centrifugal movement from the center outward, the unfolding of the dervishes's arms to release the self and embrace that which extends beyond the self, recapitulates the themes of growth and discovery that Durrell embodies in Darley and Clea. Like the great final chapter of *A Passage to India,* where the birth of Shri Krishna implies wholeness and suggests that the irreconcilability of East and West lies in the failure to unite inner and outer, conscious and unconscious in an act of creative, sympathetic, spiritual imagination,[10] this scene poses a parallel answer to the tension between the world of experience and the world of relation. Durrell's answer participates in the same metaphysics that Forster located in the fecund spiritual darkness of the Marabar Caves—unity that can be experienced when the ego no longer turns inward to commune with itself.

The last nine pages of the *Quartet* consist of two letters written by Darley and Clea, his from the island, hers from the hospital, and together they form a coda. Earlier I suggested that Darley's recognition of the relation between the above and the below, the flowering natural world and the forces of the "old dark gods of the Chthonian world", represented a profoundly important stage in his self-realization. In the present context, it also extends the holistic view of the world expressed in the epiphanic scene with the dervishes. Through a painful quest, Darley has discovered a self that is free from the distorting fictions of the premeditated life, and, just as his consciousness moved towards the healing of self, it now moves towards the healing of the war-torn world in which his roots lie buried: "My mind has been turning more and more westward, towards the old inheritance of Italy or France. Surely there is still some worthwhile work to be done among their ruins—something which we can cherish, perhaps even revive" (p. 276 C).

Clea's mind has moved in the same direction, as she explains that she too is drawn to France, and her penultimate comment recognizes the problematic of identity both she and Darley have struggled to overcome: "As for you, wise one, I have a feeling that you too perhaps have stepped across the threshold into the kingdom of your imagination, to take possession of it once and for all. Write and tell me—or save it for some small cafe under a chestnut-tree, in smoky autumn weather, by the Seine" (p. 281 C). "I wait," she concludes, "quite serene and happy, a real human being, an artist at last." Complete now as individuals and as artists, Darley and Clea, like the Mevlevi dervishes, have caught the rhythm of themselves, each other, and the universe.

In concentrating the diverse themes examined in Part I, *The Alexandria Quartet* illuminates the Apollonian character more completely than any of the earlier novels. Certainly, Durrell's exhaustive study of the formation and deconstruction of narcissistic character adds considerably to our understanding of this mode of identity. Through the examples of Darley and Clea, the *Quartet* emphasizes at length the distance between the Apollonian character's use of Romanticism and its original function in writers likes Wordsworth. The tension between centripetal and centrifugal force, between expansion and contraction of the self, places in perspective the studies of narcissism by Flaubert, Chopin, Conrad, Ford, and Fitzgerald. But while the fate of love, meaning, and identity is bleak in their novels, each of the major characters has been presented as an idealist whose attitudes and action are dominated by a kind of innocence or naiveté. Mis-

guided as they are, there is nothing consciously evil about any of
them. This is not the case in those novels I consider in Part II. In
The Immoralist, Death in Venice, and *The Blood Oranges* the
innocence of Apollo gives way to the knowledge of Dionysus,
and with the increase in the characters' knowledge and intelligence comes the possibility of conscious evil, a legacy from
Nietzsche's most radical position concerning the freedom of the
"wanderer." Under the sign of Dionysus, Romantic Imagination
becomes darker. The Apollonian will to power is destructive,
but the Dionysian is corrupt.

Part III
The Dionysian Quest

8
Romantic Decadence: *The Immoralist*

He becomes the son of Nothingness. His beginnings
are in his own self.
—Octavio Paz, *The Labyrinth of Solitude*

I

In the preface to *The Immoralist* Gide asks his readers to see the novel as an account of Michel's inner journey as well as a reflection of the age: "If certain distinguished minds have chosen to regard this drama as no more than the account of a strange case, and its hero as a sick man; if they have failed to see that some very urgent ideas of very general interest may nonetheless be found in it—that is not the fault of these ideas nor of this drama, but of the author, and I mean: of his clumsiness—though he has put in this book all his passion, all his tears, and all his care."[1] Elsewhere Gide writes that "with the exception of my *Nourritures,* all my books are *ironic* works; *they are books of criticism.*"[2] The critical position sketched in these comments suggests that *The Immoralist* reflects the philosophical spirit of nineteenth-century European thought exemplified by Nietzsche but that Nietzschean ideas are foregrounded only in so far as they lead Michel away from traditional ethics to narcissistic indulgence.[3] Actually, mislead would be a more accurate word, since Michel's fate dramatizes the inadequacy of the philosophy of radical individualism. Gide shows how this philosophy shapes Michel's consciousness, and how the Ménalquean credo Michel adopts—"I lay claim to nothing but my own nature, and the pleasure I take in an action is my clue to its propriety"— illuminates the neurotic condition Kernberg calls "pathological narcissism."[4] In the following pages I want to explore the ways Michel's pathology is linked to the ideology of individualism, expressing only in more obvious clinical symptoms the problems of self-consciousness we have already encountered.

Because Michel's self-concept is tied so closely to his attitudes towards history and social forms, I want to begin my analysis of the novel by exploring his view of the past, a view colored not only by Nietzsche but also by the Decadent Movement in late nineteenth-century French literature. In *The Romantic Agony* Mario Praz argues that "the Decadents devoted themselves to living over again the gory annals of the Eastern Empire, torn by dissentions and court hatreds, hemmed in on all sides by barbarian conquerors, a body full of bruises and decay enveloped in the symmetrical folds of a mantle of heavy gold."[5] The relationship between Praz's observation and Michel's principles should be readily apparent. Until his marriage to Marceline and their wedding trip to Africa where he is overcome by tuberculosis, Michel's life is devoted to philology. After he has begun to recover, Michel explains to his friends that his past habits of scholarly exploration should naturally have led him back to "philological research, applying myself, for instance, to determining the Goth's responsibility in the corruption of the Latin language" (p. 65). But his new sensitivity has altered Michel's view of what is valuable in the past. Now he sees that the old approach would have caused him to neglect "such figures as Theodoric, Cassiodorus, Amalswintha and their splendid passions for the sake of mere signs, the residue of their lives." Michel's attraction to the possibilities of excess symbolized by these figures requires penetration through dead signs to the "subject whose barbaric grandeur and nobility had just become evident" (p. 66). Philology is no longer an end in itself, but rather a means of entering into what Michel believes was an ancient drama of the senses.

Michel grows "increasingly enthusiastic" about the "crude morality of the Goths," particularly that of the young king Athalaric, whose "violent, voluptuous, unbridled life . . . utterly corrupted, glutted with debauchery" emerges as a model for his own apostasy from the constricting forms and conventions of society. These ideas are quickly developed into a philosophical position. At La Morinière he "sketched an ethic which would become a science of self-exploration perfected by a disciplined intelligence" (p. 72), and from this ethic he draws the controlling metaphor of his university lectures in Paris where he systematically defends what he has now come to see as the virtues of savagery:

> Discussing the decline of Latin civilization, I described artistic culture as rising like a secretion to the surface of a people, at first a symptom of plethora, the superabundance of health, then immediately hardening, calcifying, opposing any true contact of the mind with nature, concealing beneath the persistent appearance of life the diminution of life, forming a rind in which the hindered spirit languishes, withers and dies. Finally, carrying my notion to its conclusion, I said that Culture, born of life, utimately kills life. (P. 92)

Michel returns to this critique of civilization near the end of his story when he tells his friends why he is irresistibly attracted to Arab life:

> A land liberated from works of art. I despise those who can acknowledge beauty only when it's already transcribed, interpreted. One thing I admire about the Arabs: they live their art, they sing and scatter it from day to day; they don't cling to it, they don't embalm it in *works.* Which is the cause and effect of the absence of great artists. (P. 158)

These passages demonstrate how Michel, by distorting culture to fit his definition, justifies his experiments in hedonism. Secondly, in the transparency of his assertions that culture degenerates into a mere metaphor of experience and that art is corrupt because it obscures the authentic, we find Gide's judgement of Michel's ideas. The result of Michel's attempt to "live" his philosophy is revealed in the last words he speaks to his friends at Sidi b. M.—his ideas alienate him from everything and everyone, including his misconstrued "authentic being." Despite his learning, Michel is as deluded by imagination as Emma, Edna, and Jim were before him, and we will see how his isolation results from similar Romantic predilections.

II

Gide's preface encourages us to attend to the novel's philosophical underpinning, but *The Immoralist* is not primarily a *roman à thèse;* the Nietzschean elements are essentially a

means that enable Gide to penetrate the conscious and unconscious levels of Michel's mind. Consequently, I want to suggest
that *The Immoralist* is a symbolic study of self-delusion and self-
destruction[6] and that the best way to approach its psychological
nuances is through an examination of its chthonic imagery of
natural and bodily elements: desert, oasis, natural growth, water, blood. In these images, particularly those of water and
blood, we find the key to Michel's unconscious homosexuality
and his narcissism.

The first significant water image occurs soon after Michel has
reacquainted his friends with the salient facts of his past life. The
onset of tuberculosis left him "on the verge of death" (p. 20)
when he and Marceline arrived in Biskra, and the memory of
those days is hideous to him. The most vivid memory is of
Marceline's care, which he candidly acknowledges was all that
stood between him and death. Because of her attentiveness he
was finally able to perceive at least the faint possibility of survival: "And one day, finally, like a shipwrecked sailor catching
sight of land, I felt a glimmer of life awakening; I could smile at
Marceline" (p. 21). He goes on to express the shock of this
discovery: "merely being alive became quite amazing for
me. . . . Till now, I would think, I never realized that I was alive.
Now I would make the thrilling discovery of life." Convinced
that his old life as a philologist was merely a living death, Michel
associates his rebirth with the sea from which he will emerge to
discover his new life of sensation in the African oasis.

The theme of rebirth through water reappears in the first of the
Arab boys Michel is drawn to—Bachir, whose childish vitality
gives Michel strength and whose blood leads Michel to a remarkable vision of the source of life. Soon after Marceline has
brought Bachir into their house, Michel suffers another hemor-
rhage. Earlier, Bachir had cut his thumb as he whittled a piece of
wood, and the image of that accident comes back to Michel as he
contemplates his own sickness. Remembering how the child responded to his wound with delight, Michel experiences a sudden
gestalt:

> I thought of Bachir's beautiful, quick-flowing blood. And sud-
> denly I was seized by a desire, a craving, something wilder,
> more imperious than I had ever felt before: to live! I wanted to
> live. I clenched my teeth, my fists, concentrated my whole
> being hopelessly, furiously in this thirst for existence. (P. 25)

Through an act of imagination recalling his recreation of culture to suit his own ends, Michel has psychically replaced his own "ugly, blackish" (p. 25) blood with the "beautiful, quick-flowing blood" of Bachir. But Michel does more than imaginatively expropriate the boy's blood; he has fused his sense of passionate self-awareness with the first of the Arab boys encountered in Biskra and for whom, he admits at the end of his story, he returned two years later, as if to the source of life. Michel's awareness of new life in Bachir's blood repeats his sense of rebirth in the sea and this association becomes the nexus of the novel's most important symbolism. Water and blood, the sources of life in nature and human beings, both produce images of an ideal self and both suggest Narcissus' discovery of himself in the pool. Moreover, Michel's passionate desire to live, which he experiences through the *gestalt* image of the boy's blood, focuses on the vitality of another male, thus establishing a symbolic link between narcissism and his unconscious homosexuality.

The symbolic function of these chthonic images is expanded and clarified a few pages later when Michel sets out on an obsessive course of eating and drinking, fiercely determined that his health should be served with a religious devotion. The idea is so intense that he cannot sleep:

> There was a bottle of mineral water on the night table: I drank one glass, two; the third time, drinking straight from the bottle, I drained it in one gulp. I rehearsed my will like a lesson to be learned by heart; I educated my aggression, aimed it at whatever was around me; it had to struggle against everything: my salvation depended on no one but myself. (P. 28)

Michel's drinking extends the narcissistic symbolism of Bachir's blood; that is, once again he takes over (in this case ingests) the source of his own image. It also emphasizes another aspect of narcissism, for Michel is convinced that nothing good any longer exists beyond his own being, that physical salvation depends on the same absolute concentration on self that spiritual salvation will soon demand.

These images of water and blood dominate the sensuous imagery of the opening sections of *The Immoralist,* preparing the way for the erotic motif that appears as soon as Michel is well enough to explore the oasis at Biskra. Having recovered enough

to read and memorize a few lines from Homer, Michel now sets
out on an odyssey of his own into the "wonderful palm gardens
of the oasis" (p. 38) where he follows Marceline along a "strange
path, unlike any I have ever seen in other countries." The path
parallels an aqueduct which brings water to the parched desert
and to the grove hidden in the palms, from which floats the
melody of a flute. The edenic grove is infused with music and
life:

> full of silences and of rustlings: the faint noise of the water
> which flows through, irrigates the palms, and retreats from
> tree to tree; the circumspect call of the turtledoves; the tune of
> the flute a child was playing. Sitting almost naked on the trunk
> of a fallen palm, he was tending a heard of goats; he showed
> no alarm at our approach, did not run away, ceased playing
> only an instant. (P. 39)

Here the action moves on two planes at once. As pure
phenomena, the life of the grove lulls Michel into a dream-like
blissfulness. But, on the symbolic level, we see that he has jour-
neyed through the chthonic world of water and natural growth to
the very center of his unconscious.[7] There in the grove, as if
waiting for Michel, sits Lossif, an Arab Pan who represents
Michel's deep sexual identity. With Bachir, sexual interest was
entirely repressed, but the discovery of Lossif awakens Michel's
latent homoeroticism. On the following day he returns to the
grove where he meets Lossif's older brother, Lachmi, and
watches the boy climb a palm and descend "revealing under his
loose cloak a golden nakedness" (p. 41). Lachmi returns with a
flask of palm sap used in making wine: "On Lachmi's invitation I
tasted it, but the insipid flavor, raw yet syrupy, did not please
me." Thus Michel's dual journey into the oasis and his unconscious is apprehended through liquid images whose multivalency
incorporates the natural chthonic world, narcissism, and latent
homosexuality.

But the symbolism of Lachmi's gift and its significance is lost
on Michel who is conscious only of increasingly sensual experiences as he slowly awakens to his new identity. At this point in
the novel, Michel is too overwhelmed by the sensations of self to
be consciously aware of the true nature of his sexuality. Delight
in the chthonic world and in himself is sufficient for the time
being, as we see when he returns to the grove several days later

and finds it saturated and heavy with water: "I did not understand the forebearance of the African earth, submerged for days at a time and now awakening from winter, drunk with water, bursting with new juices; it laughed in this spring frenzy whose echo, whose image, I perceived within myself" (p. 45). His pleasure in the unity he perceives with the reassertion of life forces in the spring is continued after he and Marceline leave Biskra and stop for a while at Ravello. After critically examining his body and finding its pallor disgusting compared to the well-tanned peasants, Michel sets about a tanning program which increasing his confidence to the point where he can bathe in a "spring of clear water" (p. 56) high in the hills above the sea. Stretching out in the grass afterwards, he is overwhelmed by the powerful odor of mint growing nearby, whose leaves he then crushes and rubs over his skin. "I looked at myself a long time," he says, "without any more shame, with joy. I judged myself not yet strong, but capable of strength, harmonious, sensual, almost beautiful" (p. 57).

This fascination with self continues at La Morinière where Michel rediscovers the "woods full of mystery" and delights in the meadows where he finds water in "each hollow . . . pond, pool or stream; you hear a continual trickling" (p. 69). There he hunts eels with Charles in one of the pools and when he feels the water rising to his thighs addresses him with the familiar *tu*. The connection with earlier scenes linking sexuality with water is completed fifty pages later when Michel listens to Ménalque's discourse on the nature of pleasure: "Oh Michel, each joy is like manna in the desert, which spoils from one day to the next; or like water from the fountain of Ameles which Plato says no pitcher could preserve" (p. 112). Ménalque's warning about the evanescent nature of pleasure prefigures Michel's disenchantment when he returns to Biskra. At the same time, his comment introduces another element into the ironic structure of *The Immoralist*—by insisting on the temporariness of pleasure, Ménalque's metaphor clarifies the problematic nature of Michel's identity, for the very water in which Michel sees himself reflected and through which he approaches his sexual identity is doomed to disappear. The tension between Michel's conviction that what he had become is permanent and the ultimate impermanence of his "new self" is clearly revealed in the irresolvable dilemma we encounter in the novel's conclusion.

Gide's art is so highly controlled that the chthonic imagery

does considerably more than add to the novel's sensuous texture. We have seen how it symbolically reveals Michel's narcissism and uncovers his deep homosexual longings. But the
exhibits I have brought forward—and many others could easily
have been cited—also register the nature of Michel's self-
delusion as well as the psychological consequences of his increasingly solipsistic concentration on his own sensations. The
importance of Gide's chthonic imagery in the delineation of
Michel's character, particularly the psychological crisis docu-
mented by the novel, can be readily apprehended by comparing
it to a similar pattern of images in the *Alexandria Quartet* where
Durrell also links his protagonist's self-discovery to awareness
of the natural world. Darley's belated understanding of the in-
separability of above and below, nature and the spirit of the "old
dark gods of the Chthonian world,"[8] results in a holistic integration of self which is directly responsible for what appears to be
the promise of a permanent reunion with Clea. Darley's descent
into his unconscious through a sympathetic response to the natural world leads to self-forgetfulness, which Durrell posits as the
requisite for integration. Michel, on the other hand, lacks the
sense of relatedness sufficient to desire delivery from self; self-
consciousness is all he strives for. The result is that whereas
Darley experiences communion on a number of levels, not the
least with the "old dark gods," Michel ultimately loses contact
with the chthonic deity he has discovered. At the end of his
story, he speaks of this alienation: "I no longer know, now, the
dark god I serve" (p. 163). The Dionysiac figure he alludes to has
abandoned him—that is what he knows. What he is ignorant of is
that that figure was a projection of his ego-ideal and that his
intense concentration on self has lead to complete dissocation
even from his own fabricated identity. Seduced by *fin de siècle*
Romanticism, Nietzschean exhortations to destroy the past, and
his own unconscious drive toward self-destruction, Michel's
personification of Gide's "very urgent ideas" leads him to nihilism and beyond—to absolute emptiness of spirit.

III

"I am at the moment in my life past which I can no longer see
my way. Yet this is not exhaustion. The point is, I no longer
understand. I need . . . I need to speak, I tell you. The capacity

to get free is nothing; the capacity to be free, that is the task"
(p. 7). Michel's narrative opens with this expression of doubt
that "the old Adam" can sustain him. Seeing his crisis as ethical,
he wonders if he has the strength to hold out against the conventions he had violated. Yet he is oblivious to the fact that the
source of his crisis is his counterfeit "new being," rather than
traditional Protestant values. In the next few pages I want to
explore the deceptive nature of Michel's imagination, suggesting
that he has lost all ability to see clearly because his vision is
constantly turned inward.

If we return to Michel's comment quoted above, we see that
the novel begins at a point where Michel's experiments in individuality will soon reveal success or failure. That he can no
longer sustain his present precarious balance is obvious and, to
see exactly why this is the case, it is necessary to move forward
to his description of his "authentic" being and to pay particular
attention to the metaphor he uses to describe it. Michel has been
discoursing on the "immobility of death" (p. 50) he found in his
former study of history, concluding that one who has sensed his
own death sees things differently, that for him "the layers of
acquired knowledge peel away from the mind like a cosmetic
and reveal, in patches, the naked flesh beneath, the authentic
being hidden there" (p. 51). And this discovery provided him
with an occupation:

> Henceforth this was what I sought to discover: the authen-
> tic being, the "old Adam" whom the Gospels no longer ac-
> cepted; the man whom everything around me—books,
> teachers, family and I myself—had tried from the first to
> suppress. And I had already glimpsed him, faint, obscured by
> their encrustations, but all the more valuable, all the more
> urgent. I scorned henceforth that secondary, learned being
> whom education had pasted over him. Such husks must be
> stripped away.

He concludes by comparing himself to "a palimpsest":

> I shared the thrill of the scholar who beneath more recent
> script discovers, on the same paper, an infinitely more pre-
> cious ancient text. What was it, this occult text? In order to
> read it, would I not have to erase the more recent ones?[9]
> (Pp. 51–52)

Michel's habit of reversing the values of all that is convention-

ally significant reappears in his reaction against his Huguenot
roots and his assertion that the New Adam of Christ is less true
to the essence of man than the "old Adam," fallen and aware of
the sin that provides his first sense of identity. Authenticity for
Michel, it should be noted, becomes synonymous with a brooding self-consciousness that is clearly antithetical to any notion of
social interdependence.

But Michel reveals much more about himself here than
rebelliousness against traditional theology. I am especially interested in the "thrill" he mentions because his excitement makes it
easy to gloss over the ambiguity inhering in his palimpsest
metaphor. That he insists on his "authentic being" having an *a
priori* relationship to his "secondary" self exemplifies, it seems
to me, Michel's self-delusion and his victimization by his own
imagination. I would argue that Michel invents, rather than discovers, the old Adam, who can easily be seen as a compendium
of the familiar codes of naive Romanticism and the age's clichés.
His "authentic being" is only a more subtly disguised generic
descendant of Emma Bovary's magazine persona, Edna Pontellier's fantasy self who loves the photograph of the tragedian,
Jim's heroes of adventure tales.

The old Adam's fradulence is further revealed in Michel's
discourse on the necessity of dissimulation. After shaving off his
beard as a symbolic gesture toward his new identity, he suspects
that Marceline may somehow infer inner change from his altered
appearance. "It was essential," he argues, "that she not interfere
with my rebirth; to shield it from her gaze, I would have to
dissimulate" (p. 59). He points out to his listeners that he was no
longer the man Marceline had married, that his outward image
may have remained "constant and faithful," but in truth was
growing false "day by day." And the smug conclusion he draws
from deceiving his wife reflects the solipsism that will ultimately
be his ruin: "Thus, as in each instance when an initial disgust is
overcome, I ended by enjoying the dissimulation itself, savoring
it as I savored the functioning of my unsuspected faculties. And
I advanced every day into a richer, fuller life, toward a more
delicious happiness" (p. 60). If Michel's new being is *created*,
rather than the manifestation of an *a priori* identity encrusted by
convention, this obsessive secrecy registers a considerable distance between his conception of himself and reality. True, he is
not the man Marceline married—the "learned Puritan" (p. 4) is
dead—but Michel has no idea that his new being is no more

authentic than the old one, that it is only a copy, a received idea. Rather than attaining the richness of a fully-realized life as the lying old Adam, Michel is merely exploring the "already-written,"[10] as Barthes puts it.

To continue the theme of falseness, Gide conceived of Ménalque's monologue, which is delivered at a party Michel and Marceline give in their Paris apartment. Ménalque's attack on bourgeois ethics focuses on what he believes are the damaging effects of constraint:

> If there's one thing each of them claims not to resemble it's . . . himself. Instead he sets up a model, then imitates it; he doesn't even chose the model—he accepts it ready-made. People dare not—they dare not turn the page. The laws of mimicry—I call them the laws of fear. People are afraid to find themselves alone, and don't find themselves at all. I hate all this moral agoraphobia—it's the worst kind of cowardice. (P. 104)

And he concludes by arguing that in suppressing one's difference we inevitably give ourselves over to imitation. Nowhere is Gide's "criticism" more in evidence, for it is patently clear that both Ménalque and Michel are themselves exemplars of the "ready-made." Each, but especially Ménalque, has adopted a persona replete with philosophic gestures in imitation of Nietzsche, Baudelaire, and Rimbaud. Beyond that, Ménalque's parroting of received ideas is made even more outrageous by his Wildean posturings.

That neither man sees he is only repeating another kind of mimicry contributes greatly to the novel's irony. Yet the themes of mimicry and dissimulation involve more than problematic identities. The ideas Michel shares with Ménalque justify hedonistic indulgence, but they are also deeply implicated in Michel's destructiveness. This relationship between falseness and destructiveness surfaces when Ménalque dismisses Michel as being only a hedonistic dilettante. "I've tried to cut my happiness to my own measure," he tells Michel scornfully, "You keep your fireside happiness" (p. 110). To which Michel protests: "My happiness is too tight for me. Sometimes I'm almost strangled by it." Michel's ambivalence toward heterosexual relationships masks his emerging destructive attitude toward any kind of concern for others, and what he feels, Ménalque expresses in his discourse on pleasure: "I tell you, Michel, each joy still awaits us, but must find the bed empty, must be the *only one,* so that we come to it like a widower" (p. 112). The significance of this exchange to the novel's central thematic concerns becomes apparent two pages later when we learn that, as they talk, Marceline is in bed losing her child, an event that prefigures her own death, which is caused by Michel's need to return to Biskra. Michel progresses toward a "richer, fuller life" through acts which destroy both forms and people, and his evening of philosophical dalliance with Ménalque while Marceline miscarries is only the first, symbolic representation of a series of more conscious acts that follow his visit to Ménalque. Within the terms of the novel, to be false is to be destructive. In this equation we find the moral position underlying Gide's "criticism" of Michel, and the remaining pages of *The Immoralist* are given over to elaborating the self-destructiveness which results from Michel's naive and ultimately disastrous ideas.

IV

Michel begins to indulge in the more extreme forms of his doctrine after his child's death. Extremely ill, Marceline asks for her rosary, which causes Michel to remember how, when he was ill in Biskra, he rejected her desire to ask for "God's help" because that would have entailed an obligation he did not want. Now, he feels, is the time to act, to articulate his principles. "I did manage to get well myself," (p. 115) he tells her, as if he were tasting his new capacity for cruelty. Moreover, her very weakness becomes a challenge to his belief that only the strong deserve to survive and his response to her appearance is instructive: "Sickness had entered Marceline, henceforth inhabited her, marked her, soiled her. She was a tainted thing" (p. 116). Michel's repugnance may seem at odds with the numerous times he protests his love for her, but, if we look more closely at their relationship, it becomes clear that what Michel says here is in perfect accord with his "new being."

The significance of this scene to Michel's sense of his own identity can be fully appreciated by juxtaposing it to an earlier one that takes place at La Morinière in the autumn. They have gone for a walk one afternoon and finally rest on a bench overlooking the valley below. Michel remembers how Marceline looked in this tranquil setting and what he felt as she sat there, deeply aware of her pregnancy;

> Just as a breath of wind sometimes ripples smooth water, the slightest emotion could be read on Marceline's face; deep within herself she listened to the mysterious stirring of a new life; I bent over her as over a deep, clear pool which revealed, as far as one could see, nothing but love. Ah, if that was still happiness, I know I tried to hold it then, as one vainly tries to hold escaping water in one's cupped hands; yet already I sensed, close to our happiness, something besides happiness, which certainly stained my love, but as the autumn stains. . . . (P. 86)

This may be the most explicitly narcissistic scene in the novel, and it is certainly one of the most damning. I would suggest that everything Michel feels here must be understood in the context of the repetition of chthonic imagery, that the transitory nature of the pleasure he experiences returns us to Ménalque's assertion that all pleasure can only momentarily be preserved, like the "water from the fountain of Ameles." But my immediate concern lies in Michel's description of his wife's love, in which he literally sees himself. He is the source, the cause of the reflection, but the self-love he derives from Marceline's love is imperfect, and what he feels seems to be imperceptibly flowing away from him. The cause is not difficult to find—this is only one of many early manifestations of his unconscious preference for someone of his own sex. To return to the preceding scene, we see that Michel's tentative happiness in Marceline's translucent health vanishes completely when the physical image of himself dies in his child and when Marceline's illness turns her features into a death mask. As Marceline struggles to recover from her miscarriage, Michel sees nothing but a perversion of his own carefully wrought new being in her desiccated features. True to his principles, he symbolically abandons her at this point, just as he literally destroys her by forcing her to accompany him back to Africa.

By consigning Marceline to the weak, freedom becomes a possibility for Michel. While he continues to remain attentive, all his psychic and sexual energies are redirected to the farm people, in whom he senses a reality—even in the perversions of the Heurtevents—denied him by his "fireside happiness." He is especially attracted to an itinerant laborer named Pierre who

was "tall, rather handsome, not stupid but guided solely by in-
stinct; he did nothing save on the spur of the moment, yielded to
every passing impulse" (p. 120). This attraction, and the mildly
criminal diversions he indulges in during their remaining days at
the farm, are clear enough in Michel's overall plan to exploit the
possibilities of experience and require no analysis. Their primary importance is that they lead to and reinforce his decision to
return to Africa, despite Marceline's worsening condition.

In Rome Marceline appears to be steadily weakening. She
tells Michel that she understands his doctrine, that it "may be
beautiful . . . but it eliminates the weak" (p. 150), to which he
responds by saying simply—"as it should." Looking back on
these days, Michel comments on how helpless he had been before his insatiable desire: "By what aberration, what stubborn
blindness, what deliberate folly did I convince myself and above
all try to convince her that she must still have more light and
warmth, invoking the memory of my own convalescence in
Biskra?" (p. 155). He points out that "the air had grown warmer,
the bay of Palermo is a mild place, and Marceline enjoyed it.
There, perhaps, she might have . . . But was I free to choose
what I wanted, to decide what I desired?" That he was free is as
apparent to Michel as it is to his friends. Here the lineaments of
his Huguenot morality are traceable, if only faintly, on his consciousness, for the rhetorical nature of the question he poses, its
tone, reveals that he knows abdication of responsibility to his
wife (for what he argues were transcendent values) does not
release him from his fundamental responsibility for her well-
being. What this reveals about his convictions becomes clear a
few pages later.

Michel and Marceline retrace their original journey to the
south. By this time Michel has given himself over completely to
"every passing impulse," revelling in the glimpses he has of life
in the poorest sections of the cities. The sights and smells of
harbor life in Syracuse are particularly intoxicating. There, he
says, "the dregs of society were delectable company for me . . .
what need had I of understanding their speech when my whole
body savored it!" (p. 155). In what appears to be a blatant imitation of Rimbaud's African journey, Michel desires to mingle
with these men who represent the authentic—longing "to roll
under the table with them and waken only with the sad shudders
of dawn." Michel's attraction anticipates the Consul's drunken,
rhapsodic vision of the flotsam and jetsam of humanity in Mexi-

can cantinas, a much desired alternative to what he knows will be an unsuccessful attempt to make love with Yvonne. Michel's latent homosexuality forces him, like the Consul, toward an at-least-symbolic erotic experience with unknown men, and he achieves this one night at Kairouan when he sleeps among a "group of Arabs" in the open air and returns to the hotel "covered with vermin" (p. 159).

At this point, Michel breaks off his narrative. He tells his friends that:

> There's no use attempting now to impose more order on my story than there was in my life then. I've been trying long enough to tell you how I became what I am. If only I could rid my mind of this unendurable logic! . . . I feel nothing in myself except nobility. (P. 158)

It is a brilliant ploy by Gide. Michel's story is approaching its most sordid scenes and, just before making these comments, he has begun to hesitate in his speech, describing the approach to Tunis haltingly, not knowing what to say of Malta except that it was "dead white." The anger of the first sentence ("There's no use. . . .") leads to his comment about the restraints of "unendurable logic," in which he finds only a momentary, untenable excuse for what is happening to him. Until now, he has woven the events of his life into a superb, tightly-presented exposition during which he has taken pains to be as logical as possible. Now he suddenly and unexpectedly exclaims: "I feel nothing in myself except nobility." It is this last comment that provides the key to all he has just said. We remember that Michel is approaching the end of his story—which is structurally the beginning of the novel where he admitted to his friends that "I am at a moment in my life past which I can no longer see my way." What happens here on the verge of his disclosures about Marceline's death, the incident with the Arab prostitute, and his bitter disappointment with Biskra is a combination of self-defense, confusion, and un-certainty. Aware that his ethic of self-exploration has failed, he is overcome by what he must now say, and, as if to protect himself from the criticism of his listeners, he asserts pompously, absurdly, that he has achieved nobility. Here the Nietzschean superman seems much more like an adolescent, and his final examples of degradation, as well as the noticeable disintegration of his narrative, reflect with great accuracy this momentary *crise de conscience*.

At Biskra he discovers a shattered dream. While the oasis and the town remain the same, the children have undergone a hideous transformation—they have grown up. As Michel disgustedly recites their jobs and the salient events in their lives—one washes dishes, one has lost an eye, another has married—it all seems grotesque: "I realized from my unbearable sadness that *these* were the real reason I had returned to Biskra—Ménalque was right: Memory is an invention of misery" (p. 161). But one of the boys, Moktir, remains attractive and, in a frantic attempt to salvage something of the dream, Michel arranges for Moktir to accompany them to Touggourt despite Marceline's increasing weakness—or possibly because of it.

Marceline is on the verge of death when they reach their hotel in Touggourt. Although he is impatient to explore the city, Michel explains that "by a last pretense of virtue, I stayed with her until evening" (p. 165), pointing out that it had become unbearable to look at her face any longer because it had come to seem like a *memento mori*. Reassured that her situation is stable, he joins Moktir in the streets. Soon they enter a cafe where Michel is taken in hand by Moktir's mistress, who, in a room empty of everything but a low bed, draws him to her: "And I yielded to her embrace," he reports calmly, "the way you give yourself up to sleep" (p. 166). Although *The Immoralist* is filled with sensual imagery and erotic fantasies, Michel has only two sexual experiences, once with Marceline and now with the Arab woman. Each encounter follows immediately upon violence or a presentiment of death. With Marceline, Michel can express his sexuality after fighting with a drunken cab driver. With the Arab woman, he abandons himself, *as if in a dream,* shortly after leaving Marceline, who is obviously dying. Clearly, sex, violence, and death are linked in Michel's unconscious. Both passive and active sexual violence can be accounted for by his "doctrine", which embraces destruction and brutality on all levels (we need to remember his attraction to Athalaric), but Eros-Thanatos remains as unperceived as his homosexuality, which he may also be symbolically expressing by making love to Moktir through his mistress. And such an interpretation seems even more likely when we realize that Moktir remains in the room.

But there is even more involved here—nothing less, I think,

than Gide's strongest judgement of Michel's doctrine. Marceline is dying in Michel's bed even as he is making love to the Arab woman in another, and these events that are taking place simultaneously echo Ménalque's injunction that "each joy awaits us, but must find the bed empty, must be the *only one,* so that we come to it like a widower." What happens is identical in every detail to the events that occur at the end of *Under the Volcano,* where the Consul is able to have sex with the prostitute Maria while Yvonne is being trampled to death by the horse he untethered earlier outside the Farolito. In each case, sexuality is equated with degradation, dream, or delusion and successful sexual performance (perhaps even the desire for sex) can be achieved only when Marceline and Yvonne are betrayed. For at least a moment Michel has cut himself loose from all demands extrinsic to himself—he has become an immoralist.

His infidelity inspires no guilt, and, as he calmly describes Marceline's death and burial, his apparent distance from any emotion confuses the narrator: "We felt . . . that by relating it, Michel had somehow legitimized his action" (p. 169). This discomfort leads to a series of questions:

> He had completed his story without a quaver in his voice, without an inflection or a gesture to reveal that any emotion whatever disturbed him either because he took a cynical pride in not seeming moved, or because a kind of reticence kept him from moving us by his tears, or because he simply wasn't moved. I can't distinguish in him, even now, what is pride, or strength, or aridity, or reserve. (P. 169)

What the narrator cannot distinguish the attentive reader can. To put it simply, Michel is philosophically and emotionally paralyzed. We have seen the symptoms prefigured in his language, in the increased reliance on fragments and single words to convey thoughts of an order of complexity that earlier demanded and received extensive syntactical elaboration. I have already touched on one reason for this change in Michel's fluency; as his story comes closer to the present moment, he becomes increasingly disturbed by the sense of confusion that prompted him to call his friends together. Even more basic to our understanding of his crisis is the fact that the absence of inflection in his speech, even of gestures, reflects the consequences of his inner journey. I have shown how, in *Madame Bovary,* narcissism can never be more than a meditation since it is impossible to actualize fantasy. *The Immoralist* provides a more extreme example by showing that narcissism can result in psychic paralysis and raises the question: What are the limits of self-absorption? No one knows, but it is clear that Michel has, at the end of his narrative, arrived at a point where he is on the verge of being consumed by his own inwardness. The next stage in his development is autism.

All that lies between Michel and the abyss of self are the vestiges of his Protestant heritage. He wants "some reason to live" because he has discovered that his freedom is "useless." "It's not . . . that I'm tired of my crime," he says, "if that's what you want to call it; but I must prove to myself that I have not exceeded my rights" (p. 169). Moreover, he is sometimes "afraid that what I have suppressed will take its revenge" (p. 170). It is already taking its revenge. Looking into himself—that still pool which has given him back only ravishing images of what he has believed was his "authentic being"—Michel now sees, and is frightened by, a reflection of what lies behind him, the world of moral dictates, forms, and conventions he has tried to destroy. And this is where *The Immoralist* ends, with Michel poised between the world of the Psalm that stands as the epigraph to the novel—"I will praise thee, for I am fearfully and wonderfully made"—and reality. Whether he will disappear into the silence of self or somehow find a means of salvation Gide does not say. Once Michel's voice has faded into ellipsis, we are left to contemplate the corruption of his Dionysian will-to-power which reappears in *Death in Venice*.

9

The Closed Circle:
Death in Venice and the Passions of the Mind

> I well know how much in you—in all of us, despite
> Nietzsche, desite Goethe himself—rises up against the
> thought of the romantic as morbid and antagonistic to
> life. For is not the romantic the sweetest and
> wholesomest thing in the world, goodness itself, born
> as it is in the deepest depth of the folk-soul? Yes, no
> doubt. But it is a fruit, splendidly fresh and sound for
> its moment, and yet extraordinarily prone to decay;
> the purest refreshment to the spirit if enjoyed at the
> right moment, yet at the next, the wrong moment,
> spreading bitterness and corruption among men. It is a
> fruit of life, conceived of death, pregnant of dissolu-
> tion; a wonder of the soul, perhaps the highest, in the
> eye, and sealed with the blessing of conscienceless
> beauty, but on cogent grounds regarded with mistrust
> by the eye of a responsible and controlling love of life,
> and a subject for self-conquest at the definite behest of
> conscience.
> —Thomas Mann, "Nietzsche and Music"

I

The Immoralist and *Death in Venice* are two variations on the
same theme. Like Michel, Gustave von Aschenbach embarks
upon a dual journey to the South and into his unconscious. We
have seen how Michel struggles to shed the persona of his inau-
thentic self, which he believes was created by civilization and its
restraints, and how he abandons in the process the claims of
history and traditional values, which have come to seem false
and misleading. Michel's goal is the Old Adam, whose discovery
ironically leads to *accidia* rather than integration, so that at the

169

end of *The Immoralist*, desperate for a more meaningful *raison d'être* than Ali, he rather pathetically asks his friends to drag him away from Biskra, admitting that his will to act has been destroyed.

While the general features of this pattern are repeated in *Death in Venice*, Aschenbach is more aware of the consequences of his acts, even though he is equally helpless at the end. Once he has arrived in Venice and discovered Tadzio, Aschenbach too abandons the claims of social order and embraces the immoral as he acquiesces to the demands of Dionysus. Michel's discoveries are linked to the fashionable hedonism of Ménalque and the "utterly corrupted," debauched, and violent life of the young king Athalaric whose principles become the foundation of Michel's Parisian lectures. Similarly, Aschenbach discovers his authentic self through the imaginative and philosophical literature of the Western world but this is where careful distinctions must be made between Gide's hedonist and Mann's novelist. Except for those occasions where he can use it to justify his own ends, history for Michel is "dead," whereas literature is both Aschenbach's *métier* and his reality. The tragedy of *Death in Venice* springs from the predispositions of a great novelist's temperament, which increasingly confuses art with life. Moreover, the imaginative worlds of literature and music to which he responds express a romantic vision "conceived of death, pregnant of dissolution." Michel's attraction to Athalaric's nihilism becomes, in *Death in Venice,* a desire for self-destruction within a complex imaginative structure dominated by a Romanticism that is absolutely "antagonistic to life."

Michel strives to live for and in the moment of pleasure, but for Aschenbach significant moments exist in relation to the timeless vistas of art. The essence of Aschenbach's analogical approach to experience can be found in the narrator's comments shortly after Aschenbach arrives in Venice. In his room in the Hotel des Bains Aschenbach stands before one of the windows facing the sea, looking at the rhythmic action of the waves:

> A solitary, unused to speaking of what he sees and feels, has mental experiences which are at once more intense and less articulate than those of a gregarious man. They are sluggish, yet more wayward, and never without a melancholy tinge. Sights and impressions which others brush aside with a glance, a light comment, a smile, occupy him more than their

due; they sink silently in, they take on meaning, they become experience, emotion, adventure. Solitude gives birth to the original in us, to beauty unfamiliar and perilous—to poetry. But also, it gives birth to the opposite: to the perverse, the illicit, the absurd.[1]

Aschenbach will become obsessed with Tadzio because the boy embodies characteristics of mythic figures who have became Aschenbach's companions in his solitude. He *is* Hyancinthus, Eros, Narcissus, Hermes. Entering the novelist's imagination in these guises, Tadzio gives birth first to beauty, then to the illicit, which Aschenbach understands by way of the analogical process described above. Like Emma, Edna, and Jim, Aschenbach has "mental experiences" of external phenomena that mirror literary "pictures of the world." But unlike Emma and Jim, Aschenbach is aware of the direction his imagination has begun to lead him, even though he cannot do anything about it. His helplessness springs from the fact that the risks of abandonment are perceived through poetry and music—Romanticism in the broadest sense—which shape his perception of himself in irresistibly attractive heroic contexts that ultimately yield an abundant crop of the Romantic "fruit of life, conceived of death."

II

Aschenbach chooses Venice for his break from writing because, of all the places in the world, it "alone had the power to beguile him, to relax his resolution, to make him glad" (p. 369). To him, Venice is the objective correlative of Romantic "experience, emotion, adventure," the antithesis of the closed and ordered world of Munich. Specifically, the city symbolizes certain powerful literary and musical motifs that begin to emerge while he is travelling on the Pola steamer. Near the end of the crossing Aschenbach leaves the dining saloon for the open deck where he hopes for a glimpse of the city:

But sky and sea remained leaden, with spurts of fine, mistlike rain; he reconciled himself to the idea of seeing a different Venice from that he had always approached on the landward side. He stood by the foremast, his gaze on the distance, alert for the first glimpse of the coast. (P. 350)

And as he looks into the mist his anticipation is guided by the perceptions of another literary man:

> . . . he thought of the melancholy and susceptible poet who had once seen the towers and turrets of his dreams rise out of these waves; repeated the rhythms born of his awe, his mingled emotions of joy and suffering—and easily susceptible to a prescience already shaped within him, he asked his own sober, weary heart if a new enthusiasm, a new preoccupation, some late adventure of the feelings could still be in store for the idle traveller.

The melancholy poet is of course Byron, whose Childe Harold stands on the Bridge of Sighs and declaims: "I saw from out the wave her structures rise/ As from the stroke of the enchanter's wand."[2] Aschenbach's Venice also seems touched by magic— even his approach to the city is accompanied by mysterious musicians and a gondolier who seems risen from the Underworld. But the significance of these remembered lines lies more in what they tell us about Aschenbach's "prescience." His approach to Venice and the "late adventure of the feelings" awaiting him there are perceived—though only partially on the conscious level—within the context of a Byronic world and in the shadow of the Byronic hero. Like Childe Harold, Aschenbach has left behind one world for another where he will explore "a new enthusiasm, a new preoccupation." Byron once called Venice "the seat of all dissoluteness,"[3] and it is precisely such a city that Aschenbach discovers through his pursuit of Tadzio. His prescience, then, passes through the mist to the "illicit," the outlawed, the criminal—essential aspects of true Byronic heroism and the logical focus of a solitary, melancholy, Romantic mind like Aschenbach's. Thus the mist obscuring his view of Venice is both a natural phenomenon and a symbolic barrier between his conscious and unconscious. As he stands on the deck of the Pola steamer these and other correspondences are gathering force in his unconscious. They will begin to play a crucial role in his life as soon as his experience of the outer world validates his literary imagination.

Once in Venice his imagination leads him to the classical world. Lying in the shade on a warm afternoon, mesmerized by the blue of the sea, he recalls his "mountain home, the theatre of his summer labours":

There clouds hung low and trailed through the garden, violent storms extinguished the lights of the house at night, and the ravens he fed swung in the tops of the fir trees. And he would feel transported to Elysium, to the ends of the earth, to a spot more carefree for the sons of men, where no snow is, and no winter, no storms or downpours of rain; where Oceanus sends a mild and cooling breath, and days flow on in blissful idleness, without effort or struggle, entirely dedicated to the sun and the feasts of the sun. (P. 370)

Here Aschenbach refashions the fourth book of *The Odyssey* where Proteus speaks to Menelaos, assuring him that his end will not come in "horse-pasturing Argos,"

but the immortals will convey you to the Elysian
Field, and the limits of the earth, where fair-haired
Rhadamantys is, and where there is made the easiest of life
    for mortals,
for there is no snow, nor much winter there, nor is there ever
rain, but always the stream of the Ocean sends up breezes
of the West wind blowing briskly for the refreshment of
    mortals.[4]

Aschenbach's early experience of the Mediterranean is fixed by images of Homer's Apollonian world and it is in the context of such a world that Aschenbach first perceives Tadzio. In the opening sections of *Death in Venice* the city is bracketed by opposing visions: the Apollonian, which gives birth to beauty, and the Dionysian, which gives birth to the illicit. Mann leaves no doubt that Aschenbach is infinitely more susceptible to illicit Romantic adventure, which simply overpowers the restraints of Classicism, so that from the first pages of the novella we see the appeal of form give way to the appeal of chaos, intellectual order to disorder, "self-conquest" to self-indulgence.

These conflicting visions merge in the images of the sea that is always there in the background. It is apparent as early as the Pola crossing that Venice and the sea are inseparable in Aschenbach's imagination. Each implies the other and each represents a central Romantic concept announced in Aschenbach's "prescience":

His love of the ocean had profound sources: the hard-worked artist's longing for rest, his yearning to seek refuge from the thronging manifold shapes of his fancy in the bosom of the simple and vast; and another yearning, opposed to his art and perhaps for that very reason a lure, for the unorganized, the immesurable, the eternal—in short, for nothingness. He whose preoccupation is with excellence longs fervently to find rest in perfection; and is not nothingness a form of perfection? (Pp. 360–61)

The enchanted sea of Byron and the paradisal sea of Homer are contained within the eternal sea of nothingness, which is symbolically inseparable from the decadent South Aschenbach first envisioned as a "primeval wilderness world" dense with "trees, misshapen as a dream" (p. 339). Venice and the sea objectify his inner, Dionysiac journey to the Primitive and, in concert with a host of other symbols, signify the death-wish that first expressed itself in Aschenbach's jungle fantasy in Munich, which led him to feel both terror and longing for the tiger crouched in its bamboo thickets.

III

Before the Venetian holiday, Aschenbach's Romanticism was entirely subjugated to his work. Day after day he began with "a cold shower over chest and back; then, setting a pair of tall wax candles in silver holders at the head of his manuscript, he sacrificed to art, in two or three hours of almost religious fervour, the powers he had assembled in sleep" (p. 343). But once he has left Munich behind, his imagination is assaulted by a growing number of Romantic referents and it is clear that his fascination with the sea, particularly with its destructiveness, embraces the foreboding harmonies of Wagner's *Tristan.* Wagner's theme of the desire for annihilation through love expresses Aschenbach's deepest desires and provides another reason for Mann's having chosen Venice as the site of his hero's confrontation with himself. No one has summarized the significance of the relationship between Wagner and the city better than Erich Heller. Mann, he writes, "could not have chosen another scene for Aschenbach's doom. Venice is its inevitable location. For it seems a city built by the very Will to Power in honor of Death. Teeming with Life, it is yet entirely Art, the residence of Eros Thanatos, the *Liebestod,* the music of which it has inspired."[5]

Heller's eloquent rendering of the ambience of destruction accords perfectly with conscious and unconsious responses to the sea, the city, and the vision of the tiger waiting for him deep within his imagined jungle.

Music plays as large a part in Aschenbach's adventures as literature. Moreover, it carries the dominant themes of dissolution and death. Consider the scene where Aschenbach is being rowed to the Lido by the mysterious and frightening gondolier. "Even if you mean to rob me," Aschenbach thinks, "even if you hit me in the back with your oar and send me down to the kingdom of Hades, even then you will have rowed me well":

> but nothing of the sort happened. Instead, they fell in with women singing to guitar and mandolin. They rowed persistently bow for bow with the gondola and filled the silence that had rested on the waters with the lyric love of gain. Aschenbach tossed money into the hat they held out. The music stopped at once, they rowed away. (P. 354)

Much is prefigured here: the greedy immorality of the Venetians who withhold information about the cholera epidemic; the almost enchanted quality of many of the events that await Aschenbach's arrival in the city; the relationship between music and death. The more immediate importance of the scene lies in the fact that Aschenbach's arrival in Venice is heralded by the sonorous harmonies of the most romantic of instruments, the guitar, whose voice is second in importance only to Tadzio's and the lute-like sounds his name creates in Aschenbach's imagination. It is the guitar, we remember, that the laughing, leering figure of death plays near the end of *Death in Venice*. His music, laden with insinuations of decadence and destruction, is anticipated in the musician's gondola, whose songs "filled the silence that had rested on the waters"—the same waters, it should be noted, that soon inspire Aschenbach's longing for nothingness.

Aschenbach first hears Tadzio's name as a musical motif. On the beach the boy's friends shout a strange, talismanic word, which Aschenbach "was not without curiosity to learn . . . but he could make out nothing more exact than two musical syllables, something like Adgio—or oftener still, Adjiu, with a long-drawn-out *u* at the end" (p. 361). When Tadzio talks to the women in his family, "Aschenbach understood not a word he said; it might be the sheerest commonplace, in his ear it became mingled harmonies. Thus the lad's foreign birth raised his speech to music" (p. 371). Tadzio's name functions very much like the Desire motif in *Tristan,* which is played by woodwinds that seem to echo the *u*-sound that initially entrances Aschenbach.[6] And that motif in turn, expressing as it does the desire for death, nothingness, destruction of the self, becomes the dominant music of his orgiastic dream at the end of the novella. There he imagines a "long-drawn *u*-sound at the end" of the revellers' shouts, "and with all these, dominating them all, flute-notes of the cruellest sweetness, deep and cooing" (p. 391). If the flute is associated by Aschenbach with Tadzio-Eros, then the guitar and mandolin become the instruments of Tadzio-Hermes. When the sounds of these instruments are joined, the Desire motif fades into the Walpurgis-Night of his dream whose "promiscuous embraces" (p. 392) celebrate his utter degradation and the nothingness he will soon confront.[7]

IV

This preliminary assessment of Aschenbach's analogical habit of mind and of the way his innermost desires are related to literature, the sea, and music should clarify the development of his imagined relationship with Tadzio. At first Tadzio is only a "long-haired boy of about fourteen" who attracts Aschenbach's attention because of his remarkable features: "Aschenbach noticed with astonishment the lad's perfect beauty. His face recalled the noblest moment of Greek sculpture—pale, with a sweet reserve, with clustering honey-coloured ringlets, the brow and nose descending in one line, the winning mouth, the expression of pure and godlike serenity" (p. 356). At dinner in the hotel, Aschenbach meditates on the idea of harmony Tadzio inspires before moving on to occupy himself with more general esthetic questions. This initial meeting already reveals Aschenbach's tendency to relate his experience to esthetic contexts, and the sequence of events that transpires in the hotel diningroom follows very closely the sequence that unfolded on the steamer as he anticipated his first view of Venice. In this case, his immediate response is not to Tadzio as a human phenomenon, but to Tadzio's beauty that radiates correspondences to Greek sculpture and then leads into esthetic speculation. And the process continues after dinner. Aschenbach spends the evening wandering in the park, lost in pleasant speculations. Later he "passed the night in deep, unbroken sleep, visited, however, by varied and lively dreams" (p. 358). Tadzio has already touched Aschenbach's imagination, for his dreams clearly spring from his encounters with the boy and there can be little doubt that the novelist's creative faculty is at work on new material.

The process of transforming raw experience to imaginative forms is even more apparent the next day on the beach where Aschenbach watches Tadzio run into the surf:

> The sight of this living figure, virginally pure and austere, with dripping locks, beautiful as a tender young god, emerging from the depths of the sea and sky, outrunning the element—it conjured up mythologies, it was like a primeval legend, handed down from the beginning of time, of the birth of form, of the origin of the gods. With closed lids Aschenbach listened to this poesy hymning itself silently within him, and anon he thought it was good to be here and that he would stop awhile. (P. 363)

Vision, analogy, absorption—from an image Tadzio is incorporated into the context of myth, archetype, "primeval legend." It is because he conjures up mythologies that he can be taken into Aschenbach's imagination where he becomes "experience, emotion, adventure." This process is part of what by now should be a recognizable structure, for it repeats exactly what happens between Emma and Rodolphe, Edna and Robert, Michel and his Arab boys. Rodolphe, Robert, the young Arabs, and now Tadzio give birth to each protagonist's erotic fantasies—embodied in Emma's "lover," Edna's tragedian, Michel's suppressed homosexual desires, Aschenbach's "tender young god." In each case, the erotic object becomes significant only after it has been interiorized and absorbed into the self through an imaginative process.

At this point in *Death in Venice,* Aschenbach's relationship to Tadzio undergoes a complex and revealing development, for Tadzio has literally become his "new preoccupation." Rising early, Aschenbach goes to the beach every day, takes his place there as in a theater, and prepares for the boy's arrival: "Then he settled down; he had three or four hours before the sun reached its height and the fearful climax of its power; three or four hours while the sea went deeper and deeper blue; three or four hours in which to watch Tadzio" (p. 371). As these hours pass in rapt contemplation Aschenbach slowly and methodically memorizes every "line and pose" of the boy, enchanted by "the thin envelope of flesh covering the torso, . . . the delicate outlines of the ribs and the symmetry of the breast-structure" (p. 371). Not even the texture of the boy's flesh escapes his attention: "His armpits were still as smooth as a statue's, smooth the glistening hollows behind the knees, where the blue network of veins suggested that the body was formed of some stuff more transparent than mere flesh."

The psychological processes at work here encompass much more than mere ideality, for Aschenbach's attention suggests both the esthetic and the erotic, a meditation on beauty and a physical obsession for Tadzio as he stands there on the verge of nothingness. The scene reveals the deepest reaches of Aschenbach's consciousness and his conscience. If Tadzio remains only a Polish boy, then Aschenbach is only a slightly corrupt middle-aged man, but, if Tadzio can convincingly be seen as the very embodiment of Greek perfection and sensibility, then Aschenbach's homosexual attraction can be disguised as a pursuit of beauty, form, perfection. This is obvious when the obsessive attention to the details of Tadzio's body breaks off abruptly with two elegantly contrived questions that show the essence of Aschenbach's self-deception:

> And yet the pure, strong will which had laboured in darkness and succeeded in bringing this godlike work of art to the light of day—was it not known and familiar to him, the artist? Was not the same force at work in himself when he strove in cold fury to liberate from the marble mass of language the slender forms of his art which he saw with the eye of his mind and would body forth to men as the mirror and image of spiritual beauty? (Pp. 371–72)

In this esthetic formulation Aschenbach finds a temporary refuge from the disturbing attractions of Tadzio's "thin envelope of flesh." In fact, there is a sense of relief in this retreat to the analogy between the creation of human and artistic form since it allows Aschenbach a means of focusing on Tadzio that does not compromise him.

That relief expresses itself in a joyous meditation on form: "Mirror and image!" Aschenbach exclaims to himself:

> His eyes took in the proud beauty of that figure there at the

water's edge; with an outburst of rapture he told himself that what he saw was beauty's very essence; form as divine thought, the single and pure perfection which resides in the mind, of which an image and likeness, rare and holy, was here raised up for adoration. This was very frenzy—and without a scruple, nay, eagerly, the aging artist bade it come. (P. 372)

Stunned by his sudden access to the essence of the beautiful—and relieved unconsciously of the disturbing feelings Tadzio's body inspired—Aschenbach attempts to put even more distance between himself and his real desires by conjuring up an analogy between himself and Socrates. In his imagination he sees the philosopher lecturing young Phaedrus outside the city walls of Athens and in his recreation of their dialogue finds further justification for his fascination with Tadzio. Did not the philosopher speak of "the impious and corrupt, who cannot conceive beauty though they see its image, and are incapable of awe" (p. 373)? Did he not say "that the lover was nearer the divine than the beloved"? Safe in his conviction that his response to Tadzio encompasses such lofty principles, Aschenbach feels moved to write—"moreover, he would write in Tadzio's presence." Thus he avoids the real significance of Tadzio through momentary displacement—from an attractive boy he has become an esthetic inspiration.

But Aschenbach's defenses crumble the very next day. Feeling that he should speak to the boy, he misjudges the opportunity and realizes that he was on the verge of chasing him and making a fool of himself. That, at least, is the surface explanation. On a deeper level, Aschenbach is aware that speech would destroy the fantasy he has created, and so he chooses to remain silent, a choice that is repeated near the end when he is faced with the consequences of telling Tadzio's mother about the plague. Here silence signals his willful surrender to his imagination, which is crowded with images of Eros, Pan, Hyancinthus—an anthology of mythic beings who come alive for him as they never had before one night when Tadzio smiles at him, smiles as Narcissus may have smiled at himself in the pool. Overcome by Tadzio's expression and its "coquetry" (p. 378), Aschenbach seeks the symbolic darkness in the park where he can give his emotions full play. At first he is angry at the boy, but his anger quickly gives way to the emotion that has been struggling to the surface of his consciousness: " 'I love you!' he whispered."

Why should this seemingly insignificant event bring his feelings so dramatically to the surface? The answer lies in his having associated Tadzio with Narcissus, whose homoeroticism frees Aschenbach's latent homosexuality. As Narcissus, Tadzio suddenly and powerfully symbolizes the nature of the attraction Aschenbach has elaborately tried to ignore. This *gestalt* illuminates with devastating irony the consequences of Aschenbach's "late adventure of the feelings"—a new and profound awareness of self. For, while love in all its forms both increases self-awareness and diminishes it, homosexual love takes as its object the other who mirrors the self. Aschenbach's destruction cannot be linked to any single event that befalls him during his sojourn in Venice, but one of the major causes springs from the interiority of his love, which never expresses itself outside of his imagination.

While he continues to see Tadzio in Classical manifestations, his homosexual desire for the boy and his need to express the "illicit" aspects of Byronic-Wagnerian Romanticism lead Aschenbach further and further into himself. Interiority and self-indulgence now define his *métier* as Aschenbach's increasing obsession with self becomes clearly evident in his response to the unhealthiness pervading Venice. At one point he finds substantial evidence of the severity of the plague in the German newspapers:

> "It ought to be kept quiet," he thought, aroused. "It should not be talked about!" And he felt in his heart a curious elation at these events impending in the world about him. Passion is like crime: it does not thrive on the established order and the common round; it welcomes every blow dealt the bourgeois structure, every weakening of the social fabric, because therein it feels a sure hope of its own advantage. (P. 380)

And this sense of disorder gives him a "dark satisfaction":

> The city's evil secret mingled with the one in the depths of his heart—and he would have staked all he possessed to keep it, since in his infatuation he cared for nothing but to keep Tadzio here, and owned to himself, not without horror, that he could not exist were the lad to pass from his sight.

Having entered with a vengeance the "illicit," chaotic world of Romantic Imagination, Aschenbach now becomes increasingly preoccupied with his own sensations, concerned solely with himself and ignoring, at the same time, Tadzio's welfare. But these psychological effects carry with them only part of the passage's significance; Aschenbach's solipsistic obsession, and the "dark satisfaction" it breeds, resonate with the destructive implications of Romantic literature, the sea, and the death music of the *Liebestod*. It is the attraction of the chaotic within the attraction of passion that satisfies Aschenbach.

By now Aschenbach has abandoned all interior pretenses concerning his relationship to Tadzio. Venice has become a place of assignations as he pursues the boy through its streets, his imagination "drunk with passion," (p. 381) his dignity in shreds. Once, following Tadzio and his family through the canals into the very heart of the city, Aschenbach experiences a revelation. Assaulted by images of gardens, crumbling walls, intricate lattices, beggars, cheats, it is as if he sees the city for what it is for the first time. "Yes," he muses,

> this was Venice, this the fair frailty that fawned and that betrayed, half-fairy-tale, half snare; the city in whose stagnating air the art of painting once put forth so lusty a growth, and where musicians were moved to accords so weirdly lulling and lascivious. Our adventurer felt his senses wooed by this voluptuousness of sight and sound, tasted his secret knowledge that the city sickened and had its sickness for love of gain, and bent an ever more unbridled leer on the gondola that glided on before him. (P. 381)

This is the realization of "the late adventure of the feelings" Aschenbach so confidently hoped for as he left behind the demands of his art and the restrictions it had imposed for years. Venice has come at the "wrong moment," late in the life of a man whose mind has been saturated in imagined worlds and whose melancholy temperament finds its most acute expression in a longing for destruction. What should have been a "love of life," as Mann defines it in his essay on "Nietzsche and Music," has become an obsession with death as it appears in the guise of Aschenbach's love of Tadzio-Eros-Narcissus. Aschenbach left Munich and found himself embroiled in a relationship that could have provided the means of escape from the tyranny of self, if only for a while. But, as the possibility of release from self collapses, *Death in Venice* begins to describe a circle symbolic of Aschenbach's return to his own self-contained and self-containing world, a circle that will be completed with his death.

V

Aschenbach uncovers the truth about the cholera epidemic, completely unaware that in doing so he will soon expose the truth about himself. Having ferreted out the details from a polite clerk at the English travel bureau, he leaves the office possessing knowledge not only of the plague, but also of the blockade that is imminent. Outside in the sunny Piazza, he "strode up and down the spacious flags, feverishly excited, triumphant in possession of the truth at last, but with a sickening taste in his mouth and a fantastic horror at his heart. One decent, expiatory course lay open to him" (p. 389). Aschenbach has reached the point in his moral existence where his response to that "expiatory course" will either save or damn him.

But, despite the "sickening taste in his mouth" and the "horror" he feels, "he knew that he was far indeed from any serious desire to take such a step. It would restore him, would give him back himself once more; but he who is beside himself revolts at the idea of self-possession" (p. 390). Suddenly images of the Munich graveyard impinge upon his consciousness, and he sees again the gravestones on which were inscribed statements about the after-life that had arrested his attention, sees, too, the strange pilgrim who had initiated the sequence of thought that led him to flee the city. Though his life is hanging in the balance here, Aschenbach is perfectly conscious of the choice he will arrive at momentarily. These images and others force him to confront the possibility of following the "expiatory course" of leaving Venice for his mountain retreat. But the very thought of "reason, self-mastery, an ordered existence . . . the old life of effort" is repellent to him: "the bare thought made him wince with a revulsion that was like physical nausea." His choice made, Aschenbach repeats the very phrases that first came to his lips when he became aware of the epidemic: " 'It must be kept quiet,' he whispered fiercely. 'I will not speak!' " His decision is intensely private, secret, guarded, whispered just as he whispered his confession of love for Tadzio. Aschenbach, the moralist, scourge of the abyss and human weakness, must keep his knowledge of his own degradation to himself, for what he most desires now he found in the center of the city: the lascivious and voluptuous: "His art, his moral sense, what were they in the balance beside the boons that chaos might confer?" (p. 390). Like Faustus, Tristan, Lowry's Consul, Aschenbach chooses to plunge headlong toward his own damnation, helpless but far from despairing before the lurid visions spreading out in his imagination.

But his choice involves much more than abjuring his "old ordered existence." By electing to remain silent, he reverses the Romantic code that places the well-being of the beloved above life itself, a reversal implied earlier in the first Socratic dialogue where Aschenbach savoured the notion that the lover is exalted over the beloved. However, important as these considerations are, the central issue here has to do with morality, not solipsism. In choosing to remain silent so that he can experience the irresistible appeal of chaos, Aschenbach consciously, willfully denies his "moral sense" and in doing so destroys his conscience. Faced with the option of saving Tadzio by losing him forever, Aschenbach can think only of the ecstasy continued pursuit of the boy will bring. In giving himself over to the "fantastic horror" in his heart, to the "snare" of chaos, he abdicates his responsibility as a member of the human community.

This rupture with humanity is completed that night with his orgiastic dream, which Mann presents as a psycho-drama taking place within Aschenbach's soul. In his dream, the arrival of Dionysus, the "Stranger God" (p. 391), is announced by the counterpointed musical motifs of Tadzio's name and sensuous "flute-notes." These "sweet and wild" harmonies accompany Aschenbach as he imagines himself joining the promiscuous phallic celebration in the midst of which "he tasted the bestial degradation of his fall." And it is after this inner recognition of his debased morality that he can alter his appearance with a visit to the hotel barber, who transforms him into the double of the repellent old man on the Pola steamer. As he adds the final touches to his creation, the barber says with wonderful irony, "Now the signore can fall in love as soon as he likes" (p. 393), and Aschenbach "went off as in a dream," with the ludicrous primary colors of black hair and strawberry-red lips reflecting symbolically the blood and death into which he had dreamed himself on that fateful night.

Aschenbach continues to follow Tadzio through the streets and byways of Venice, absolutely contemptuous of his own well-being. Once he pauses, exhausted, and, to slake his thirst, buys strawberries which he eats greedily, either unaware or unconcerned that they might carry the disease. Finally, he rests on the steps of a well in a little out-of-the-way square. "There he sat," the great writer who renounced "all sympathy with the abyss and the troubled depths of the outcast human soul" (p. 395):

> There he sat. His eyelids were closed, there was only a swift, sidelong glint of the eyeballs now and again, something between a question and a leer; while the rouged and flabby mouth uttered single words of the sentences shaped in his disordered brain by the fantastic logic that governs our dreams.

Aware that the lasciviousness of Venice has become his own, that he has been reduced to nothing more now than his own lust for Tadzio, Aschenbach retreats into his literary imagination and conjures up the pristine grassy slopes outside the walls of Athens. His "disordered brain" returns to the *Phaedrus,* because Socrates' counsel offers a justification for his fate. The artist, Socrates tells the young man, cannot avoid knowledge of the abyss since his medium is in itself sensuous and thus corrupt and corrupting. And at the center of this attempt to justify his degredation is the notion that Aschenbach has been victimized by his art, that his talent and the severe discipline necessary for its expression betrayed him. "But detachment," he imagines Socrates saying,

> and preoccupation with form lead to intoxication and desire, they may lead the noblest among us to frightful emotional excesses, which his own stern cult of the beautiful would make him the first to condemn. So they too, they too, lead to the bottomless pit. Yes, they lead us thither, I say, us who are poets—who by our natures are prone not to excellence but to excess. (Pp. 395–96)

Nowhere in the course of the events preceding or following this scene is Aschenbach's self-deception more evident, for to believe in what he has imagined would require him to also believe that choice, restraint, and morality do not exist. To deny, in other words, the central preoccupation of his art.

The conclusion of *Death in Venice* is juxtaposed to this scene, whose ironies continue to reverberate until the end. Mann has now shifted the action to the beach "once so full of colour and life, look[ing] now autumnal, out of season; it was nearly deserted and not even very clean. A camera on a tripod stood at the edge of the water, apparently abandoned; its black cloth snapped in the freshening wind" (p. 396). The camera symbolizes Aschenbach's art and life, recalls the coffin-like gondolas and especially all that has been implied in the musical motifs that call up the *Liebestod,* for that black cloth snapped by the wind is also the black sail signaling disaster in *Tristan.* It is a remarkably vivid sign, and we can hear the cloth snapping back and forth as Aschenbach's eyes greedily follow the movement of the boy slowly making his way out into the sea. Moments before he dies, "it seemed to him the pale and lovely Summoner out there smiled at him and beckoned; as though, with the hand he lifted from his hip, he pointed outward as he hovered on before into an immensity of richest expectation" (p. 397). The love of death and the love of self are merged in this final vision of Tadzio in his two mythic guises, Narcissus and Hermes.

Thus Aschenbach follows the dream, just as Stein predicted Lord Jim would, until the end. It is an imagination of excess consuming itself under the sign of Dionysus that Mann shows us, as Aschenbach looks expectantly towards the radiant image of Tadzio beckoning him to the nothingness of the sea. While Gide's Michel at least feared the unknown consequences of his experimentation, Aschenbach's pact with Romantic death reveals no compromise, hesitation, or questioning. The self-corrupting effect of such unchecked Dionysian vitality is continued in *The Blood Oranges,* where we encounter an even more extreme form of narcissism and uses of imagination that go beyond the boundaries tested by Gide and Mann.

10
"What Country, Friends, Is This?": The Inner Terrain of *The Blood Oranges*

> . . . so full of shapes is fancy,
> that it alone is high fantastical.
> —William Shakespeare, *Twelfth Night*

> But even in the most paradisial of the worlds I've
> created, the roses conceal deadly thorns.
> —John Hawkes to Robert Scholes[1]

I

In Gide and Mann we witnessed the birth of Michel and Aschenbach as narcissists. Michel begins as a precocious philologist, newly married, immersed in a bourgeois world. Only after a vacation from his work, which leads to illness, the gradual discovery of his body, and the more crucial discovery of the values he associates with the Old Adam does he enter into the domain of imagination I have been exploring. Similarly, Mann's novella opens with Aschenbach deeply engaged in the art of fiction. Needing relaxation, he sets off for the Mediterranean coast. As with Michel, there is a sense of suspension in which we see a powerful mind at repose but active enough to sieze on the merest suggestions. Unlike *The Immoralist* or *Death in Venice*, *The Blood Oranges* begins in the realm of imagination. Here are Cyril's first words:

> Love weaves its own tapestry, spins its own golden thread, with its own sweet breath breathes into being its mysteries— bucolic, lusty, gentle as the eyes of daisies or thick with pain. And out of its own music creates the flesh of our lives. . . . See me as a small white porcelain bull lost in the lower left-hand corner of that vast tapestry, see me as a great white creature

horned and mounted on a trim little golden sheep in the very center of Love's most explosive field.[2]

The gradual inward movement of the preceding novels from the world of everyday reality to the richer but problematic interiority of the protagonists has simply been skipped over by Hawkes. Here the reader is plunged into a powerful imagination's controlling metaphor, which evokes associations with courtly Romance, a snare for the careless, a mirror of himself, the creative process. Cyril's virtuosity dazzles, but his seductiveness, like Circe's, can distract us from the limitations of his vision.

An esthetician of the senses, Cyril believes he has brought into being[3] the edenic world referred to in the epigraph taken from *The Good Soldier,* that "terrestrial paradise where, amidst the whispering of the olive-trees, people can be with whom they like and have what they like and take their ease in shadows and in coolness." The center of this world is Cyril's mind, its suburb the Mediterranean island where he sets out once again to prove his doctrine that our "sexual selves . . . are merely idlers in a vast wood." "Need I insist," he argues, "that the only enemy of the mature marriage is monogamy? That anything less than sexual multiplicity (body upon body, voice on voice) is naive" (p. 209)? Cyril's doctrine rests on this *idée fixe* which is coded: "sexual extension." For Cyril, Eros is the essence of life; all emotion not directly related to sexuality is the shadow of Thanatos. That he is related through this conception to Gide's Michel goes without saying, but there is a difference: Cyril is completely uninhibited; he is the better hedonist.

At the same time, Cyril differs considerably from Michel in that he is both narcissistic and unbounded, protean. On the first page of *The Blood Oranges* he explains that "I have always allowed myself to assume whatever shape was destined to be my own in the silken weave of Love's pink panorama" (p. 1). After the affair with Catherine has been established, he asks himself why she does not "know . . . that I am enough, that she is enough, that we are all interchangeable" (p. 121). His belief in interchangeability extends to the natural world, for, when he notices that the mimosa tree has blossomed, he embraces it: "Slowly I opened my mouth and arched my tongue, pushed forward my open mouth and rounded expectant tongue until my mouth was filled and against all the most sensitive membranes of tongue and oral cavity I felt the yellow fuzzy pressure of the flowering tree" (p. 54). And, in his conclusion that "in the midst of the kiss I thought I heard Fiona's giggle, Catherine's sigh," nature and Eros are elided. An even more important example of Cyril's boundlessness occurs when he wonders if Hugh will discover evidence of his presence in Catherine's bedroom: "Would he find my tennis shoes? Would he begin to understand that there could be no limits on our exchange and that in the circumscribed country of Illyria a grassy wind was bound to blow away the last shreds of possessiveness" (p. 155)? As creator of Illyria and director of all that happens there, Cyril denies himself nothing, incorporates everything, and sees himself mirrored in his lovers as well as in nature. What we have here, then, is a case of psychic decomposition, for Cyril's ego spreads out to encompass all that is external to it.[4] And, in examining this fragmentation of self, it becomes possible for us to understand the particular qualities of Cyril's narcissistic personality, qualities that are similar to, but distinct from, those of Michel and Aschenbach.

Behind Cyril's obsession with interchangeability is the psychoanalytic concept of the double, which both Freud and Rank see as the product of repressed narcissistic impulses. Among the many effects manifested in literary texts by doubling or decomposition is, as Patrick Brantlinger argues, the suggestion that "two or more characters are parts of a single self, the process of whose disintegration the tale shadows forth."[5] From this perspective, the tapestry metaphor, constantly defined by Cyril in terms of dreams and romance, symbolizes the regressive nature of fantasy—in this case, Cyril's belief that he is part of everything and everyone around him. That Cyril locates his narcissistic personality within the frame of romance clarifies even further the essentially regressive nature of his beliefs for, as Brantlinger puts it, "like dreams, the romance form symbolically carries us backwards down the path of [the] process of maturation, promising us a temporary reprieve from inhibition and repression."[6] Promising too, I would add, the static quality Frye sees as central to his typology of naive Romance.[7] If we append to these conceptions the facts that Cyril is "already two or three long leaps beyond middle age" (p. 16), and his insistence that "vintage sap" (p. 17) is more potent than the passions of the young ("jaunty, spritely people with trim bodies and unclouded eyes"), we have a reasonably detailed profile of a narcissistic middle-aged man who denies change through a symbolic regression to the timeless, edenic world of Romantic fantasy: a "terrestrial paradise."

To put it another way, Cyril sees himself as a satyr. Whether he engages in sex with Fiona or Catherine, remembers the "roster of . . . girls and women, from young to old and old to young" whom he took "whenever the light was right or the music sounded" (p. 2), takes the flowering mimosa blossom into his mouth, or swallows the plump grapes in his arbor, Cyril always tends his sexual needs and he clearly suffers from the same kind of auto-eroticism that afflicted Emma Bovary and Michel. Obsessed with self, Cyril loves himself as much as they love themselves, but what he loves most is himself functioning as a sexual being.

Cyril's narcissistic self-indulgence exacts a high price from all those who find themselves within his field. Each of the novels I have examined shows that an act of mind separates the protagonist from reality, but that his interiority nevertheless forces itself on others. For example, whether Hugh should or should not cling to the traditional sexual mores he believes in is less important to the novel than the fact that Cyril forces his vision onto Hugh and in doing so kills him—and drives Catherine mad in the bargain. There is really no difference between this moral myopia and the disastrous results attendant on Michel's conscious and unconscious manipulation of Marceline, Gatsby's of Daisy, Edward's of Nancy. When Hugh begins to crack under the pressure of Cyril's theory, or when Catherine is driven into the silences of psychotic withdrawal, Cyril ignores Hugh's pain and cannot accept responsibility for Catherine's condition because he sees both cases as aberrations, neither of which would have happened if his ideas had been heeded. The tragic results of his doctrine never surface in his consciousness, not even when his tapestry seems to be in tatters at the end.

The Blood Oranges is thus the most problematic of our novels because of what appears to be the absence of a recognizable ethical center, some character like Marlow who offers at least a partial alternative to Cyril's views, or some ironic tension in the narrative, similar to that of *Madame Bovary, Death in Venice,* or *The Immoralist,* which creates ethical perspective as the novels unfold. I think that this dilemma can be resolved by responding to the total structure of Hawkes's book, and that includes a response to its epigraph that links the world of Ford's "good people" to the one Cyril creates for himself. But a basis for this comparison must first be established by attending to the general symbolic design of *The Blood Oranges*.

II

Cyril's "high fantastical" world reflects what Hawkes calls "totality of vision or structure. And structure—verbal and psychological coherence—is . . . my largest concern as a writer. Related or corresponding events, recurring image and recurring action, these constitute the essential substance or meaningful density of my writing."[8] Now that substance, as I have already tried to suggest, focuses on the problematics of Romantic imagination which Georg Lukács, in another context, defines as "the nostalgia of the characters for utopian perfection, a nostalgia that feels itself and its desires to be the only true reality."[9] But much of the novel's irony can ultimately be traced to the fact that Cyril *feels* no nostalgia; he believes that utopian perfection lies in the warp and woof of his tapestry. Opposed to the longings of Emma, Edna, Jim, and the others is his sense of achievement, even of satiety. With this distinction in mind, I now want to look more closely at the "psychological coherence" of Cyril's nostalgia-free imagination that creates a centripetal force among his "quartet," pulling everyone inward toward the center of his will.

The action of *The Blood Oranges* properly begins with a *tableau vivant*. Cyril and Fiona have been investigating an old church when they are suddenly disturbed by the clanging of an alarm bell. Rushing outside, they follow the natives to a car wreck, where they find Hugh, Catherine, and their children who have appeared as suddenly on the island as Viola does in Shakespeare's play. These new arrivals from over the mountains are immediately confronted by the "sex singer" and his wife as they emerge from the fetid canal into which their bus has plunged, emerge as in a rebirth into the lemon-scented sunshine of Cyril's imagination. When they reach the embankment Fiona, the novel's Aphrodite to Cyril's Pan, "suddenly kissed the gaunt stony cheek of this tall hero. . . . I knew then," Cyril adds, "that we were due for some kind of new adventure, Fiona and I. What else could it be?" (p. 34). This immediate expropriation of Hugh and Catherine to their design prepares us for virtually everything that follows. Most characteristic is the narrowing of options, a

reduction of reality to the predetermined frame of "sexual extension"—that is, the shape of Cyril's tapestry.

Two examples confirm this narrowing effect. When Cyril,
Fiona, Hugh, and Catherine take the sun on the beach some time
later, Fiona whispers: "Do you know where we are, baby? Tell
me quick":

> Surprised at her sudden and atypical desperation, but laughing
> and aiming my mouth toward the hint of white cartilage buried
> like an arrow in the now violent cream- and sable-colored hair:
> "Sure," I shouted, "we're in Illyria." (P. 119)

Soon afterwards Cyril imagines the sexual tensions among them
as a "little invisible white goat" (p. 90), which then magically
appears. "Look, baby," Fiona cries out, "a little goat" (p. 92)!

> Could it be that one of my speechless creatures of joy and
> sentiment had torn itself loose from the tapestry that only I
> could see? Was it now bearing down upon us with blue eyes
> and the wind in its hair? Was the little goat that had danced
> among us in my mind now going to leave its little hoofprints in
> the center of Fiona's blanket or come rushing and butting
> between our legs? It did not seem possible. But of course it
> was. (P. 93)

Cyril is ecstatic to find that "the goat was real":

> At first glance he was in the air, hanging suspended at the
> height of his second leap from the gloomy pines, and even
> from where we stood we could see his bright blue eyes and the
> nubile horns embedded in soft down.

Once the moment is recorded and the ideal arc of the little goat
transferred to the imagination, Cyril's fiction-making and fiction-
perceiving mind (which can stop action like a movie camera)
allows real time and movement in space to begin once more:
"Then he sprang, leapt, danced his soaring stiff-legged dance,"
his essence safely caught up in the tapestry's threads. In each
example, the narrowing of phenomena in reality (the island and
the goat) has come about through strict control, and they are
made to respond to concepts (the ideality of Illyria, the sexuality
of the goat) carefully predetermined by Cyril.

Later that day when the "sun was setting, sinking to its pre-

destined death . . . to the four of us, or at least to me, that
enormous smoldering sun lay on the horizon like a dissolving
orange suffused with blood. . . . Together we sat with legs out-
stretched, soles of our feet touching or nearly touching, a four-
pointed human starfish resting together in the last livid light of
day" (p. 37). The novel's title is inscribed in this scene, but as an
ironic sign of Cyril's habit of constricting reality, rather than as
an unequivocal symbol of pleasure. In describing his title,
Hawkes has been careful to define its two qualities:

> The fruit is sweet, but it's streaked with the color of blood,
> which to me is a paradox. It means that the blood is real but
> also sweet; it means that no sweetness is ephemeral but on the
> contrary possesses all the life-drive seriousness of the rich
> black flow of blood itself. It suggests wound invading desire,
> desire "containing" agony.[10]

Structurally, the scene brings forward the initial expropriation of
Hugh and Catherine to Cyril's and Fiona's design; the "new
adventure" has literally begun. Symbolically, it registers in a
balanced, geometrical shape Cyril's concept of interchangeability. This is obvious when, sensing the prospect of another exploration of "sexual extension," Cyril removes Fiona's bra. The act
makes Hugh uncomfortable, but he remains passive, "unmus-
ical" (p. 43) as Cyril puts it. But Catherine, after considerable
hesitation, "acted in her own behalf" by removing her own bra
without Hugh's help. Acted, as Cyril triumphantly says, "delib-
erately and in large part for me" (p. 44). The magic of his imagination works; he has almost brought Catherine into its "pink
field."

And so the "small white porcelain bull" is prepared to spring.
All that remains is a final symbolic act, for rituals are incumbent
upon everyone who comes within Cyril's vision and that evening, in the cool arbor from whose lattices depend bunches of
ripe grapes, Cyril initiates his test of sexual potential, the grape-
tasting game. Uneasy after the sun-drenched titillation earlier in
the day, Hugh is immediately wary: "No grapes for me, boy. No
thanks" (p. 184). But Catherine is willing and capable of understanding the game's significance:

> So up went Catherine on tiptoe and with her eyes open, her
> mouth open, her jaw thrust forward. But as soon as she en-
> countered the first grape, felt the first grape bouncing with a

will of its own against her upraised chin, Catherine shuddered, stumbled, looked at me with a long soft look of unmistakable recognition. Was this what I was thinking? Was the sensation she had just experienced the same as mine? (P. 185)

Catherine's acquiescence to the Illyrian *rite de passage* culminates later than night with Cyril's making love to her in the villa next door. Almost effortlessly, he has woven her into his tapestry, his "map of Love" (p. 167), acquainting her with "its contours, its monuments, its abandoned gardens, its narrow streets."

Her place in the tapestry is even further defined some time later when Cyril takes her into the village where they witness a boat launching. Nowhere is his manipulative power more evident than in the narrow streets and on the beach. Built on the "high edge of the village" (p. 124), the finished boat is moved down the rough streets by means of rolling it over blocks of wood greased with animal blood. When it has been rolled, pushed, and tugged to the shore, the villagers gather for the christening and it is then that Cyril perceives a symbolic opportunity to secure Catherine in "Love's tapestry."

On the beach a young man plays an "archaic heart-shaped stringed instrument" (p. 128) whose "Eastern music" fills the "festive air," and an "old goat-faced man" offers then a ritual drink, which Cyril is careful to share with Catherine. Then, as the boat is launched, he asks: "Remind you of anything?" (p. 130). And Catherine's hesitation is nothing before his design: "Catherine," he insists, "doesn't it remind you of a wedding?" (p. 131). With the association made, they move into the water with the old man, who soon manages to climb into the boat and crouch on hands and knees in its prow, a naked goat-man beautifully expressive of the symbolic moment, the mock wedding willed into being by Cyril:

> The stern was at the top of its arc, Catherine and I were staring up into the orange brilliance of the old man's aged nakedness, and his shanks were dripping, his buttocks were dripping, his obviously unspent passion was hanging down and rotating loosely like a tongue of flame. (P. 133)

At that moment Catherine's eyes meet Cyril's, she smiles, and the wedding is complete: "At last," he thinks, "we had come under the aegis of the little crouching goat-faced man half naked at the end of the day. What more could we ask?" With this evidence of imagination's power, Cyril is free to explore the "vast tapestry" with even more abandon, for he has given Catherine an acceptable context for their relationship—they now make love under the sign of the old goat-man, priest of Eros.

III

Cyril's victory is offset at first by Fiona's failure to bring Hugh into the "pink field." Despite her obvious charms and Cyril's machinations, Hugh balks, refusing to enter the field out of fear inspired by his moral "medievalism" and his unwillingness to surrender Catherine even temporarily to Cyril's design. Fiercely possessive, Hugh's spirit clings to the world beyond Illyria. And as his inability to hear the sensual music of Illyria becomes evident, Cyril associates him with the cold rigidity of stone, until Hugh seems to become an effigy linked to the squat church and the old fortress which lie off the coast of the island. This association was prefigured in Cyril's first glimpse of Hugh's face as he was making his way up from the half-submerged bus: "Its exact replica, an image of Saint Peter that was perfect except for the broken ears, had been chiselled along with the head of Saint Paul into the granite arch of the entrance to the squat church" (p. 31). Impelled by Hugh to explore the fortress (he has dreamed of something significant lying within its structure), Cyril finds his hagiography takes on a more definite shape as the "quartet" descends the stone staircase. In the darkness he wishes that "Hugh's poor torch would discover a real effigy with a stone cowl, stone feet, stone hands pressed together and pointed in prayer" (p. 205). And that wish is symbolically answered as Hugh casts about the flotsam and jetsam of the lowermost room where he finally discovers the chastity belt. Carrying it back into the sunlight, Hugh places the object on a "cracked and fluted pediment . . . [an] . . . improvised altar upon which lay what appeared to be only a thin circlet of pitted iron—frail, ancient, oval in shape, menacing" (p. 206). Cyril, Fiona, and Catherine immediately identify Hugh with the belt, disavowing any connection with this symbol of old morality by swimming out to sea as if to cleanse themselves. As he looks back to shore, Cyril "saw Hugh stretched out on the black pebbles with one knee raised and his good hand beneath his head, the little black iron trinket visible on his white chest" (p. 208).

In the end, Fiona does have her way with Hugh who, for a while, experiences the "sex-song" directly, rather than through his photographs of nude peasant girls. One morning when Cyril returns from an assignation with Catherine, Fiona triumphantly takes him by the hand and leads him into their bedroom where Hugh lies asleep: "Isn't he beautiful?" (p. 259) she whispers. He "had proven my theories," Cyril thinks, "completed Love's natural structure, justified Catherine's instincts, made Fiona happy when she had given up all her hopes for happiness. What more could I ask?" (p. 260). But later that day Hugh hangs himself and it appears as if the threads of the tapestry have begun to unravel.

Although he had grudgingly been dragged into the field by Fiona, the theory of interchangeability was ultimately too far removed from Hugh's morality, and he could only kill himself to escape from the power of Cyril's vision. But Cyril interprets Hugh's motives differently. After Hugh's death Fiona leaves to mother Catherine's children somewhere beyond Illyria, while Cyril stays to undertake "Catherine's recovery as if she were my wife instead of Hugh's" (p. 210)—stays, he insists, to "renew" their love. Speaking to the silent Catherine, who has remained totally withdrawn after collapsing during Hugh's funeral, Cyril

> insisted on the accidental nature of Hugh's death, explained to Catherine that Hugh's death was an accident inspired, so to speak, by his cameras, his peasant nudes, his ingesting of the sex-song itself. It was not their shared love that had triggered Hugh's catastrophe. It was simply that his private interests, private moods had run counter to the activities of our foursome, so that his alien myth of privacy had established a psychic atmosphere conducive to an accident of that kind. (P. 211)

Always persuasive, Cyril's measured words seem to have something of a beneficial effect on her as the Illyrian idyll draws to a close. Moreover, at the end Cyril is so deeply immersed in what he has created that he responds to Hugh's death, Catherine's withdrawal, and Fiona's disappearance as only momentary setbacks to his Saturnalia. After all, the maid Rosella may become aware of his sexual presence, Catherine may recover. And so the music of love still sounds, if only faintly, and Cyril remains within the realm of the "high fantastical" as the novel draws to its close.

IV

"What country, friends is this?" Viola asks the sailors who bring her to the Illyria of *Twelfth Night,* and the same question must now be asked of *The Blood Oranges.* First of all, it is much more than a novel that teases our accepted ideas about sexual morality; Hawkes's serious exploration of imagination and interiority clearly reveals the destructive consequences of a mind that can only respond to the environment it has created for itself. Secondly, in a number of important ways it mirrors *The Good Soldier,* and I have already tried to suggest some of the relationships between these works. By doing so I have not intended to suggest imitation, but affinity, and that is exactly what Hawkes himself pointed out to Robert Scholes in an interview he gave a year after *The Blood Oranges* was published.

In the interview, Hawkes explained how he had been thinking about Ford's novel "for a long while, [as well as about] the validity of the moral vision of *The Lime Twig*" in which "what Cyril would call sexual extension is punished by death and total cataclysmic collapse, which is the mighty backlash of my own Puritan upbringing."[11] He then describes the quandary he faced when confronted by a student's question about that moral vision. I think it is worth quoting his comments at length for the illumination they provide about the connections he perceives between his work and Ford's:

> When the student, who happened to have been a marvelous girl, said, 'Why can't Michael Banks in *The Lime Twig* simply have sex with all those women and go on living in an ordinary way?' I really had no answer. Similarly, I've heard students resist *The Good Soldier* because of the convention of adultery which is essential to that book. Once again, this is a fiction that I admire enormously but which portrays an enormously bleak future for any love that seeps out of the rigidities prescribed by marriage. When I began *The Blood Oranges* I was quite aware of trying to write a fiction that would offer a somewhat different version of Ford Madox Ford's novel and that would give me an alternative to *The Lime Twig.*

Hawkes was partially successful in his attempt. There is no question that Cyril's fate provides an "alternative" to Michael Banks's—the world he creates for himself remains immune to the influence of the "mighty backlash" of Puritanism—but the "totality of vision" of *The Blood Oranges* discloses a perspective that is finally no more sanguine about interchangeability than what we find in Ford's novel. This is the case because in both works the "rigidities prescribed by marriage" are essentially secondary concerns; the primary ethical questions arise from the disastrous consequences of naive Romantic Imagination, the personal cost of Edward's and Cyril's manipulations of Leonora, Nancy, Catherine, and Hugh—which transcends, in my view, the "convention of adultery."

This congruence of views can be traced to structural and symbolic points of contact between the novels. Most of the action in *The Good Soldier* takes place at the German spa, Bad Nauheim, an idyllic spot for "heart" patients, which reflects Cyril's conception of Illyria. The characters in both novels are all close in age. "When we first met," Dowell writes, "Captain Ashburnham . . . was thirty-three; Mrs. Ashburnham—Leonora—was thirty-one. I was thirty six and poor Florence was thirty."[12] Similarly, at "the height of our season," Cyril remarks, "Fiona and Hugh were almost forty, Catherine had passed that mark by several years, while I was already two or three long leaps beyond middle age" (p. 16).[13] In Hawkes's "quartet," Cyril becomes a version of Edward, Hugh of Dowell, Fiona of Florence, and Catherine of Leonora. Each novel is narrated by one member of the foursome who reconstructs their communal past while alone with a woman who is no longer rational. And there have also been suicides: Florence's, Edward's, Hugh's. The major difference in structure is that the narrators occupy opposite ends of the sexual spectrum: Cyril's "sex singing" is reversed in Dowell, who has been denied consummation of his marriage with Florence for the better part of a decade. But this difference is balanced by Dowell's belated understanding of the true relationships in his "coterie" and a growing understanding of himself. His is the informed vision, grounded in an awareness of human tragedy that is beyond Cyril, who remains isolated and incapable of such knowledge.

There are also thematic correspondences that go beyond those suggested by Hawkes's epigraph. For example, *The Good Soldier* begins with Dowell wistfully longing for the permanence of an ideal world, and his nostalgia must be seen in the light of Cyril's conviction that he has found such a place. In addition, music permeates the atmosphere of both novels, providing each narrator with a metaphor for his experience. For Dowell, it is as if his "coterie" moved with the measured form and grace of the minuet through the spas and points of interest in Florence's Baedeker. As he prepares himself for the task of recounting his shattered life, he is momentarily incredulous when he remembers how beautifully synchronized they had all been. "No," he says to himself, "you can't kill a minuet de la cour . . . The mob may sack Versailles; the Trianon may fall, but surely the minuet—the minuet itself is dancing itself away in the furthest stars, even as our minuet of the Hessian bathing places must be stepping itself still."[14]

The apparent timelessness of that existence has such purchase on his imagination that he finds it inconceivable to accept its extinction: "Isn't there any nirvana pervaded by the faint thrilling of instruments that have fallen into the dust of wormwood but that yet had frail, tremulous and everlasting souls?" Following immediately upon this question is his recognition that there is no such place, that what held the "coterie" together was "false," "not a minuet . . . but a prison." Dowell's ideal world, which moved to the measured beat of the Kur orchestra, was overcome by "agonies" inherent in a world subject to the vagaries of time and change. To be more specific, it was defeated by its own illusoriness, defeated, that is, by the "prison" of imagination. On the other hand, for Cyril music contains no dissonances. He is the "sex-singer" whose lyric "creates the flesh of our lives" (p. 1), a lyric filled with "spoken tones of joy and desire" (p. 3), the "bell-like sound of the mating game bird," the "brass voice" (p. 230) of his sexual relationship with Catherine. Cyril's music is always harmonious, always played in his imagined nirvana, which Dowell characterizes as being "false," a "prison." (There is, of course, an interesting and complex relationship between Edward and Cyril which should not need explanation other than to point out that Edward's sentimental, solipsistic approach to experience is reflected in great detail by Cyril.)

The preceding discussion of structural and thematic parallels should return us to the beginning of both novels, and I want to emphasize that every comment Dowell and Cyril make must be understood in relation to where they are and what they are doing in the fictive present. *The Blood Oranges* opens with a lyric: "Love weaves its own tapestry;" *The Good Soldier* with an expression of regret: "This is the saddest story I have ever heard." Although Fiona has disappeared, Hugh is dead, and Catherine is lost in psychotic withdrawal, Cyril cheerfully explains that he remains "patient" and "faithful," that "perhaps one day I will reach out and close my fingers on Rosella's thigh, perhaps my last mistress may again become my mistress. It is possible. We shall wait and see" (p. 3). Although Dowell is faced by a similar situation—Florence is dead, Edward has killed himself for love of Nancy Rufford, and Nancy, whom Dowell loves, is mad—his response could not be more opposed to Cyril's. Explaining that he sits across the table from her in the evenings, Dowell goes on to say that "she will say that she believes in an Omnipotent Deity or she will utter the one word, 'shuttlecocks,' perhaps. It is very extraordinary to see the perfect flush of health on her cheeks, to see the lustre of her coiled black hair, the pose of the head upon the neck, the grace of the white hands—and to think that it all means nothing—that it is a picture without a meaning."[15]

It is from this context of Dowell's concern and Nancy's psychic devastation that the epigraph of *The Blood Oranges* emerges. Summing up his experiences, Dowell writes:

Well, it is all over. Not one of us has got what he really wanted. Leonora wanted Edward, and she has got Rodney Bayham. . . . Florence wanted Branshaw, and it is I who have bought it from Leonora. I didn't really want it; what I wanted mostly was to cease being a nurse-attendant. I am a nurse-attendant. Edward wanted Nancy Rufford and I have got her. Only she is mad. It is a queer and fantastic world. Why can't people have what they want?

Having seen the devastation wrought by Edward's romantic temperament and Florence's chronic promiscuity, Dowell then asks the questions of the epigraph, questions whose irony informs both *The Good Soldier* and *The Blood Oranges:*

Is there then any terrestrial paradise where, amidst the whispering of the olive-trees, people can be with whom they like and have what they like and take their ease in shadows and in coolness? Or are all men's lives like the lives of us good people—like the lives of the Ashburnhams, of the Dowells, of the Ruffords—broken, tumultuous, agonized, and unromantic lives, periods punctuated by screams, by imbecilities, by deaths, by agonies? Who the devil knows?

Remembering Hawkes's comment that his title expresses a similar dialectic ("desire 'containing' agony"), it should be clear that Cyril's "terrestrial paradise" has also been invaded by "deaths, by agonies." His "constellation," like Dowell's "coterie," has disintegrated, and his weekly visit to Catherine mocks, even while it mirrors, Dowell's characterization of himself as a "nurse-attendant."

Dowell's "terrestrial paradise" metamorphoses into a "queer and fantastic world" symbolized by Nancy's beautiful blankness. The "Ashburnham tragedy" is concentrated in her madness. While Cyril's "paradisial" world has finally revealed its "deadly thorns" to us, Cyril has learned nothing, feels nothing but the presence of his design, desires nothing but another opportunity to test his theory. He responds to Catherine, and remembers Fiona and Hugh, only as elements within his tapestry, not as human beings who have been tragically affected by his manipulations. To Michel's weak but nevertheless real recognition of a shadowy morality—"Sometimes I'm afraid that what I have suppressed will take its revenge"—Cyril would answer: "Everything coheres, moves forward. I listen for footsteps. In Illyria there are no seasons" (p. 271). The irony of course is that Dowell finally understands the consequences of Edward's sentimental longing for the freedom of Courtly Romance, while Cyril, the sexual esthetician, sees no impediment to his own theory. Though he is unaware of it, at the end Cyril is lord only of the ruins created by his sex-song. There is no total collapse, no backlash, only the absence of understanding and the persistence of an inner world that denies meaning to the reality of other lives.

Arching back through all the writers I have discussed, Hawkes's exploration of Cyril's "pure exercise of the imagination" emphasizes how the mirror of the narcissist's mind not only shows him a false image of himself, but also distorts his vision of others to the point where they become unrecognizable as individuals and function only as secondary images of himself. Unlike Michel and Aschenbach, who abandon Apollo for Dionysus, Cyril believes that, through his tapestry, he has balanced the Apollonian energy that gives form to thought with the Dionysian that gives expression to feeling. Like everything else in *The Blood Oranges,* his conviction is dissonant with what he has created, for Hawkes subtly reveals the inherent destructiveness of Dionysian excess in Cyril's moral chaos. The inadequacy of the Romantic Imagination in either of its guises has been my central concern, and I now want to conclude this study by returning to the general question of narcissism's significance to human love.

Conclusion

The preceeding chapters have charted Narcissus's metamorphosis from the time of the Romantics, who thought he symbolized the virtues of self-observation and the powers inherent in the self, to the Modernist and Post-Modernist concentration on his sterility. Regardless of date, national origin, or subsidiary themes, the presentation of narcissistic consciousness in these novels consistently exemplifies Freud's chillingly ironic observation about solipsistic isolation: "The return of the object-libido to the ego and its transformation into narcissism represents, as it were, a happy love once more."[1] Freud's comment recalls the epigraph at the beginning of this book, a portion of which I now want to bring forward for the insights it offers into what happens when the narcissist's ego has absorbed his object-libido:

> What you seek is nowhere,
> And if you turn away, you will take with you
> The boy you love. The vision is only shadow,
> Only reflection, lacking any substance.
> It comes with you, it stays with you, it goes
> Away with you, if you can go away.

Earlier I argued that the narcissist's identity was analogous to the shadowy reflections in Plato's cave. Now that we have seen Narcissus in his various avatars in modern fiction, it is possible to go farther and say that he is literally trapped in his own reflection, that his choice of withdrawing his love from another in order to more fully commune with himself intensifies Ovid's qualification of his vision as "shadow." In these last few pages I want to show that the poetics of narcissism reside in Ovid's substanceless darkness.

Wordsworth helps us to understand this shadow-vision when he observes that "the food of hope/ Is meditated action; robbed of this/ Her sole support, she languishes and dies." The line cogently describes the evanescent nature of the hope which drives the narcissist towards the inevitable dissolution of his dream. But to fully appreciate the irony of this dissolution requires an awareness of the discourse the narcissist employs to communicate with the object of his desire, since the defining feature of narcissistic consciousness is the language which embodies the "hope," or fantasy, at the center of his mind.

In *A Lover's Discourse,* Roland Barthes offers an anatomy of narcissistic desire in his analysis of the lover's language. His conclusions about the discourse the lover uses in his internal colloquy with the beloved need only the slightest adjustment to illuminate the narcissist's discourse, since Barthes convincingly demonstrates how the apparent interior dialogue between lover and beloved is, in fact, a monologue devoted to a carefully crafted fantasy of the self. My point is that, for both Barthes' "subject" and the narcissist, the beloved (or the object-libido) is internalized and thus displaces the lover's or narcissist's consciousness. Now the consequences of this displacement become clear at the moment the narcissist realizes that the hope he has invested in "meditated action" has vanished. When, like Barthes's subject, he recognizes his failure to achieve the object of his desire, he feels trapped, "doomed to total destruction." "I have projected myself into the other," Barthes writes, "with such power that when I am without the other I cannot recover myself, regain myself: I am lost, forever."[2] That loss, we remember, is identical to Narcissus's, who died, on the bank of the pool, in the shadow of his own image.

The nature of the illusion which leads to this loss can be further clarified by attending to the narcissist's quest, which reveals what Todorov calls, in his remarks on Jamesian narrative, "the search for an absence." In his discussion of the enigmatic qualities in certain of James's stories, Todorov observes that "the tale consists of the search for, the pursuit of . . . the . . . primal essence. . . . On one hand there is an absence (of the cause, of the essence, of the truth), but this absence determines everything; on the other hand there is a presence (of the quest), which is only the search for an absence."[3] Barthes's lover's discourse and the narcissist's quest for an ideal self are inscribed in the pursuit Todorov describes; each is limited to prospective possibilities, "meditated" actions which can ultimately surface only as absences, Ovidian shadows. For the lover and the narcissist, there is always a wild misperception of the relationship between fantasy and reality, between the hope of the passionate discourse and the vacancy it signifies. Thus the narcissist's quest, his hope, finally appears as a nothingness which is synonomous with his essence. This nothingness is precisely what Conrad's Stein meant to reveal to Marlow in his analysis of Jim's sea-dream, and it is always present in the novels I consider in the controlling metaphors of sea, labyrinth, barranca, minuet, darkness, and tapestry.

Now this theme of absence, of nothingness, is most apparent in the conclusion of each novel, as epitomized in Nick's final observation in *The Great Gatsby:* "So we beat on, boats against the current, borne back ceaselessly into the past." The figure of the old writer in *Krapp's Last Tape* is the logical extension of Nick's elegy to Gatsby's (and the narcissist's) fate, for in Beckett's play we see the essence of the modern narcissist, the aged Krapp, engaged in a dialogue with a gone self, alone in his dark den. Gone now are the literary sources, the Nietzschean ideals, the chivalric, Romantic, and erotic models which briefly enabled the narcissist's illusions. The object Krapp desires, like Emma's adulterous heroine, or Michel's Athalaric, is absent, yet he is fascinated by that absence and we see him bent forward, attentive to the recording of his own voice made thirty years before, which begins with him boasting of having intellectually achieved, on his thirty-ninth birthday, the "crest of the wave":

Celebrated the awful occasion, as in recent years, quietly at the Winehouse. Not a soul. Sat before the fire with closed eyes, separating the grain from the husks. . . . Good to be back in my den. . . . The new light above my table is a great improvement. With all this darkness round me I feel less alone. (Pause.) In a way. (Pause.) I love to get up and move about in it, then back here to . . . (hesitates) . . . me. (Pause.) Krapp.[4]

The darkness of Krapp's den is the center of the play. It has been pointed out that the dark is the source of Krapp's talent, an opaque sign of the mind "separating the grain from the husks," and we must judge the life briefly brought back from the past against it.[5] For the darkness, for his own creative potentialities, Krapp gave up the girl in the boat. Even though he still carries with him a haunting image of her eyes, what they meant was not compelling enough to replace his self-imposed isolation, so that he was able to say to her, even at the one moment on the tape when he was tied to another and to nature ("under us all moved, and moved us, gently, up and down, and from side to side" (p. 23), that "it was hopeless and no good going on" (p. 27). The sensation of self, the "fire" in Krapp thirty years before, was better than the "chance of happiness" (p. 28), and so he gave her up for himself, and the self's literal and metaphorical darkness. Krapp, on stage, is trapped in the past, in another, and his situation thus repeats the narcissist's, who is also left, at the end of the novels, without a self. Like Krapp's, the narcissist's quest is based on an illusion. Each novel shows how his efforts to fictionalize himself, and by so doing to become the object of his desire, are finally thwarted. And the parallels between these characters I have considered and Krapp move even more deeply into irony when we remember that Krapp and the narcissist forfeit life for fiction—Krapp's work failed ("seventeen copies sold") just as the narcissist's work of himself does.

Seen from this perspective, Krapp's tape becomes a synecdoche for the narcissist's desire. Consider Emma's mirror, which, at the penultimate moment before her death, reveals the lie of her dream; or Jim's sea-dream, which he followed "until the end"; or Gatsby's "Platonic conception of himself." Each represents visual or philosophical shadows invoked time and again within the darkness of the self. Moreover, the final sentence of Beckett's play ("The tape runs on in silence") epitomizes the narcissist's collective fate, the lover's destruction, the quest's vacancy. Krapp does not make his last tape because he has nothing to say—that is, his life, his experience over the last thirty years (which could have provided new material for the last tape had he chosen the girl's eyes over himself) has been absorbed by the dark. The silence at the end, interrupted only by occasional mechanical noise from the tape (which we might well hear in the theater), is nothing less than the narcissist's dream, the repetition of nothing.

Notes

Chapter 1. Narcissistic Consciousness

1. See Louise Vinge's *The Narcissus Theme in Western Literature Up To The Early 19th Century* (Lund: Gleerups, 1967). Her book provides an exhaustive account of the myth's development.

2. Paul Zweig, *The Heresy of Self-Love: A Study of Subversive Individualism* (New York: Basic Books, 1968), p. v. Hereafter cited in the text. Insightful comments on the evolution of literary consciousness treated in this chapter may be found in John Foster, *Heirs to Dionysus: A Nietzschean Current in Literary Modernism* (Princeton, N.J.: Princeton University Press, 1981); Eric Kahler, *The Inward Turn of Narrative,* trans. Richard and Clara Winston (Princeton, N.J.: Princeton University Press, 1973); Richard Terdiman, *The Dialectics of Isolation* (New Haven: Yale University Press, 1976), and Linda Hutcheon, *Narcissistic Narrative: The Metafictional Paradox* (Canada: Laurier University Press, 1980). In addition, Nancy K. Miller, *The Heroine's Text* (New York: Columbia University Press, 1980) provides interesting feminist perspectives on the role of romance in novels focusing on female characters.

3. Here I am indebted to James McFarlane's fine essay, "The Mind of Modernism," in *Modernism 1890–1930,* ed. Malcolm Bradbury and James McFarlane (New York: Penguin Books, 1976), p. 79.

4. Franz Kuna, "The Janus-faced Novel: Conrad, Musil, Kafka, Mann," in *Modernism 1890–1930,* p. 446.

5. Walter Kaufman, *Nietzsche: Philosopher, Psychologist, Antichrist* (Princeton, N.J.: Princeton University Press, 1950), p. 25.

6. For a more detailed description, see the Introduction to *Nietzsche: A Collection of Essays,* ed. Robert Solomon (Garden City, N.Y.: Anchor Books, 1973), pp. 1–3.

7. Malcolm Bradbury, "The Name and Nature of Modernism," in *Modernism 1890–1930,* p. 40.

8. Bradbury, p. 40.

9. Bradbury, p. 41.

10. *The Modern Tradition: Backgrounds of Modern Literature,* ed. Richard Ellmann and Charles Feidelson, Jr. (New York: Oxford University Press, 1965), p. 540.

11. Friedrich Nietzsche, *The Birth of Tragedy and The Genealogy of Morals,* trans. Francis Golffing (New York: Doubleday Anchor Books, 1956), p. 19.

12. Nietzsche, p. 22.

13. Nietzsche, p. 25.

14. Nietzsche, p. 31.

15. Karl Jaspers, "Man as His Own Creator," in *Nietzsche: A Collection of Critical Essays,* ed. Robert C. Solomon (Garden City, N.Y.: Doubleday Anchor Books, 1973), p. 153.

16. Jaspers, p. 144.

17. René Girard, *Deceit, Desire, and the Novel: Self and Other in Literary Structure,* trans. Yvonne Frecero (Baltimore, Md.: The Johns Hopkins University Press, 1965), pp. 2, 4.

18. For a similar idea see Fritz Senn, "Nausicaa," in *James Joyce's Ulysses: Critical Essays,* ed. Clive Hart and David Hayman (Berkeley, Calif.: University of California Press, 1974), p. 290.

19. Tzvetan Todorov, *The Poetics of Prose,* trans. Richard Howard (Ithaca, N.Y.: Cornell University Press, 1977), p. 145.

20. James Joyce, *Ulysses* (New York: Vintage Books, 1961), p. 356. Hereafter cited in the text.

21. Quoted in Frank Kermode, *The Genesis of Secrecy* (Cambridge: Harvard University Press, 1979), p. 76.

22. Lawrence Durrell, *Clea* (New York: Dutton, 1961), p. 55.

23. Douglas Day, *Malcolm Lowry: A Biography* (New York: Oxford University Press, 1973) provides an exhaustive analysis of these and other aspects of the Consul's character. Some of my observations are indebted to his pioneering work.

24. Day, p. 326.

25. Day, p. 327. Day points out that these images are reminiscent of "Dante's Malebolge, the eighth ring of the Inferno; the dwelling place of Prometheus, where he is tormented daily by his attendant vulture; of Ixion, tied for all eternity to his spinning infernal wheel; and of Shelley's Alastor, 'the dark magician in his visioned cave.'"

26. Day, pp. 329–30.

27. Malcolm Lowry, *Selected Letters of Malcolm Lowry,* ed. Harvey Breit and Margerie Bonner Lowry (New York: Capricorn Books, 1969), p. 58.

28. Malcolm Lowry, *Under the Volcano* (London: Jonathan Cape, 1967), p. 6.

29. Lowry, *Under the Volcano,* p. 52.

30. Octavio Paz, *The Labyrinth of Solitude: Life and Thought in Mexico,* trans. Lysander Kemp (New York: Grove Press, 1961), p. 20.

31. Day, p. 331 and pp. 347–48.

32. Ralph Harper, *The Seventh Solitude: Man's Isolation in Kierkegaard, Dostoevsky, and Nietzsche* (Baltimore, Md.: The Johns Hopkins University Press, 1965), p. 13.

33. Sigmund Freud, *Collected Papers,* vol. 4, trans. Joan Riviere (New York: Basic Books, 1959), p. 46.

34. George Eliot, *Middlemarch* (Boston: Houghton Mifflin, 1957), p. 156.

35. Patrick Brantlinger, "Romances, Novels, and Psychoanalysis," in *The Practice of Psychoanalytic Criticism,* ed. Leonard Tennenhouse (Detroit, Mich.: Wayne State University Press, 1976), p. 19.

36. Brantlinger, p. 21.

37. Brantlinger, p. 25.

38. Erich Auerbach, *Mimesis: The Representation of Reality in Western Literature,* trans. Willard R. Trask (Princeton, N.J.: Princeton University Press, 1968), p. 489.

39. Brantlinger, p. 36.

40. Sigmund Freud, *The Standard Edition of the Complete Works of Sigmund Freud,* trans. James Strachey (London, 1966), vol. 23, p. 58.

41. Robert Rogers, *A Psychoanalytic Study of the Double in Literature* (Detroit, Mich.: Wayne State University Press, 1970), p. 18.

42. Jan Miel, "Jacques Lacan and the Structure of the Unconscious," in *Structuralism,* ed. Jacques Ehrmann (New York: Doubleday Anchor Books, 1970), p. 99.

43. Michael Balint, *The Basic Fault: Therapeutic Aspects of Regression* (London: 1968), p. 55.

44. Heinz Kohut, *The Analysis of the Self* (New York: International Universities Press, 1971), p. 3.

45. Otto Kernberg, *Borderline Conditions and Pathological Narcissism* (New York: Jason Aronson, 1974), p. 315.

Chapter 2. The Fairest of Them All: Modes of Vision in *Madame Bovary*

1. Gustave Flaubert, *Madame Bovary*, ed. and trans. Paul deMan (New York, 1965) p. 59; hereafter cited in the text.

2. Tzvetan Todorov, *The Fantastic: A Structural Approach to a Literary Genre*, trans. Richard Howard (Cleveland: Press of Case Western Reserve Univ., 1973), p. 121.

3. I am indebted to Christopher Prendergast's fine study of *idées reçues* in Flaubert, "Writing and Negativity," *Novel* 8 (1975): 197–213. Prendergast offers an elaborate definition of *endoxon* as it applies to *Madame Bovary:* "The consensus of received opinion which a given society assumes and offers as Reality . . . is what Aristotle called *endoxon* ('current opinion') and, following Aristotle, we may perhaps call the discourse which repeats and reinforces consensus knowledge the endoxal discourse, the language of common-sense, the language of the stereotype, whose function is to cover a world historically produced with the mantle of the universal and the permanent and of which the classic forms are the maxim, the proverb, the platitude, the *idée reçue" (p. 207).*

4. Roland Barthes, *S/Z: An Essay,* trans. Richard Miller (New York: Hill and Wang, 1974), p. 21.

5. Erich Auerbach, *Mimesis: The Representation of Reality in Western Literature,* trans. Willard Trask (New York: Doubleday, 1953), p. 483.

6. John C. Lapp explores this congruence in "Art and Hallucination in Flaubert," in *Flaubert: A Collection of Critical Essays,* ed. R. Girard (Englewood Cliffs, N.J.: Prentice-Hall, 1964), pp. 75–88.

7. Lapp, pp. 76–7.

8. Robert Rogers, in *A Psychoanalytic Study of the Double in Literature* (Detroit: Wayne State Univ. Press, 1970), makes a similar observation about Narcissus's self love (p. 20). He also defines narcissism in a way I have found useful: "Narcissism is a kind of love, but it is misleading to translate the concept into what is known commonly as 'self-love.' Self-love in the everyday sense of 'egotism' is a metaphorical expression. In narcissism, the self-love is literal. The only difference between this kind of love and the erotic love of another person is in the object. Narcissism paradoxically involves a relationship, a relationship of self to self in which one's self is regarded as though it were another person" (p. 18). In addition, *Romanticism and Consciousness,* ed. Harold Bloom (New York: Norton, 1970), contains several outstanding essays that touch on the relationship between narcissism and Romanticism. Bloom's "The Internalization of Quest-Romance" (pp. 3–24) is especially good on the Freudian view of this subject. See also J. H. van den Berg's "The Subject and His Landscape" (pp. 57–65) and Paul de Man's "Intentional Structure of the Romantic Image" (pp. 65–77).

9. This is true not only for Emma and her prototype, Don Quixote, but also for Conrad's Lord Jim, Ford's Edward Ashburnham, Fitzgerald's Jay Gatsby. Each character's death is closely linked to this aspect of the language of Romanticism.

10. Roland Barthes, *The Pleasure of the Text,* trans. Richard Miller (New York: Hill and Wang, 1975), p. 17. Here is the relevant *prose:* "How can we take pleasure in a

reported pleasure (boredom of all narratives of dreams, of parties)? How can we read criticism? Only one way: since I am here a second-degree reader, I must shift my position: instead of agreeing to be the confidant of this critical pleasure—a sure way to miss it—I can make myself its voyeur: I observe clandestinely the pleasure of others, I enter perversion; the commentary then becomes in my eyes a text, a fiction, a fissured envelope, the writer's perversity (his pleasure in writing is without function), the doubled, the trebled, the infinite perversity of the critic and of his reader."

11. Quoted in Prendergast, p. 213.

Chapter 3. *The Awakening:* A Political Romance

1. Kate Chopin, *The Awakening,* ed. Margaret Culley (New York: Norton, 1976), p. 15. Hereafter cited in the text.

2. Gustave Flaubert, *Madame Bovary,* ed. Paul de Man (New York: Norton, 1965), p. 58.

3. In *The American 1890's: Life and Times of a Lost Generation* (New York: Viking, 1966), Lazar Ziff makes the following comments about Creole society: "The community about which she wrote was one in which respectable women took wine with their dinner and brandy after, smoked cigarettes, played Chopin sonatas, and listened to the men tell risqué stories. It was, in short, far more French than American. . . . [T]hese were for Mrs. Chopin the conditions of civility, and, since they were so French, a magazine public accustomed to accepting naughtiness from that quarter and taking pleasure in it on those terms raised no protest. But for Mrs. Chopin they were only outward signs of a culture that was hers and had its inner effects in the moral make-up of her characters" (p. 297). For a more general examination of the social contexts of fiction than I can explore in this space see Georg Lukács, *The Historical Novel* (London: Merlin Press, 1962), and Ian Watt, *The Rise of the Novel* (Berkeley, Calif.: University of California Press, 1965).

4. Tzvetan Todorov, *The Fantastic: A Structural Approach to a Literary Genre,* trans. Richard Howard (Cleveland, Ohio: The Press of the Case Western Reserve University, 1973), p. 26.

5. Todorov, p. 33.

6. Margaret Culley, "Edna Pontellier: 'A Solitary Soul,' " in *The Awakening,* p. 228.

7. Culley, p. 228.

8. Ziff, p. 304.

9. C. G. Jung, *Psyche and Symbol,* ed. Violet S. de Laszlo (New York: Doubleday Anchor Books, 1958), p. 7.

Chapter 4. "So Fine As He Can Never Be": *Lord Jim* and the Problem of Imagination

1. Joseph Conrad, *Lord Jim,* ed. Thomas Moser (New York: Norton, 1968), p. 208. Hereafter cited in the text.

2. Conrad, *Nostromo,* (New York: Holt, Rinehard & Winston, 1961), p. 413.

3. Conrad, *Under Western Eyes,* (New York: Anchor Books, 1963), p. 16.

4. See David Thorburn's *Conrad's Romanticism* (New Haven, Conn.: Yale University Press, 1974) for an excellent discussion of the "light literature" of Conrad's day.

5. Norman Holland, "Unity Identity Text Self," *PMLA* 90 (October 1975):817.

6. Herman Melville, *Moby Dick,* ed. Harrison Hayford and Hershel Parker (New York: Norton, 1967), p. 140.

7. Ian Watt, *Conrad and the Nineteenth Century* (Berkeley, Calif.: University of California Press, 1979), p. 322.

8. Watt, p. 323.

9. Gustav Morf, *The Polish Heritage of Joseph Conrad* (London: Sampson, Low, Marston, 1930), p. 158. Albert Guerard, *Conrad the Novelist* (Cambridge: Harvard University Press, 1966), p. 151, agrees with Morf, saying that "the emphasis Morf gives to half-conscious and unconscious identification is, I am now persuaded, correct."

10. See Jocelyn Baines, *Joseph Conrad: A Critical Biography* (London: Weidenfeld and Nicolson, 1960), pp. 415–52.

11. Joseph Conrad, *Conrad's Prefaces,* ed. Edward Garnett (London: J. M. Dent, 1937), p. 208.

Chapter 5. "A Queer and Fantastic World": Romance and Society in *The Good Soldier*

1. Ford Madox Ford, *The Good Soldier* (New York: Vintage Books, 1955), p. 5. Hereafter cited in the text.

2. Arnold Kettle, *An Introduction to the English Novel* (London: Hutchinson University Library, 1951), vol. 1, p. 31. James Trammel Cox presents a considerably different argument from mine or Kettle's in "Ford's 'Passion for Provence' " *ELH* 18 (December 1961): 383–98.

3. John Meixner, "The Saddest Story," *Kenyon Review* 22 (Spring 1960): 235.

4. Ezra Pound, "Peire Vidal Old," in *Personae* (New York: New Directions, 1926), p. 32.

5. Ford Madox Ford, *Henry James* (London: Martin Secker, 1913) p. 153.

6. Hugh Kenner, "Conrad and Ford," in *Gnomon* (New York: McDowell, Obolensky, 1958), p. 168.

7. Ezra Pound, "Homage to Ford Madox Ford," in *New Directions in Prose and Poetry* (Norfolk: New Directions, 1942), p. 480.

8. Ford Madox Ford, *Parade's End* (London: The Bodley Head, 1924), vol. 3, p. 29.

Chapter 6. F. Scott Fitzgerald's "Universe of Ineffable Gaudiness"

1. F. Scott Fitzgerald, *The Great Gatsby* (New York: Scribners, 1953), p. 112. Hereafter cited in the text.

2. For a concise summary of these influences see Frederick J. Hoffman, *The Great Gatsby: A Study* (New York: Scribners, 1962).

3. Frank MacShane, ed., *Critical Writings of Ford Madox Ford* (Lincoln: University of Nebraska Press, 1964), p. 43.

4. Edward Crankshaw, *Joseph Conrad: Some Aspects of the Art of the Novel* (New York: Russell and Russell, 1963), p. 87.

5. Hoffman, p. 167.

6. Arthur Mizener, *The Far Side of Paradise* (Boston: Houghton Mifflin, 1949), p. 60.

7. Eliot's influence has been traced in various places. Among the most useful is John W. Bicknell, "The Waste Land of F. Scott Fitzgerald," *Virginia Quarterly Review* 30 (Autumn 1954): 556–72.

8. Erich Auerbach, *Mimesis,* trans. Willard R. Trask (Princeton: Princeton University Press, 1953), p. 489.

9. See my essay, "Ford Madox Ford and The Great Gatsby", *Fitzgerald/Hemingway Annual* (1975): 57–74.

10. Hugh Kenner, *A Homemade World* (New York: William Morrow, 1975), chapter 2, "The Promised Land," pp. 20–50, is endlessly provocative.

11. *The Letters of F. Scott Fitzgerald,* ed. Andrew Turnbull (New York: Scribners, 1963), p. 358.

12. Hoffman, p. 169.

13. F. Scott Fitzgerald, *The Crack Up* (New York: New Directions, 1956), p. 70.

14. Marius Bewley, "Scott Fitzgerald's Criticism of America," in Hoffman, p. 269.

15. Bewley, p. 284.

16. Joseph Conrad, *Lord Jim* (New York: Norton, 1968), p. 136.

17. Tzvetan Todorov, *The Fantastic* (Cleveland: Case Western Reserve University Press, 1973), p. 92.

18. T. S. Eliot, "Ulysses, Order, and Myth," in *The Modern Tradition,* ed. Richard Ellman and Charles Feidelson, Jr. (New York: Oxford University Press, 1965), p. 681.

Chapter 7. Narcissism and Selflessness in *The Alexandria Quartet*

1. Lawrence Durrell, *Clea* (New York: Dutton, 1961), pp. 202–3. Further passages from *Clea, Justine, Balthazar* and *Mountolive* in the Dutton edition will be cited in the text accompanied by the following abbreviations: *Justine,* J; *Balthazar,* B; *Mountolive,* M; *Clea,* C.

2. Geoffrey Hartman, "Romanticism and 'Anti-Self-Consciousness,'" in *Romanticism and Consciousness,* ed. Harold Bloom (New York: Norton, 1970), p. 51.

3. Robert Langbaum, *The Mysteries of Identity: A Theme in Modern Literature* (New York: Oxford University Press, 1977), pp. 25–51.

4. John Unterecker, *Lawrence Durrell* (New York: Columbia University Press, 1964), p. 39, constructs a typology of symbols for the *Quartet:* ". . . just as *Justine* is most conspicuously the book of mirrors, *Balthazar* the book of masks, and *Mountolive* the book of intrigue—the first two volumes offering private false faces and the third offering the public false faces of political action—*Clea* must take its place . . . as Durrell's book of wounds . . ."

5. Leon Edel, *The Modern Psychological Novel* (New York: Grosset and Dunlap, 1964), p. 187.

6. Sigmund Freud, *Collected Papers,* vol. 4, trans. Joan Riviere (New York: Basic Books, 1959), p. 46.

7. Jan Miel, "Jacques Lacan and the Structure of the Unconscious," in *Structuralism,* ed. Jacques Ehrmann (New York: Anchor, 1970), p. 99.

8. Quoted in J. Hillis Miller's *Poets of Reality: Six Twentieth-Century Writers* (New York: Atheneum, 1969), p. 3.

9. Miller, p. 3.

10. See Wilfred Stone's *The Cave and the Mountain: A Study of E. M. Forster* (Stanford: Stanford University Press, 1966), chapter 12, pp. 298–347.

Chapter 8. Romantic Decadence: *The Immoralist*

1. André Gide, *The Immoralist,* trans. Richard Howard (New York: Vintage Books, 1970), p. xiv. Hereafter cited in the text.

2. Quoted by Jean Hytier in his essay, "The Recits," in *Gide: A Collection of Critical Essays,* ed. David Littlejohn (Englewood Cliffs, N.J.: Prentice-Hall, 1970), p. 73.

3. Albert Guerard makes the point succinctly: "Michel's revolt reflects his age (the age

of Nietzschean hopes and destructions). . . . Already the psychological realism of *L'Im-moraliste* seems more important than its critique of individualism; its anticipation of Freud more valid than its oblique reflection of Nietzsche," in *André Gide* (Cambridge: Harvard University Press, 1969), p. 100.

4. Otto Kernberg, *Borderline Conditions and Pathological Narcissism* (New York: Jason Aronson, 1975).

5. Mario Praz, *The Romantic Agony,* trans. Angus Davidson (New York: Meridian Books, 1967), p. 383.

6. Guerard is very persuasive on this point in chapter 3, "The Early Novels," pp. 93–139.

7. Murray Krieger calls the scene in the oasis a "subdued Apollonian vision," (p. 27) but does not deal with the chthonic imagery as a means of understanding Michel's unconscious. Nevertheless, his essay on *The Immoralist* in *The Tragic Vision* (New York: Holt, Rinehart & Winston, 1960) offers a provocative view of the novel.

8. Lawrence Durrell, *The Alexandria Quartet* (New York: Dutton, 1961): *Clea,* p. 274.

9. See Jacques Derrida, *Of Grammatology,* trans. Gayatri Chakravorty Spivak (Baltimore: The Johns Hopkins University Press, 1976), p. xiv. Michel's naiveté in thinking that he can effectively erase his inferior self parodies the Derridean problem of erasure, the difference being that Derrida knows that the word (Michel's conventional being) is necessary, even though it is inaccurate.

10. Roland Barthes, *S/Z: An Essay,* trans. Richard Miller (New York: Hill and Wang, 1974), p. 21.

Chapter 9. The Closed Circle: *Death in Venice* and the Passions of the Mind

1. Thomas Mann, *Death in Venice in Classics of Modern Fiction: Ten Short Novels,* ed. Irving Howe, 2nd., (New York: Harcourt Brace Jovanovich, 1972), p. 355. All subsequent citations cited in the text.

2. Lord Byron, "Childe Harold's Pilgrimage," Canto 4, Stanza 1.

3. Quoted by André von Gronicka, "Myth Plus Psychology: A Stylistic Analysis of *Death in Venice*" in *Thomas Mann,* ed. Henry Hatfield (Englewood Cliffs, N.J.: Prentice-Hall, 1964), p. 50.

4. Homer, *The Odyssey of Homer,* trans. Richmond Lattimore (New York: Harper Torchbooks, 1967), p. 79. See von Gronicka, p. 60, for a more elaborate explanation.

5. Erich Heller, *Thomas Mann: The Ironic German* (New York: Meridian Books, 1961), p. 105.

6. Elliott Zuckerman, *The First Hundred Years of Wagner's "Tristan"* (New York: Columbia University Press, 1964), p. 138.

7. See Robert Martin Adams's discussion of Wagner in *Nil: Episodes in the Literary Conquest of the Void During the 19th Century* (New York: Oxford University Press, 1966), pp. 177–97.

8. See Heller, pp. 109–10 where he presents a different view.

Chapter 10. "What Country, Friends, Is This?": The Inner Terrain of *The Blood Oranges*

1. John Hawkes and Robert Scholes, "A Conversation on *The Blood Oranges,*" *Novel* (Spring 1972): 198.

2. John Hawkes, *The Blood Oranges* (New York: New Directions, 1970), p. 1. Hereafter cited in the text.

3. In the *Novel* interview, an interesting exchange between Hawkes and Scholes focuses on this point:

SCHOLES: ". . . if one has the creative power one can somehow or other bring Illyria into being around one, at least to a certain extent."
HAWKES: "Illyria doesn't exist unless you bring it into being."   (203)

4. See Robert Rogers, *A Psychoanalytic Study of The Double in Literature* (Detroit: Wayne State University Press, 1970), p. 4.
5. Patrick Brantlinger, "Romances, Novels, and Psychoanalysis," in *The Practice of Psychoanalytic Criticism,* ed, Leonard Tennenhouse (Detroit: Wayne State University Press, 1976), p. 33.
6. Brantlinger, p. 36.
7. Northrop Frye, *Anatomy of Criticism: Four Essays* (Princeton, N.J.: Princeton University Press, 1957), p. 186: "At its most naive (romance) is an endless form in which a central character who never develops or ages goes through one adventure after another until the author himself collapses."
8. Quoted by Tony Tanner in *City of Words: American Fiction 1950–1970* (New York: Harper & Row, 1971), p. 203.
9. Georg Lukács, *The Theory of the Novel* (Cambridge: M.I.T. Press, 1971), p. 70.
10. *Novel* interview, p. 202.
11. *Novel* interview, pp. 200–201.
12. Ford Madox Ford, *The Good Soldier* (New York: Vintage Books, 1955), p. 4.
13. John Kuehl makes a similar observation in *John Hawkes and the Craft of Conflict* (New Brunswick, N.J.: Rutgers University Press, 1975), p. 148.
14. *The Good Soldier,* p. 6.
15. *The Good Soldier,* p. 254.

Conclusion

1. Sigmund Freud, "On Narcissism," *The Standard Edition of the Complete Psychological Works of Sigmund Freud,* trans. by James Strachey, vol. 14, p. 100.
2. Roland Barthes, *A Lover's Discourse,* trans. Richard Howard (New York: Hill and Wang, 1978), p. 49.
3. Tzvetan Todorov, *The Poetics of Prose,* trans. Richard Howard (Ithaca: Cornell University Press, 1977), p. 145.
4. Samuel Beckett, *Krapp's Last Tape and Other Dramatic Pieces* (New York: Grove Press, 1970), p. 15.
5. Robert Langbaum, *The Mysteries of Identity* (New York: Oxford University Press, 1977), p. 130.

Bibliography

Adams, Robert Martin. *Nil: Episodes in the Literary Conquest of the Void During the 19th Century.* New York: Oxford University Press, 1966.

Auerbach, Eric. *Mimesis: The Representation of Reality in Western Literature.* Translated by Willard R. Trask. Princeton, N.J.: Princeton University Press, 1968.

Baines, Jocelyn. *Joseph Conrad: A Critical Biography.* London: Weidenfeld and Nicolson, 1960.

Balint, Michael. *The Basic Fault: Therapeutic Aspects of Regression.* London: Tavistock Publications, 1968.

Barthes, Roland. *A Lover's Discourse.* Translated by Richard Howard. New York: Hill and Wang, 1978.

———. *The Pleasure of the Text.* Translated by Richard Miller. New York: Hill and Wang, 1975.

———. *S/Z: An Essay.* Translated by Richard Miller. New York: Hill and Wang, 1974.

Beckett, Samuel. *Krapp's Last Tape and Other Dramatic Pieces.* New York: Grove Press, 1970.

Bicknell, John. "The Waste Land of F. Scott Fitzgerald." In *Virginia Quarterly Review* 30 (Autumn 1954): 556–72.

Bloom, Harold. "The Internalization of Quest-Romance." In *Romanticism and Consciousness.* Edited by Harold Bloom. New York: W. W. Norton, 1970.

Bradbury, Malcolm. "The Name and Nature of Modernism." In *Modernism 1890–1930.* New York: Penguin Books, 1976.

Bradbury, Malcolm, and McFarlane, James, editors. *Modernism 1890–1930.* New York: Penguin Books, 1976.

Brantlinger, Patrick. "Romances, Novels, and Psychoanalysis." In *The Practice of Psychoanalytic Criticism.* Edited by Leonard Tennenhouse. Detroit, Mich.: Wayne State University Press, 1976.

Chopin, Kate. *The Awakening*. Edited by Margaret Culley. New York: W. W. Norton, 1976.

Conrad, Joseph. *Conrad's Prefaces*. Edited by Edward Garnett. London: S. M. Dent, 1937.

————. *Lord Jim*. Edited by Thomas Moser. New York: W. W. Norton, 1968.

————. *Nostromo*. New York: Holt, Rinehart, and Winston, 1961.

————. *Under Western Eyes*. New York: Anchor Books, 1963.

Cox, James Trammel. "Ford's Passion for Provence." In *ELH* 17 (December 1961): 383–98.

Crankshaw, Edward. *Joseph Conrad: Some Aspects of the Art of the Novel*. New York: Russell and Russell, 1963.

Culley, Margaret. "Edna Pontellier: A Solitary Soul." In *The Awakening*. Edited by Margaret Culley. New York: W. W. Norton, 1976.

Day, Douglas. *Malcolm Lowry: A Biography*. New York: Oxford University Press, 1973.

de Man, Paul. "Intentional Structure of the Romantic Image." In *Romanticism and Consciousness*. Edited by Harold Bloom. New York: W. W. Norton, 1970.

Derrida, Jacques. *Of Grammatology*. Translated by Gayatri Chakravorty Spivak. Baltimore, Md.: The Johns Hopkins University Press, 1976.

Durrell, Lawrence. *The Alexandria Quartet*. New York: Dutton, 1961.

Edel, Leon. *The Modern Psychological Novel*. New York: Grosset and Dunlap, 1964.

Eliot, George. *Middlemarch*. Boston: Houghton Mifflin, 1957.

Eliot, T. S. "Ulysses, Order, and Myth." In *The Modern Tradition: Backgrounds of Modern Literature*. Edited by Richard Ellman and Charles Feidelson. New York: Oxford University Press, 1966.

Ellman, Richard, and Feidelson, Charles, editors. *The Modern Tradition: Backgrounds of Modern Literature*. New York: Oxford University Press, 1965.

Fitzgerald, F. Scott. *The Crack Up*. New York: New Directions, 1956.

————. *The Great Gatsby*. New York: Charles Scribner's Sons, 1953.

————. *The Letters of F. Scott Fitzgerald*. Edited by Andrew Turnbull. New York: Charles Scribner's Sons, 1963.

Flaubert, Gustave. *Madame Bovary*. Translated by Paul de Man. New York: W. W. Norton, 1965.

Ford, Ford Madox. *Parade's End*. London: The Bodley Head, 1924.

————. *The Good Soldier*. New York: Vintage Books, 1955.

———. *Henry James*. London: Martin Secker, 1913.

———. *Critical Writings of Ford Madox Ford*. Edited by Frank Mac-Shane. Lincoln, Neb.: University of Nebraska Press, 1964.

Foster, John. *Heirs to Dionysus: A Nietzschean Current in Literary Modernism*. Princeton, N.J.: Princeton University Press, 1981.

Freud, Sigmund. *The Standard Edition of the Complete Psychological Works of Sigmund Freud*. Translated by James Strachey. London: Hogarth Press, 1953–1974.

———. *Collected Papers*. Authorized translation under the supervision of Joan Riviere. New York: Basic Books, 1959.

Frye, Northrop. *Anatomy of Criticism: Four Essays*. Princeton: Princeton University Press, 1957.

Girard, René. *Deceit, Desire, and the Novel*. Translated by Yvonne Frecero. Baltimore: The Johns Hopkins University Press, 1965.

Gide, André. *The Immoralist*. Translated by Richard Howard. New York: Vintage Books, 1970.

Guérard, Albert. *Andre Gidé*. Cambridge: Harvard University Press, 1969.

———. *Conrad the Novelist*. Cambridge: Harvard University Press, 1966.

Harper, Ralph. *The Seventh Solitude: Man's Isolation in Kierkegaard, Dostoevsky, and Nietzsche*. Baltimore: The Johns Hopkins University Press, 1965.

Hartman, Geoffrey. "Romanticism and 'Anti-Self-Consciousness.'" In *Romanticism and Consciousness*. Edited by Harold Bloom. New York: W. W. Norton, 1970.

Hawkes, John. *The Blood Oranges*. New York: New Directions, 1970.

Hawkes, John, and Scholes, Robert. "A Conversation on *The Blood Oranges*." In *Novel* 5 (Spring 1972).

Heller, Erich. *Thomas Mann: The Ironic German*. New York: Meridian Books, 1961.

Hoffman, Frederick S. *The Great Gatsby: A Study*. New York: Charles Scribner's Sons, 1962.

Holland, Norman. "Unity Identity Text Self." In *PMLA* 90 (Oct. 1975).

Homer. *The Odyssey of Homer*. Translated by Richard Lattimore. New York: Harper Torchbooks, 1967.

Hutcheon, Linda. *Narcissistic Narrative: The Metafictional Paradox*. Canada: Laurier University Press, 1980.

Hytier, Jean. "The Recits." In *Gide: A Collection of Critical Essays*. Edited by David Littlejohn. Englewood Cliffs, N.J.: Prentice-Hall, 1970.

Jaspers, Karl. "Man as His Own Creator." In *Nietzsche: A Collection of Critical Essays*. Edited by Robert C. Solomon. Garden City, N.Y.: Anchor Books, 1973.

Joyce, James. *Ulysses*. New York: Vintage Books, 1961.

Jung, C. G. *Psyche and Symbol*. Edited by Violet S. de Laszlo. New York: Anchor Books, 1958.

Kahler, Eric. *The Inward Turn of Narrative*. Translated by Richard and Clara Winston. Princeton: Princeton University Press, 1973.

Kaufmann, Walter. *Nietzsche: Philosopher, Psychologist, Antichrist*. Princeton: Princeton University Press, 1950.

Kenner, Hugh. *Gnomon*. New York: McDowell, Obolensky, 1958.

———. *A Homemade World*. New York: William Morrow, 1975.

Kermode, Frank. *The Genesis of Secrecy: On the Interpretation of Narrative*. Cambridge: Harvard University Press, 1979.

Kernberg, Otto. *Borderline Conditions and Pathological Narcissism*. New York: Jason Aronson, 1974.

Kettle, Arnold. *An Introduction to the English Novel*. London: Hutchinson University Library, 1951, Volume I.

Kohut, Heinz. *The Analysis of the Self*. New York: International University Press, 1971.

Krieger, Murray. *The Tragic Vision*. New York: Holt, Rinehart and Winston, 1960.

Kuehl, John. *John Hawkes and the Craft of Conflict*. New Brunswick: Rutgers University Press, 1975.

Kuna, Franz. "The Janus-faced Novel: Conrad, Musil, Kafka, Mann." In *Modernism 1890–1930*. Edited by Malcolm Bradbury and James McFarlane. New York: Penguin Books, 1976.

Langbaum, Robert. *The Mysteries of Identity: A Theme in Modern Literature*. New York: Oxford University Press, 1977.

Lapp, John C. "Art and Hallucination in Flaubert." In *Flaubert: A Collection of Critical Essays*. Edited by René Girard. Englewood Cliffs, N.J.: Prentice-Hall, 1964.

Lowry, Malcolm. *Under the Volcano*. London: Jonathan Cape, 1967.

———. *Selected Letters of Malcolm Lowry*. Edited by Harvet Breit and Margerie Bonner Lowry. New York: Capricorn Books, 1969.

Lukács, Georg. *The Historical Novel*. London: Merlin Press, 1962.

———. *The Theory of the Novel*. Cambridge: MIT Press, 1971.

McFarlane, James. "The Mind of Modernism." In *Modernism 1890–1930*. Edited by Malcolm Bradbury and James McFarlane. New York: Penguin Books, 1976.

Mann, Thomas. *Death in Venice*. In *Classics of Modern Fiction: Ten Short Novels*. Edited by Irving Howe. New York: Harcourt Brace Jovanovich, 1972.

Meixner, John. "The Saddest Story." In *Kenyon Review* 22 (Spring 1960).

Melville, Herman. *Moby Dick*. Edited by Harrison Hayford and Hershel Parker. New York: W. W. Norton, 1967.

Miel, Jan. "Jacques Lacan and the Structure of the Unconscious." In *Structuralism*. Edited by Jacques Ehrmann. New York: Anchor Books, 1970.

Miller, J. Hillis. *Poets of Reality: Six Twentieth-Century Writers*. New York: Atheneum, 1969.

Miller, Nancy K. *The Heroine's Text*. New York: Columbia University Press, 1980.

Mizener, Arthur. *The Far Side of Paradise*. Boston: Houghton Mifflin, 1949.

Morf, Gustav. *The Polish Heritage of Joseph Conrad*. London: Sampson, Low, Marston, 1930.

Nietzsche, Friedrich. *The Birth of Tragedy and the Genealogy of Morals*. Translated by Francis Golffing. New York: Anchor Books, 1956.

Paz, Octavio. *The Labyrinth of Solitude: Life and Thought in Mexico*. Translated by Lysander Kemp. New York: Grove Press, 1961.

Pound, Ezra. "Homage to Ford Madox Ford." In *New Directions in Prose and Poetry*. Norfolk: New Directions, 1942.

————. "Peire Vidal Old." In *Personae*. New York: New Directions, 1926.

Praz, Mario. *The Romantic Agony*. Translated by Angus Davidson. New York: Meridian Books, 1967.

Prendergast, Christopher. "Writing and Negativity." In *Novel* 8, 1975.

Rogers, Robert. *A Psychoanalytic Study of the Double in Literature*. Detroit: Wayne State University Press, 1970.

Senn, Fritz. "Nausicaa." In *James Joyce's Ulysses: Critical Essays*. Edited by Clive Hart and David Hayman. Berkeley and Los Angeles: University of California Press, 1974.

Solomon, Robert, editor. *Nietzsche: A Collection of Essays*. Garden City: Anchor Books, 1973.

Stone, Wilfred. *The Cave and the Mountain: A Study of E. M. Forster*. Stanford: Stanford University Press, 1966.

Tanner, Tony. *City of Words: American Fiction 1950–1970*. New York: Harper and Row, 1976.

Terdiman, Richard. *The Dialectics of Isolation*. New Haven: Yale University Press, 1976.

Thorburn, David. *Conrad's Romanticism*. New Haven: Yale University Press, 1974.

Thornton, Lawrence. "Ford Madox Ford and *The Great Gatsby*." In *Fitzgerald/Hemingway Annual*, 1975.

Todorov, Tzvetan. *The Fantastic: A Structural Approach to a Literary Genre*. Translated by Richard Howard. Cleveland: Case Western Reserve Press, 1973.

Todorov, Tzvetan. *The Poetics of Prose*. Translated by Richard Howard. Ithaca: Cornell University Press, 1977.

Unterecker, John. *Lawrence Durrell*. New York: Columbia University Press, 1964.

Van den Berg, J. H. "The Subject and His Landscape." In *Romanticism and Consciousness*. Edited by Harold Bloom. New York: W. W. Norton, 1970.

Vinge, Louise. *The Narcissus Theme in Western Literature Up To The Early 19th Century*. Lund: Gleerups, 1967.

von Gronicka, André. "Myth Plus Psychology: A Stylistic Analysis of Death in Venice." In *Thomas Mann*. Edited by Henry Hatfield. Englewood Cliffs, N.J.: Prentice Hall, 1964.

Watt, Ian. *The Rise of the Novel*. Berkeley and Los Angeles: University of California Press, 1965.

————. *Conrad and the Nineteenth Century*. Berkeley and Los Angeles: University of California Press, 1979.

Ziff, Lazar. *The American 1890's: Life and Times of a Lost Generation*. New York: Viking Press, 1966.

Zweig, Paul. *The Heresy of Self-Love: A Study of Subversive Individualism*. New York: Basic Books, 1968.

Index